Street Commerce

THE CITY IN THE TWENTY-FIRST CENTURY

Eugenie L. Birch and Susan M. Wachter, Series Editors

A complete list of books in the series is available from the publisher.

Street Commerce

Creating Vibrant Urban Sidewalks

Andres Sevtsuk

PENN

University of Pennsylvania Press
Philadelphia

Copyright © 2020 University of Pennsylvania Press

All rights reserved. Except for brief quotations used for purposes of review or scholarly citation, none of this book may be reproduced in any form by any means without written permission from the publisher.

Published by
University of Pennsylvania Press
Philadelphia, Pennsylvania 19104-4112
www.upenn.edu/pennpress

Printed in the United States of America on acid-free paper
10 9 8 7 6 5 4 3 2 1

Library of Congress Cataloging-in-Publication Data

Names: Sevtsuk, Andres, author.
Title: Street commerce: creating vibrant urban sidewalks / Andres Sevtsuk.
Other titles: City in the twenty-first century book series.
Description: 1st edition. | Philadelphia : University of Pennsylvania Press, [2020] | Series: The city in the twenty-first century | Includes bibliographical references and index.
Identifiers: LCCN 2019045118 | ISBN 9780812252200 (hardcover)
Subjects: LCSH: Stores, Retail. | Store location. | Street life. | Retail trade. | City planning—Economic aspects. | City planning—Social aspects.
Classification: LCC HF5429 .S48 2020 | DDC 711/.5522—dc23
LC record available at https://lccn.loc.gov/2019045118

Contents

Introduction   1

Chapter 1. The Predictability, and Unpredictability, of Street Commerce   11

Chapter 2. The Survival of Individual Stores   32

Chapter 3. How Stores Cluster   77

Chapter 4. Coordinated Clustering: Business Improvement Districts, Co-ops, and Malls   93

Chapter 5. Location, Location, Location: How Retailers Gravitate to Homes, Workplaces, and Pedestrians   119

Chapter 6. How Urban Design and Building Typologies Affect Retail Location Patterns   144

Chapter 7. How Demographic Shifts and E-Commerce Are Reshaping the Retail Landscape   172

Conclusion   195

Appendix   209

Notes   213

Index   231

Acknowledgments   239

Introduction

On a sunny Sunday morning in London, my wife and I were having coffee and making plans for the day. We both had to take care of some shopping—she needed a dress from a store she likes, I had looked up some shoes and jeans online but wanted to try them on in person. We thought of having brunch in a park with friends and doing something fun in the afternoon.

Leaving the house, we walked through our neighborhood to Upper Street, the nearest high street, as they call main streets in the UK. We figured we should be able to take care of all the shopping there, given the choice of numerous clothing stores and a small urban shopping center at Angel Station. Sure enough, after checking Google Maps on our phones, we found a number of stores that she trusted for dresses and I for jeans and shoes. We walked by an eclectic mix of businesses, including a flower store, a local ice-cream maker, and a pop-up designer boutique—as well as several pubs full of Arsenal fans, whose home stadium wasn't far away. Within half an hour of browsing, we had both nailed what we were looking for. We then decided to grab some coffee to go from Coffee Works and caught a bus to Victoria Park, where there is a charming café called the Pavilion that reminds me of the Boat House in New York's Central Park with a more casual atmosphere. On a Sunday morning, it attracts joggers, parents pushing strollers, and occasional bohemians.

To celebrate our shopping success, we met up with our friends who lived close by for brunch. At some point, the conversation drifted to a new Russian film our friends had recently read about called *Leviathan*. It had just won the Palm d'Or in Cannes. We started wondering whether any theater in London would be screening it. As an independent festival film, it was not one you would expect to find in Odeon, Vue, or AMC-type theaters. Reaching again for Google in our pockets, we learned, to our surprise, that five different theaters were playing it that very afternoon in London.

We picked out the Curzon Theater in SoHo, which we had never visited before, but which had a screening in 45 minutes and seemed perfect. We walked to the Central Line, and within thirty minutes or so, we got off at Tottenham Court Road, a few hundred yards from the theater, and made it just in time for the opening titles.

It was a good film. At the end, it took us some time to get out, since the plot had sunk us both deep into thought about the intractable scale of corruption in post-Soviet Russia. As we finally made our way past the bar, out onto Shaftesbury Avenue, my wife suddenly remembered that she had also wanted to get some Erik Satie scores for piano. "Should we look up music stores in SoHo or head home? We have guests coming over for dinner soon," she said. We decided to head home, noticing that the 38 bus stop, which would take us right back, was just down the block. As we turned the corner and walked along Charing Cross Road to the bus, we came across Foyles—a popular bookstore in the UK. Because it was right at the bus stop, we decided to pop in and ask if they had any piano scores. If they did, we thought to ourselves, we would be unlikely to find Satie's, but at least they might be able to suggest where else to look.

The lady behind the counter told us to check the music section on the third floor. We took the stairs, walking past two floors packed with literature from all over the world, and arrived on the third, full of music-related publications. Another clerk pointed us to a set of large-format metal drawers at the end of the room, which looked promising. I walked over and opened a drawer. It was full of Bach and Brahms scores. The next one was full of Chopin. A few cabinets down, there were Rachmaninoff, Tchaikovsky, Tubin. And then, under "S," I discovered a whole collection of Satie scores. This was completely unexpected. My wife had only thought of Satie five minutes earlier and neither of us imagined coming across a whole collection right there. She chose her favorite pieces, and with the scores in hand, we descended back down to Charing Cross Road and caught the bus home.

As we stared through the front window on the bus's upper deck, we passed through tree-lined streets bustling with businesses and people of all ethnicities and backgrounds. We discussed our amazement that we had been able to find all we needed within a few hours in the city—we both found the garments we were looking for; *Leviathan* was playing not only in Curzon, but in four other theaters; we stumbled upon a store selling Satie scores; we encountered interesting people and businesses we hadn't seen before along the way; each bus or train that we took was no more than a couple of blocks away; and we still planned to stop by a vegetable stall near our house to pick up tomatoes, peaches, and fresh dates from Iran for dinner. We wondered whether all this had something to do with London's claim to being the greatest city in the world.

Napoleon is said to have called England a nation of shopkeepers. The shops and services that London offers, and the convenience with which they are connected on foot and by public transit, certainly capture in a very palpable manner the convenience, diversity and all-around quality of life that the city offers. I have seen a shop dedicated to umbrellas in London—hundreds and hundreds of different umbrellas—a store selling only hats, and a taxidermy store selling full-scale mounted animals. There are restaurants that specialize in Georgian, Burmese, Ethiopian, Nepalese, or Singaporean cuisine, as well as fancy department stores such as Fortnum & Mason or Harrods that attract people from all over the world.

But this wide-ranging choice of merchandise and services is not all that street commerce offers. Our stroll along streets rich in people and businesses in London that morning allowed us not only to run errands efficiently and conveniently, it also put us in contact with lots of different experiences we had not planned on encountering—people of different backgrounds and interests, businesses selling odd things, poignant smells from colorful restaurants, unexpected sights and conversations. During our brunch in Victoria Park, we overheard a conversation from a neighboring table about someone inheriting a trust fund. Walking through our neighborhood, my wife and I had peeked into people's houses and admired their kitchen furniture and tall ceilings. On the way out of the cinema, we had a brief conversation with someone from Russia.

Bustling streets, rich in amenities, are social condensers that pull people together regardless of their race, class, age, or religious belief, even if only for brief moments. Unlike the workplaces, families, political organizations, or faith groups that we are either born into or choose to be part of, the people and businesses we encounter walking down city streets are not united around shared kinship ties, interests, or beliefs. Bustling streets put us in touch with "others" who do not necessarily share the same beliefs, interests, or values with us. By fostering dialogic social exchange, streets are part of the glue that holds an urban society together.[1] The more they make us interact, the more we understand and appreciate each other.

In a famous sociological article published in 1977, Mark Granovetter demonstrated the importance of "weak" ties in urban societies.[2] By strong ties he meant the connections we have through our families, colleagues, or other groups we meet on a daily or weekly basis. Weak ties, on the other hand, describe people we meet or talk to only a couple of times a year—at a conference, an event, or just serendipitously on the street. Granovetter demonstrated that weak social ties are more important for social mobility and for spreading information across society than strong ties. For example, he showed that people are more likely to find a job through someone they meet once or twice a year than through someone they see every day.

Experiencing the city on foot along its streets helps generate weak ties—it provides the opportunity for serendipitous encounters with members of our social networks we do not see very often. Furthermore, a walk down a street full of diverse amenities and people also produces what might be called "latent" ties—social connections that do not preexist, but which can sprout from casual encounters, unplanned conversations, or simply eye contact. Some of these first-time encounters can lead to exchanges that grow into weak or even strong ties over time. Just think of the conversations you have started with strangers in a store, restaurant, hair salon, or on the street. This happens more commonly on main streets and other urban retail clusters than on quiet residential streets because these environments attract a lot more users and offer public spaces that are configured to encourage interaction. Streets lined with commerce and amenities thus produce a double benefit for city dwellers—they not only serve the utilitarian function of supplying the urban consumer class with shops, amenities, and services, but they are also instrumental in spurring latent ties and social awareness.

Street commerce can also generate economic and environmental benefits for a city. Smaller and sometimes locally owned stores along city streets tend to produce greater economic benefits for a town than do national big-box chains. A significant share of the revenues generated by small, locally owned stores reverberate back into the local economy via subcontracting from local providers, payments to local employees, and improvements made in the public infrastructure around stores, as well as through indirect investments into employee health and retirement benefits. By purchasing food products from local suppliers, furniture and office supplies from local sellers, or by using local transportation, construction and maintenance contractors can produce a strong, positive multiplier effect on a local economy. One study that compared economic multiplier effects of local versus chain bookstores found that for every dollar spent at a local store, 45 cents circulated back into the local economy. A chain store, on the other hand, spread three times less—13 cents—back to the local economy.[3] Retail transactions typically directly represent around 7% of the local economy,[4] but when combined with those from the various suppliers that support shops and food, beverage, and personal service providers in a town, a more significant share of the local economy is affected. The more integrated a local economy is, the more its wealth passes around to its inhabitants.

From an environmental perspective, retail clusters accessible by foot and by public transit reduce a city's energy bill, contribute to cleaner air, and improve public health. Having a higher proportion of visitors arrive without a car helps lower traffic congestion, encourages exercise, and reduces per capita fossil fuel consumption. According to the 2009 National Household Travel Survey, 70% of all trips in the United States are for shopping, other family or personal errands, or social and recreational trips.[5] If the bulk of trips can occur on foot or public transit, not too far from one's home or workplace, then palpable strides can be made toward reducing both greenhouse gas emissions and energy consumption, while enabling more urban land to be converted from roads and parking lots to functional economic destinations, public spaces, and recreational areas. And when development densities are too low to support street commerce on a local basis, coordinated public transit can facilitate car-free arrival from surrounding districts.

Yet relatively little has been written to explain how the patterns of stores and amenities that make cities so convenient, serendipitous, economically robust, and socially interdependent come to be. What are the forces that shape the amenity clusters that line a city's streets? What determines how much commerce we find in San Francisco as opposed to London? Why do some streets specialize in bookstores and others in only restaurants? Why are some streets used for social and recreational activities that go well beyond shopping or dining? And what can planners, urban designers, and public officials do to foster streets that produce these amenities and interactions? This book tries to address these questions.

A lot has been written about retail location and retail economics. But much of scholarly research on retailing in the 20th century focused on shopping centers, a highly coordinated form of retailing that differs in important ways from the street-based shopping that I am referring to here. Shopping centers are rarely embedded in dense urban neighborhoods, making them less dependent on the sociospatial context that immediately surrounds them. They tend to cater to customers from a whole metropolitan area, who predominantly arrive by car rather than on foot or public transit, leading to a more predictable and less diverse set of encounters.

More importantly, retail space inside shopping centers, whether urban or suburban, is typically jointly owned, enabling them to behave as a single, coordinated entity. "A shopping center is not a building but a management concept, a way common management causes separately owned businesses to behave as one," explained John T. Riordan, a longtime head of the International Council for Shopping Centers (ICSC).[6] In contrast to independent stores competing with or complementing each other in uncoordinated urban main streets, shopping centers leverage the financial benefits of joint management, synchronized leasing, detailed design, and operating guidelines that all stores in a mall must follow. Developers buy the land, develop the structures, and lease them out at variable rates to carefully picked stores, depending on how many customers they are expected to bring in. The goal is to orchestrate an optimal mix that maximizes profits for the center as a whole and establishes tailored financial incentives for individual stores to join the cluster. Stores that bring in the highest number of customers—the anchors—often pay no rent at all or even get multi-million-dollar subsidies in the form of construction, parking, signage, and priority access routes. These anchors, in turn, bring in a lot of customers and spend large sums on marketing and advertising. Smaller stores, which benefit from customer spillovers from the anchors, pay steep leases for these gains. The whole entity operates like a fine-tuned machine. When the output does not match the owner's expectations, individual stores can be immediately adjusted, bringing performance right back to where management wants it.

Street commerce works differently. With numerous independent landlords, no coordinated management structure in place, and no financial incentives to lure in large anchor stores, street commerce behaves less like a machine and more like a farmer's market. There, certain rules apply, but beyond that each store can sell whatever it pleases, whenever it pleases, while paying its landlord whatever it can negotiate. Public spaces between stores—the sidewalks, roads, squares, and pocket parks—are typically owned by a municipality and are regulated by a public legal code that bars private landlords from restricting who can enter or what activities are and are not allowed. What we know about retail economics and planning strategies in shopping centers is thus inadequate for explaining the retail patterns we observe on city streets. The specific factors affecting urban retail environments remain poorly understood among planners.

In the chapters that follow, I try to bring together knowledge that lies in different disciplinary silos to explain how economic, organizational, and spatial forces together shape these shifting retail and service establishment patterns in cities. Contrary to some economists' belief that urban retail environments are shaped purely by market forces, I argue that street commerce is molded by planning and urban-design decisions as much as by the "invisible hand" of the market. I also argue that an array of design and policy tools can be used to enhance street commerce in broadly sustainable and equitable terms. The initiative for their mobilization can emerge from grassroots and civil society organizations, city leaders, developers, or planning professional, but in each case, understanding what mechanisms are available to improve street commerce is a prerequisite. To support this argument, I demonstrate how several successful commercial streets have benefited from deliberate planning and argue that there is a growing need for such efforts as city centers continue to densify and a new generation of downtown inhabitants call for more vibrant city life.

The pattern of street commerce in a city is a good example of what complexity scientists would call an *emergent* phenomenon. The pattern of stores we observe is a result of many interacting forces that exert their influence in non-deterministic ways, yet they produce a recognizable pattern that we encounter from one city to another. Urbanist Jane Jacobs, for example, described use patterns in city parks like this:

> How much a park is used depends, in part, upon the park's own design. But even this partial influence of the park's design upon the park's use depends, in turn, on who is around to use the park, and when, and this in turn depends on the uses of the city outside the park itself. Furthermore, the influence of these uses on the park is only partly a matter of how each affects the park independently of the others; it is also partly a matter of how they affect the park in combination with one another, for certain combinations stimulate the degree of the influence from one another among their components. . . . No matter what you try to do to it, a city park behaves as a problem in organized complexity, and that is what it is.[7]

Street commerce also depends in part on the configuration of the built environment around it—the ways in which a network of streets, public spaces, buildings, land uses, and transportation lines are distributed in the city. These qualities of the built environment enable stores to access more customers in some parts of the city than others. But the influence of the built environment also depends on who lives in, works in, or occupies the buildings and spaces around stores.

Aside from the influence exerted by the external environment around stores, shops within retail clusters also position themselves strategically with respect to other shops. These endogenous interactions pull some stores together while pushing others apart, depending on the degree of competition or complementarity between them. The pattern of stores we encounter at any point in time is, in fact, a snapshot of a complex dynamic process that continuously shifts. It is impossible to explain the pattern of stores we encounter through the exogenous qualities of the built environment or endogenous economic interactions between stores alone—both play a role simultaneously.

Within a year, some businesses will thrive, some will just break even, and others will be forced to close due to insufficient revenue. In neighborhoods where things are going well, stores prosper, new shops open, and developers launch new real estate ventures. In others, visits decline, revenues fall, and shops go out of business. Some stores are replaced while others are vacated and boarded up until times improve.

Scholars in a number of fields have studied these dynamics and have influenced this book. The branch of economics that deals with spatial phenomena is typically called urban or real estate economics, and retail economics forms a part of that. Human and economic geographers have developed ways to map and spatially analyze how retailers distribute themselves across cities, states, and regions. And public policy scholars and political scientists have examined how government oversight and organizational frameworks affect business owners and their location decisions. Scholars in each of these fields have contributed knowledge that can help us explain the retail landscape we observe.

Somewhat surprisingly, urban planning and design literature has exhibited relatively little interest in urban retail clusters. The scholarship that does exist is outdated[8] or focused on very specific aspects of retailing, such as business improvement districts or main street revitalization strategies. With a few notable exceptions,[9] current planning literature also appears to address commercial development in a reactive manner, for example, observing negative externalities, such as food deserts in underinvested neighborhoods.[10] The current generation of planning professionals has been trained to think that retail and service projects belong to the realm of the private sector, and very few planning programs offer courses on commercial planning. The American Planning Accreditation Board guidelines for curricula currently do not require any specialized courses on commercial planning as part of program accreditation. Students thus graduate with a relatively poor understanding of environments and policies that allow street commerce to thrive.

By discussing different factors that shape street commerce, I will address what it takes for shops and service establishments to remain viable, how agglomeration effects and inter-store externalities affect colocation and patronage, how different merchant organizations affect coordination between stores, how location affects store accessibility and visibility, how building types and urban design regulations affect the opportunities for commercial mixed-use ground floors, what planners and policy makers can do to support street commerce, and how e-commerce is likely to influence brick-and-mortar stores. Planning commercial environments requires an inherently multidisciplinary approach—in order for retail clusters to work; their location has to work; interactions between stores and even online sellers have to work; building typologies have to work; access, parking, and pedestrian flows have to work; and organizing agreements between stores as well as public-sector partners have to work. No one of these prerequisites alone is sufficient for achieving sustainable urban street retail and commercial clusters; they all need to align in concert.

In the chapters that follow, I bring the various levers of urban street commerce together for one particular group of influencers—urban planners and designers. When moving from descriptive to normative discussion on how to improve street commerce, I thus generally refer to strategies, tactics, and tools useful to urban planners and designers. There is also plenty of relevance for real-estate development and public policy.

I also suggest that new and innovative strategies are needed to generate equitable street commerce, where gentrification or lack of investment threaten to harm the amenities and spaces that communities depend on. Just like inclusionary housing policies were developed in response to market failures, we need to create inclusionary retail policies to ensure that urban amenities are available for everyone's benefit. Retail establishments that deliver affordable goods and services not only benefit lower-income populations but serve a broader clientele across socioeconomic levels. Cities need not only to address declining main streets and downtowns reactively, but to become more proactive in using financial subsidies, zoning, urban design, and policy tools to foster equitable street commerce.

Street commerce is also currently going through important social and technological changes. Demographic shifts in the United States are producing more unmarried and single-person households, who have different living and shopping preferences than the nuclear suburban family that helped proliferate car-oriented malls across the nation. E-commerce is creating even cheaper and more convenient alternatives to big-box discount stores, driving many such establishments out of business. More flexible work schedules are increasing the share of time people spend on recreational activities and are bringing younger urbanites back to city streets, looking for new types of experiences. I explore these transitions in the penultimate chapter of the book and propose some strategies and tactics that planners and urban designers can use to cope with the new realities of brick-and-mortar retailing.

The book is organized as follows. Chapter 1 starts with a big-picture overview of how retail and services clusters are distributed across US cities. Borrowing insights from recent work on urban scaling laws, I explore how predictable, as opposed to unique, the spatial pattern of stores actually is. The chapters that follow examine the different factors that explain these patterns. Chapter 2 provides a microeconomic perspective, exploring the factors that affect the economic sustainability of individual stores and limit the density of competing stores. Chapter 3 discusses why stores tend to cluster and the forces and dynamics that lead complementary or competitive businesses to locate next to one another and how such decisions can make stores better off. Chapter 4 also discusses clustering, but from the perspective of how a number of businesses together can decide to organize around business improvement districts or associations to further common interests. Chapter 5 discusses how location affects street commerce, examines what qualities of the built environment retailers are most attracted to, and describes how retail agglomerations work as a system—how changes in one cluster are bound to affect other clusters around it and vice versa. Chapter 6 explores how architectural typologies and urban street design affect stores—qualities that zoning and urban design can directly affect. Chapter 7 explores how both e-commerce and changing demographics are shaking up brick-and-mortar commerce today, and the Conclusion summarizes key takeaways and discusses the role of street commerce in making cities more diverse, equitable, and walkable in the 21st century.

I illustrate the spatial patterns of street commerce with several examples. I use Cambridge and Somerville, Massachusetts, both part of the Boston metropolitan area, as examples of historic East Coast cities with rich legacies of street commerce that have been shaped by British colonial street patterns as well as streetcar lines in the early parts of the 20th century. Los Angeles, California, offers a counterexample—it is a fairly new city, dominated by the car, but still rich in walkable street commerce. The island city-state of Singapore offers lessons from the perspective of a strong state using top-down planning, which can at times produce remarkable results in urban development but also risks dampening private initiative and diversity. Post-Soviet towns in Estonia offer a natural example to explore the relationship between urban design, transportation policy, and retail development—they exemplify how a sudden departure from a state-controlled socialist economy to a liberal market economy played out in retail location patterns. The Indonesian city of Solo offers insights into retail development in increasingly pervasive conditions of rapidly developing cities in the Global South, where the economy is characterized by semiformal actors, weak government institutions, and rapid growth.

These examples come from different spatial, historical, political, geographical, and cultural contexts. They do not constitute comprehensive case studies of any place in particular but are instead meant to offer grounded illustrations of specific cultural, historic, architectural, and economic factors that shape street commerce in different contexts around the world. They illustrate how street commerce is not only shaped by environment and context but also conscientious policy, planning, and design.

The structure of the book is thus itself similar to the experience of wandering through bustling streets rich in encounters and experiences—not so different from the experience I recounted from the streets of London at the beginning of this Introduction. Rather than a linear, predictable trajectory of getting into a vehicle and driving to a predetermined destination, the story weaves past serendipitous, occasionally surprising, and hopefully richer experiences than you might have initially expected when you set out and picked up the book. The forces shaping street commerce are multidisciplinary and complex, and so is the order of their appearance throughout the chapters.

The various examples used throughout the book also emphasize that making street commerce work is not a uniquely American, European, or Western challenge, but indeed an issue for cities around the world. Opportunities for developing streets with vibrant commercial clusters exist everywhere. Recognizing and capitalizing on these opportunities requires a better understanding of how street commerce works and what city planners and urban designers can do to help it thrive.

CHAPTER 1

The Predictability, and Unpredictability, of Street Commerce

Despite the enormous variation in towns, neighborhoods, and businesses that one finds across the United States, a new field of urban science, pioneered by theoretical physicists who have turned to investigating cities as the new frontier for complexity research, is suggesting that there is surprising consistency to the pattern of commerce in any city or metropolitan area. Despite differing architectural styles, variations in businesses, and the unique characters of public spaces that frame them, these scientists suggest that the patterns of shops and services in different cities are actually systematic and predictable.

I am referring, in particular, to the work on urban scaling laws that has come out of the Santa Fe Institute for Complexity Studies and by scholars such as Luis Bettencourt, Jeffrey West, Jose Luis Lobo, and their colleagues.[1] In a 2007 paper published by the *Proceedings of the National Academy of Sciences* entitled "Growth, innovation, scaling, and the pace of life in cities," Bettencourt and his colleagues claimed to have discovered universal laws that describe how material urban infrastructure and immaterial socioeconomic outputs vary with city size. They discovered that as urban populations double, the per capita provisions of physical infrastructure, including the number of shops and services that cities offer, do not. Larger cities obviously require more total miles of paved streets, longer linear networks of sewage pipes, and more retail stores than smaller cities, but if we compare these provisions per capita, then larger cities actually require fewer of them than smaller cities, suggesting that efficiencies and economies of scale come to play.

This "sublinear" scaling of infrastructure and amenities can be described with a precise trend line, which suggests that despite local architectural differences, characters, and flavors, the number of businesses in Keene, NH, and Concord, MA, is, in fact, quite predictable. The system of stores in a midsize city, such as

Albuquerque, NM, is just a smaller scalar version of the same system in large metropolitan areas, such as New York or Los Angeles. Once we understand the properties of this pattern, we can develop an educated guess about how many businesses a town has just from knowing its population.

Besides scaling laws that predict the number of businesses in any town, scholars have found that businesses arrange themselves into clusters of predictable sizes. And recent data science work has additionally pointed out how regularly these clusters tend to locate with respect to each other.[2]

This chapter looks at macro patterns of retail and service establishments and discusses the regularities of these patterns across American cities. I will also discuss the limits of these regularities and illustrate how individual cities often deviate from the norm. Just as there are statistical commonalities in any group of human organizations, such commonalities are present in the macroscopic retail landscapes. But there are also unique traits that distinguish every retail cluster and metropolitan pattern of retail clusters from one another, which not only result from their unique historic, geographic, or climatic circumstances, but also from conscious policy, planning, and design choices that towns have adopted over time.

Different Scales of Street Commerce

Business establishments in the United States are officially tracked by North American Industry Categories, commonly known as NAICS codes. NAICS is the standard used by federal agencies for classifying business establishments for the purpose of collecting, analyzing, and publishing statistical data related to the US economy. The number of NAICS category digits indicates the level of detail in the establishment description. While the two-digit code "44" refers to the highest-level description, called "retail trade," a three-digit code can distinguish "441"—"Motor Vehicle and Parts Dealers"—from "442"—"Furniture and Home Furnishings Stores." A four-digit code, "4413," goes into further detail, representing "Automotive Parts, Accessories, and Tire Stores." The system goes all the way up to eight digits.

At the four-digit level, there are 36 codes that make up street commerce—27 establishment categories that fall under "retail trade," 3 categories that fall under "food services and drinking places," 3 trades that fall under "personal and laundry services," and another 3 trades under "repair and maintenance services" (Table 1). When I refer to "street commerce" in this book, I generally refer to these 36 NAICS categories, which represent the types of stores and services that anyone on the street can readily walk into to purchase goods or services without having to make

Table 1. Thirty-six retail, food, and service categories that typically constitute street commerce.

#	NAICS	Description
1	4411	Automobile Dealers
2	4412	Other Motor Vehicle Dealers
3	4413	Automotive Parts, Accessories, and Tire Stores
4	4421	Furniture Stores
5	4422	Home Furnishings Stores
6	4431	Electronics and Appliance Stores
7	4441	Building Material and Supplies Dealers
8	4442	Lawn and Garden Equipment and Supplies Stores
9	4451	Grocery Stores
10	4452	Specialty Food Stores
11	4453	Beer, Wine, and Liquor Stores
12	4461	Health and Personal Care Stores
13	4471	Gasoline Stations
14	4481	Clothing Stores
15	4482	Shoe Stores
16	4483	Jewelry, Luggage, and Leather Goods Stores
17	4511	Sporting Goods, Hobby, and Musical Instrument Stores
18	4512	Bookstores and News Dealers
19	4521	Department Stores
20	4529	Other General Merchandise Stores
21	4531	Florists
22	4532	Office Supplies, Stationery, and Gift Stores
23	4533	Used Merchandise Stores
24	4539	Other Miscellaneous Store Retailers
25	4541	Electronic Shopping and Mail-Order Houses
26	4542	Vending Machine Operators
27	4543	Direct Selling Establishments
28	7223	Special Food Services
29	7224	Drinking Places (Alcoholic Beverages)
30	7225	Restaurants and Other Eating Places
31	8111	Automotive Repair and Maintenance
32	8112	Electronic and Precision Equipment Repair and Maintenance
33	8114	Personal and Household Goods Repair and Maintenance
34	8121	Personal Care Services
35	8123	Dry Cleaning and Laundry Services
36	8129	Other Personal Services

an appointment. This definition of street commerce does not include office buildings and a series of other service-oriented establishments, such as legal, financial, or consulting businesses. It also does not include cultural amenities, such as theaters, cinemas, or concert houses, which function at specific times with advance ticketing. The categories cover shopping, eating, and personal services that are generally open for walk-ins during business hours and constitute some of the most common destinations for nonwork, school, or recreational trips in cities.[3]

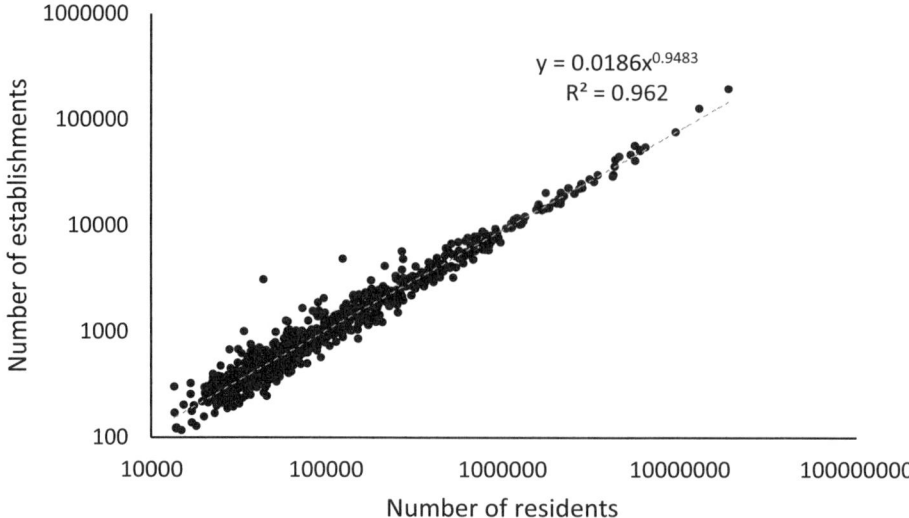

Figure 1. Log-log scatter plot of retail, food, and service establishments versus population size in 273 US metro areas where population is greater than 40,000 people.

To illustrate how the provision of these amenities scales up with metropolitan population, in Figure 1 I have plotted the number of amenities that fall into these 36 types in each US metropolitan area on the vertical axis and the corresponding 2010 population on the horizontal axis. Each black dot denotes one core-based statistical area (CBSA), which consists of an urban center of at least 10,000 people plus adjacent counties (or equivalents) that are socioeconomically tied to the urban center by commuting. There are over 900 CBSAs in the United States. In smaller cities, they tend to cover a single municipality, but in larger cities they often include several towns. Since CBSA sizes vary drastically between New York City, NY, Los Angeles, CA, or Chicago, IL, on the larger end, and Pahrump, NV, and Blackfoot, ID, on the smaller, I have plotted both axes on the graph in logarithmic scale—a scale where each successive mark on each axis is 10 times greater than the previous mark. The numbers on the axes therefore do not increase linearly as they move further from zero, but exponentially, each time multiplying the previous number by 10. This allows us to spread out all the varying town sizes along the graph instead of having a dense cluster of small towns on the left side and a few large metro areas on the right. The two topmost points on the right-hand side represent the New York-Northern New Jersey-Long Island CBSA, with a population of 18.9 million, and the Los Angeles-Long Beach-Anaheim CBSA, with a population of 12.8 million.

There is strikingly little scatter in the graph—the number of retail, food, and service businesses in most metro areas correspond closely to the area's population. As the number of residents increases, so does the number of amenities. The exponent 0.94, which characterizes the slope of the trend line, tells us that the relationship is sublinear, just like the physicists predict. An exponent of "1" would mean that when you double the population you also double the amenities. The slightly lower value of 0.94 tells us that when you double the population, the number of amenities does not quite double—commercial amenities exhibit economies of scale in larger cities.

The trend line allows us to predict the number of retail, food, and personal service businesses in specific cities from just their population size. For instance, the population of the Washington-Arlington-Alexandria metro area was 5.582 million in 2010. The trend line in Figure 1 predicts that a metro area of this size should have 46,505 retail, food, and personal service establishments. The actual number was 41,453. Population in the Atlanta-Sandy Springs-Marietta metro area was 5.27 million, which should produce approximately 44,000 such businesses. The actual number was close to 47,000. Metropolitan population is indeed a strong predictor for the number of retail, food, and services businesses—96% of variation in the number of amenities in the graph is, on average, explained by metropolitan populations.

But of course, being able to estimate the number of businesses doesn't mean that the spatial pattern of businesses from town to town are similar. How these businesses locate on the ground—clustering in one huge center or scattering around many smaller ones, stringing along public main streets or crowding in shopping malls—shapes much of our perception of a town. Can scaling laws that use just an area's population also tell us the size of a town's largest retail cluster or how amenities are clustered in centers of different sizes?

Distribution of Retail Clusters

In 1949, the American linguist George Kingley Zipf (1902–1950) came across something odd about how often people use words in a given language. He found that people used a small number of words all the time, while they used a vast majority very rarely. When ranking words in order of popularity, he found a striking pattern. People used the number one ranked word ("the") twice as frequently as the second rank word ("be"), and three times as frequently as the third rank word. He called this a rank versus frequency rule—the frequency of any word is inversely proportional to its rank in the frequency table. Later dubbed Zipf's Law, the rank versus frequency rule also works if you apply it to the sizes of cities in a country, and—surprisingly—to retail clusters in cities. Zipf's Law helps us understand how retail clusters distribute themselves into predictable patterns with very few large centers and a plethora of smaller ones. But before I apply Zipf's

Law to retail clusters, we need to take a small detour and start with a basic question: How do we define a retail cluster?

Do 2 stores make a cluster? How about 5? Or 55? And even if we have 55 stores on a street, when can we say that the stores actually form a cluster? There are many more than 55 stores along Wilshire Boulevard that cuts east-west across Los Angeles, but most of us would not say that all of Wilshire's stores are part of a single cluster.

Several techniques have been developed to define spatial clusters. Some scholars have suggested that a good starting point is to find the largest cluster in town, which is usually in the central business district (CBD), such as the agglomeration of stores along Magnificent Mile in Chicago, IL. One can then identify the second largest cluster, and the third, and so on until we have found most of the city's largest centers.[4] According to this approach, we stop counting clusters when we have reached a minimum density limit. Say we define a cluster as a place where at least 10 stores are found per acre. This approach would help us pick out clusters of any size as long as the minimum number per acre is respected. We could also define clusters as census tracts with a density of more than 10 stores per acre or a certain number of retail jobs.[5] Or we could use relative cutoff criteria and define clusters as zones with a higher commercial density than the metropolitan area average, containing at least 1% of a city's commerce.[6] Setting the cutoff relative to the city's total retail stock helps ensure that we do not evaluate retail clusters in small towns with the same yardstick as in large cities. But there is some evidence to suggest that the lower limit of perceivable cluster size does not depend on city size—survey respondents in both small and large towns tend to agree that the smallest recognizable retail cluster must have at least a few stores in close proximity.[7]

Whichever number of stores we choose as our cutoff, proceeding this way would require that we choose where to draw the boundaries of the spatial units of analysis—whether we use acres, census tracts, or square miles. Shifting the lens can easily modify the number of stores we capture.[8] And even when stores are located within the same acre or same census tract, it is not clear whether they might actually *feel* part of the same cluster from a visitor's perspective.

In a shopping mall, the concentration of stores found under a single roof certainly feels like one large cluster to most visitors. On a main street, or high street, a linear collection of individual shop fronts can also feel like a cluster. Two critical variables in both of these examples, which we often put together in our heads without really thinking about them, help us define them as clusters: first, a cluster needs to have a minimum number of businesses. A single shop does not make a cluster. Two shops also usually don't feel like a cluster. But 4 or 5 shops could start feeling like a cluster, and most people agree that 25 neighboring stores certainly feel like a cluster.

The second important variable describes the distance between stores in a cluster. How far can a store be from other stores to still be considered a member of that cluster? If 5 stores are right next to each other, say 10 yards apart, they would probably feel like a cluster. But what if the stores are 100 yards from each other? Or what if 1 store at the end of the cluster is 200 yards away from its nearest neighboring store, but the remaining 4 stores are right next to each other? Then the 4 stores might feel like a cluster without the 5th. Whether or not we define all 5 stores as a cluster now depends on the first criterion—the minimum number of stores that we accept to make a cluster.

Taking the minimum number of stores that make a cluster and the maximum allowable distance to the nearest neighbor in the cluster and measuring distances along street networks allows us to detect clusters in a consistent way, close to the way that people perceive them on real streets and neighborhoods. This is the method I will use to define retail clusters below. Figure 2 shows how this approach is applied to actual retail location data by setting the minimum number of stores in a cluster to 25, and the maximum walking distance to the nearest neighboring store in the cluster as 100 meters along the street network. In Figure 2, 31 stores surrounding a street intersection create a single cluster, while a number of other stores in the area are not considered part of a cluster because they either don't have enough members or the members are too far apart from each other. This approach for defining an individual cluster can be scaled up to a whole landscape of retail clusters in a city. In Figure 3, I apply the same methodology to detect retail clusters in Los Angeles, CA, and a bit of a buffer area surrounding its administrative area. Instead of drawing out every individual business that falls in a cluster, I show entire clusters as single black circles, setting the radius of the circle to correspond to the number of amenities in that cluster. The largest detected cluster in Los Angles is an agglomeration of 4,375 shops, located downtown. The second largest cluster runs along Hollywood Boulevard, consisting of about 600 stores. All in all, 280 clusters are detected in Los Angeles, many of which correspond to agglomerations that are well-known to the city's residents: Downtown, Koreatown, Venice, Hollywood, Sherman Oaks, La Brea, etc. Figures 4–8 show retail clusters in a selection of other American cities: Atlanta, Boston, Chicago, Washington, San Francisco, and Miami.

Now let us look at what happens when we apply the same approach to all retail and service establishment clusters across the continental United States. Figure 10 shows that the country has 8,308 retail clusters, with the biggest ones located in major cities. The 10 largest metro areas (out of 945 in the country), with populations over 4.5 million people, whose primary cities include New York, Los Angeles, Chicago, Dallas, Philadelphia, Houston, Miami, Atlanta, Washington, and Boston, account for 40% of all clustered retail and service amenities in the nation.

Comparing the distribution of these retail clusters to the distribution of residential population in the 2010 census suggests that easy access to retail and service

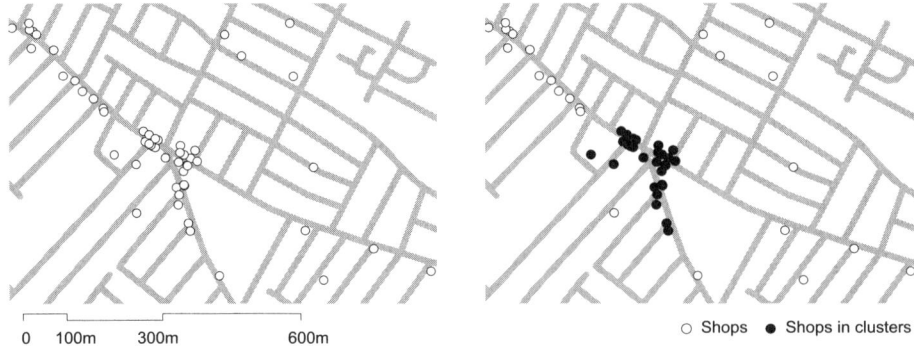

Figure 2. Defining retail clusters as agglomerations, where a minimum number of stores coexist and where the distance between stores is less than a given limit. Left: original store location data. Right: detected retail cluster.

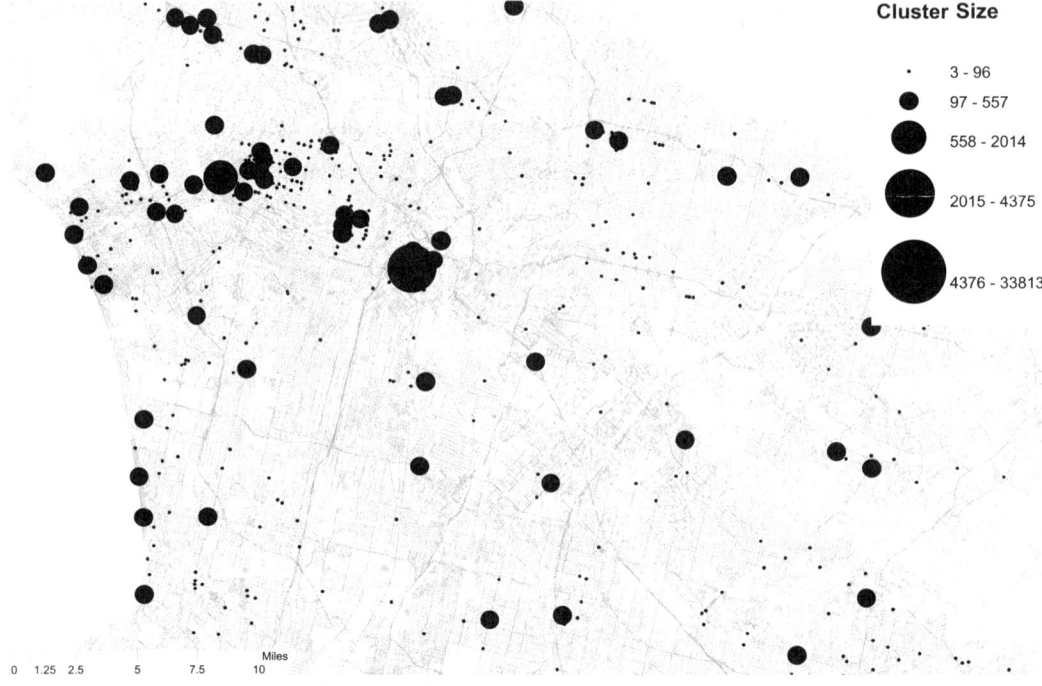

Figure 3. Retail clusters in and around Los Angeles, CA, where clusters are defined as agglomerations of at least 25 stores and where each store must lie within 100 meters from its nearest neighboring store. Each cluster is marked with a circle, located at the centroid of the cluster, with the radius corresponding to the number of amenities in the cluster. Data Source: Infogroup 2010 Business Listings, provided as part of ESRI Business Analyst software.

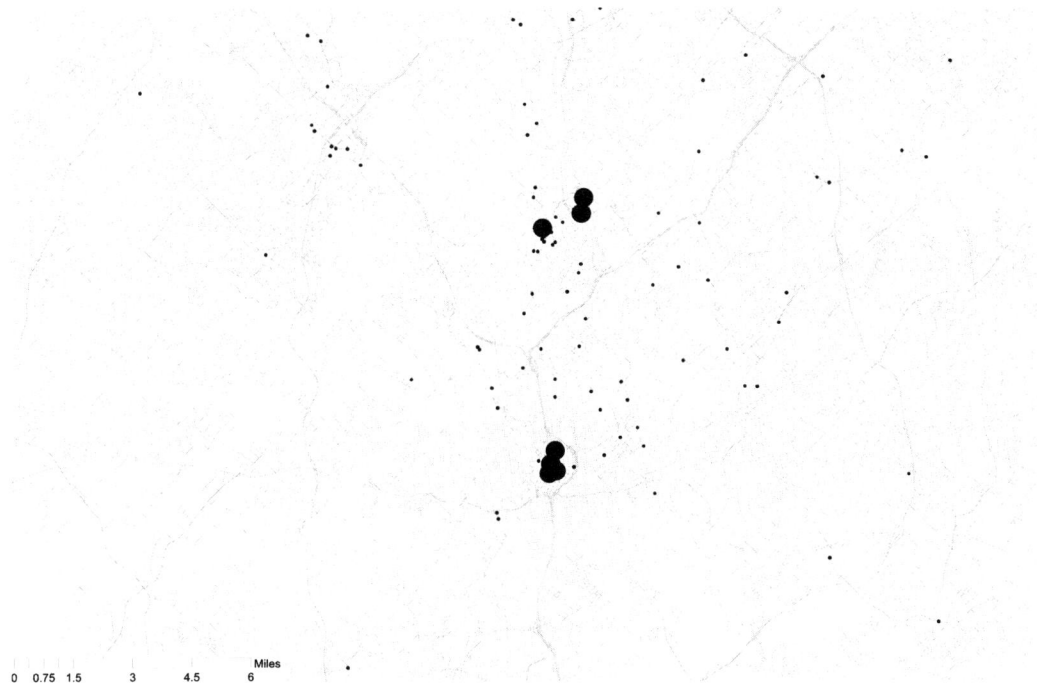

Figure 4. Retail clusters around Atlanta, GA. Data Source: Infogroup 2010 Business Listings, provided as part of ESRI Business Analyst software.

Figure 5. Retail clusters around Boston, MA. Data Source: Infogroup 2010 Business Listings, provided as part of ESRI Business Analyst software.

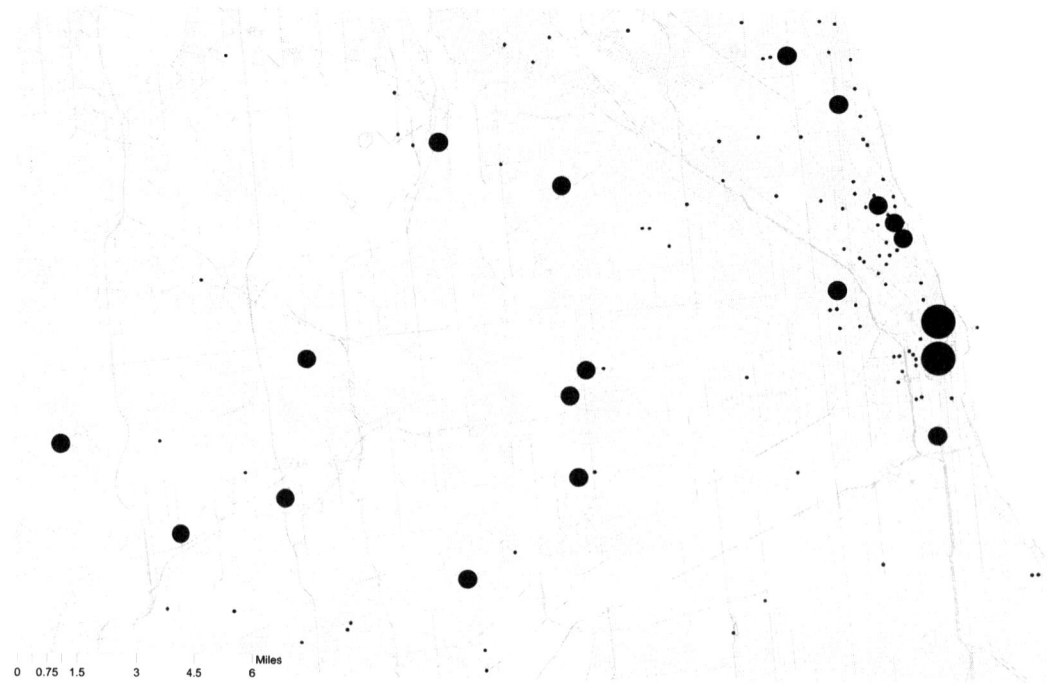

Figure 6. Retail clusters around Chicago, IL. Data Source: Infogroup 2010 Business Listings, provided as part of ESRI Business Analyst software.

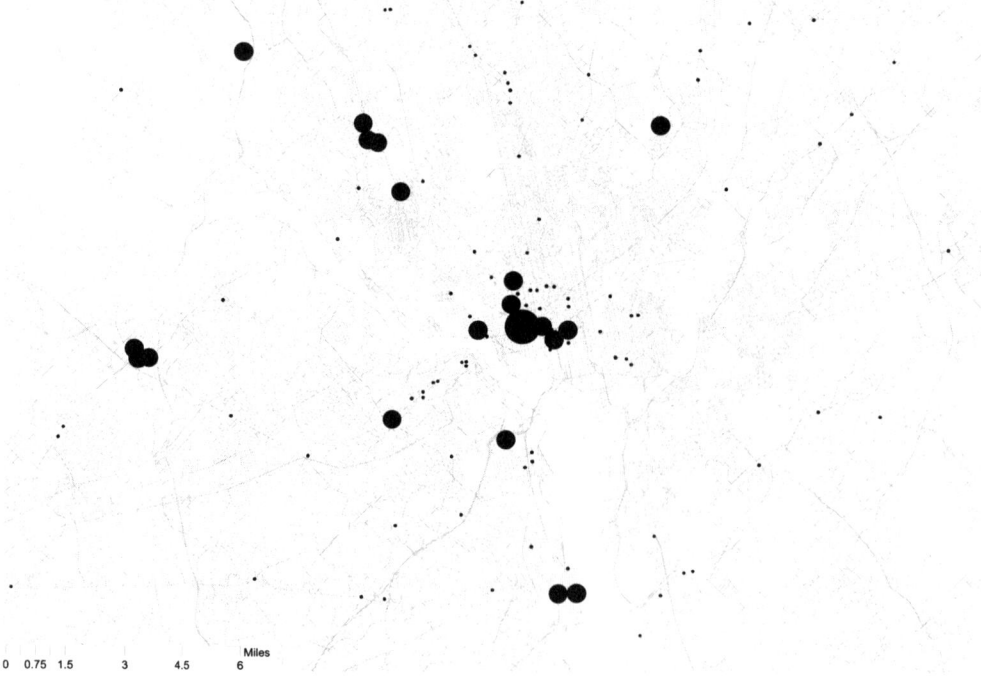

Figure 7. Retail clusters around Washington, DC. Data Source: Infogroup 2010 Business Listings, provided as part of ESRI Business Analyst software.

Figure 8. Retail clusters around San Francisco, CA. Data Source: Infogroup 2010 Business Listings, provided as part of ESRI Business Analyst software.

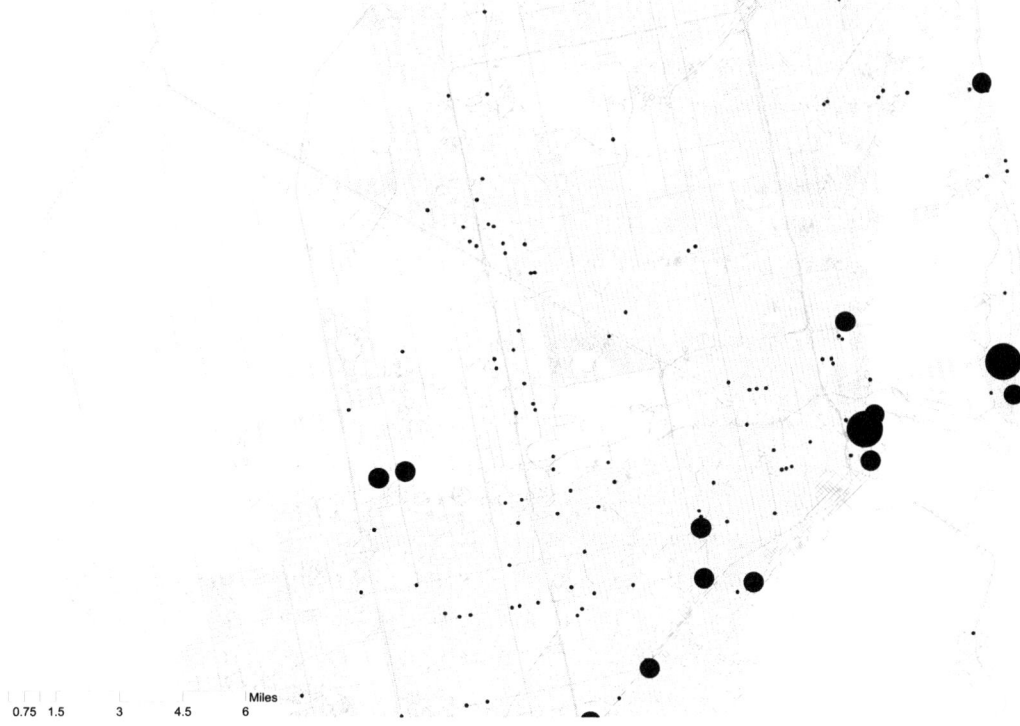

Figure 9. Retail clusters around Miami, FL. Data Source: Infogroup 2010 Business Listings, provided as part of ESRI Business Analyst software.

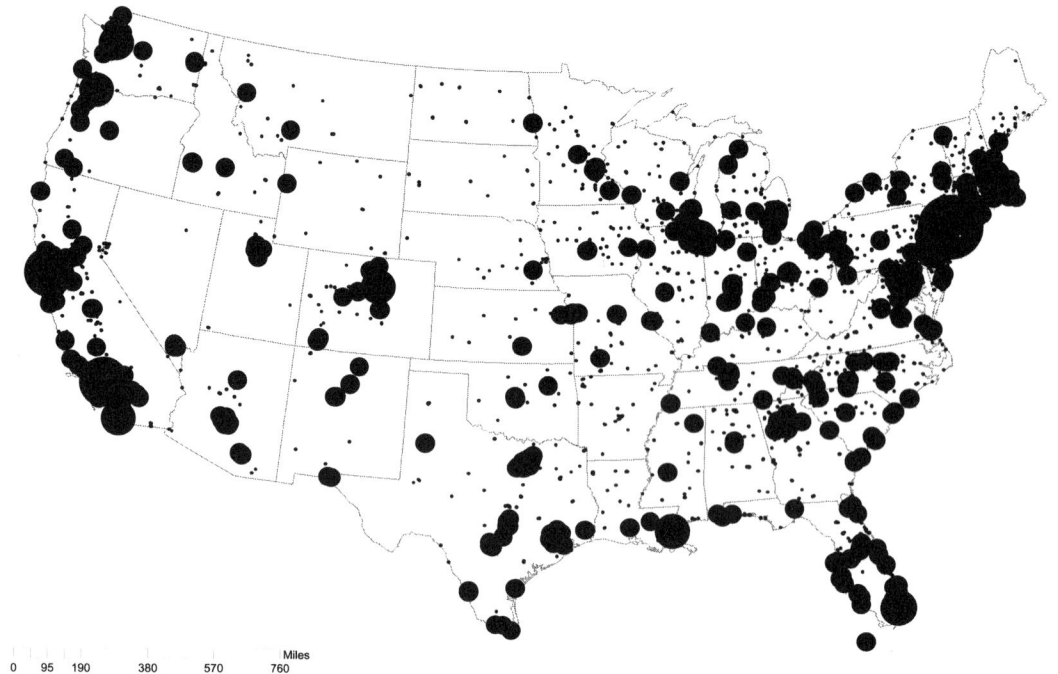

Figure 10. Retail clusters in the United States. Data Source: Infogroup 2010 Business Listings, provided as part of ESRI Business Analyst software.

amenities is unevenly distributed. Across the whole country, only 14.76% of the population lived within a 15-minute walk (1,000 meters) from at least one of these retail clusters.[9] Of all US residents, 56.53% had at least one cluster within 3 miles of their home, and 19.07%—a larger share than those who have one within a 15-minute walkshed—didn't have any retail clusters within 10 miles of their home, attesting to the large numbers of low density suburbs, exurbs and rural areas around the country.[10] Only 1 in 6.7 people was able to conduct errands, meet friends, or spend a weekend amid street commerce on foot, without having to rely on a car or transit system for getting there.

Table 2 shows the share of the population that lives within a 15-minute walk from a retail cluster in all US cities with populations larger than 350,000. The city with the highest proportion of residents within a 15-minute walk from at least one retail cluster is, unsurprisingly, New York City (88%), followed by San Francisco (84%), Boston (69%), Miami (67%), and Honolulu (62%).[11] Convenient pedestrian access to street commerce in these cities reflects their density and age, as well as an urban form that predates the automobile. In Manhattan—the densest of the five New York City boroughs—all residents (100%) have a retail cluster within a 15-minute walk from their home.

Table 2. Percent of population living within 1,000 meters of at least one retail cluster of more than 25 establishments in cities with populations over 350,000 inhabitants.

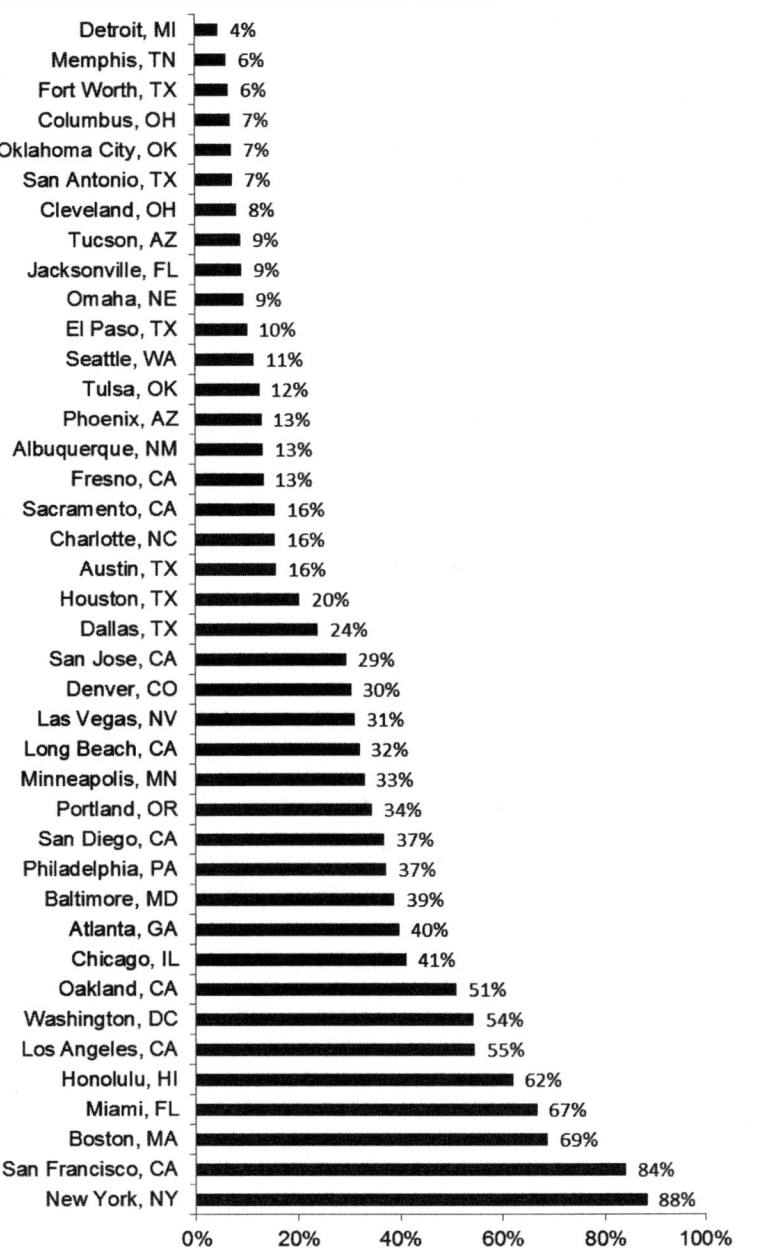

The benefit of living close to retail clusters is also demographically skewed. Whites outnumbers all other racial groups within a 15-minute walkshed around retail clusters (51% of the total). But this is largely due to the overall dominance of the white population in the United States (74%). When examined proportionately, within each group, a different picture emerges. Of all residents who identified themselves as Asian in the 2010 census, 30.5% lived within a 15-minute walk from a retail cluster, followed by "other" (23.6%), Hispanic (22.3%), and Pacific Islanders (19.9%). Among those who identified themselves as "white," only 12.6% lived within walking distance of a retail cluster. Access to street commerce, relative to the racial breakdown of the US population, is therefore highest among the Asian and Hispanic populations. The relatively low share of whites near retail clusters probably reflects white flight from inner cities, suburbanization, higher car ownership, and racial segregation over the course of the 20th century. At the same time, a higher share of minority populations near retail and service amenities could also reflect cultural preferences of living in ethnic communities, close to amenities.

In order to test how well Zipf's Law captures the actual distributions of retail clusters in American cities, we need to first explore the size of the largest cluster in each city. This will provide a benchmark to see whether smaller clusters follow according to an exponential frequency increase, as Zipf predicts. To do so, I have broken down all US cities into seven population brackets, using Jenks' natural breaks, which finds the best arrangement of city sizes into a given number of groups (Table 3).[12] The first bracket is formed of only the two largest cities in the country—New York and Los Angeles. But each successive bracket includes more cities. For example, the fourth bracket, which contains populations between 173,514 and 439,040 people, has 85 municipalities, including Virginia Beach, VA, and Atlanta, GA. I have measured the size of the largest retail and service cluster in each of the roughly 1,000 cities that fall into these seven brackets, shown in the fifth column of Table 3. A cluster must have at least 25 members and each member must be no more than 100 meters from at least one other member in that cluster.

The share of all businesses in the largest cluster in town varies considerably. In the largest cities, the dominant retail cluster tends to absorb a larger share of all businesses in town. On average, 24% of retailers in the first tier made up of New York and Los Angeles are located in the largest downtown agglomeration. In tier-two cities, this share drops to 6%, and in tier-three cities to 5%. But the proportional size of the largest retail cluster also tends to be bigger in smaller towns, where the largest cluster is sometimes the only cluster in town. In tier-seven cities, which have fewer than 14,000 inhabitants, 29% of all commerce is found, on average, in the largest cluster.

Table 3. Average share of all retail establishments contained in the largest retail cluster across US cities in seven population brackets.

Population tier	Minimum population	Number of cities	Example cities	Average max. cluster share	Std. dev. max. cluster share
1	3,792,621	2	New York, NY; Los Angeles, CA	24%	14%
2	790,300	11	Chicago, IL; Houston, TX	6%	8%
3	439,041	23	Columbus, OH; Fort Worth, TX	5%	8%
4	173,514	85	Virginia Beach, VA; Atlanta, GA	4%	3%
5	55,081	359	Overland Park, KS; Garden Grove, CA	10%	11%
6	14,538	609	Bowie, MD; Elyria, OH	18%	18%
7	243	502	Greece, NY; Tenafly, NJ	29%	21%

These averages also conceal a great deal of variation between individual cities, as the standard deviations in Table 3 suggest. Across different population tiers, deviations among individual cities from the tier-wide mean is typically as large as the mean itself, suggesting that tier averages are not necessarily useful for predicting the sizes of largest clusters in specific cities—a nuance that partly accounts for why some cities appear to have more vibrant street commerce than others.

Part of these deviations are explained by the morphological differences between cities. For instance, the proportional size of the largest retail cluster particularly depends on the density of the city. Denser cities, which are typically older and less car-oriented, tend have larger primary retail clusters with respect to their size than less dense cities. In other words, denser cities have more robust commercial downtowns.

Table 4 lists the largest cluster sizes for 10 specific cities—2 from each of the five largest population tiers. The left side of the table shows the primary cluster size for the largest *dense* city in each population tier—a city with a higher than average population density. The right side of the table shows the largest *sparse* city in each population tier—a city with a lower than average population density in that tier. In denser cities, the relative size of the largest cluster tends to be bigger. In New York City, which has an average population density of around 22,000 people per square kilometer, 33% of all stores are found in the largest cluster. Included within this massive cluster is a 32-block district of big boxes and shopping centers around Penn Station.[13] In Los Angeles, which is also a tier-one city, but which has a considerably lower average population density (8,484 people per square mile), the largest cluster only contains 14% of the city's commerce. A similar pattern holds in smaller cities. Among the second-tier populations, the largest retail cluster in Chicago, IL, which is a relatively dense city, contains around 7% of all retail and service amenities in the city. Chicago grew around railroads rather than automobile highways, which gave it a denser and more walkable urban form. In Houston, TX, which falls into the same population tier but has a considerably lower population density, only 1% of all retail and service amenities in the city are found in the largest cluster. I will explore the effect of density on retail patterns more in the next chapter.

Having worked out a way of defining retail clusters and having measured the sizes of retail clusters in each city, we can come back to Zipf's Law, which describes the rank versus frequency rule of retail clusters in a city. Zipf's Law predicts how frequently we should expect to see large, medium, and small clusters in cities. Just like with the most frequently used words in the English language, it predicts that the most commonly encountered cluster—the smallest retail agglomeration—should occur about twice as frequently as the second most commonly encountered cluster, about three times as frequently as the third most commonly encountered cluster, and so on.

Listing and ranking each city's retail clusters by their sizes allows us to test how closely their rank-size hierarchy corresponds to Zipf's Law. This can be done by plotting the natural log of clusters' rank to the natural log of their size and fitting the results in a scatter plot. The better the resulting scatter plot fits to a linear trend line, the closer the fit to Zipf's Law.

For instance, Table 5 lists the actual ranks and sizes of retail clusters in Virginia Beach, VA, where 13 clusters were found. The logarithms of cluster ranks are then plotted on the vertical axis in Figure 11, with the logs of cluster sizes on the horizontal axis. The fact that the rank-size pattern conforms quite closely to a linear

Table 4. Percentage of all retail establishments found in the largest retail cluster of the city. The left side of the table shows the largest city in each population bracket with a higher than average population density. The right side of the table shows the largest city in each population bracket with a lower than average population density in that bracket.

DENSER				*SPARSER*			
City	Tier	Pop/ sq. m	Biggest cluster	City	Tier	Pop/ sq. m	Biggest cluster
New York, NY	1	28,211	33%	Los Angeles, CA	1	8,484	14%
Chicago, IL	2	11,883	7%	Houston, TX	2	3,842	1%
Boston, MA	3	13,943	36%	Columbus, OH	3	3,960	2%
Miami, FL	4	12,645	4%	Omaha, NE	4	3,517	2%
Portland, ME	5	3,141	21%	Jacksonville, NC	5	1,457	4%

Table 5. Retail cluster sizes and ranks in Virginia Beach, VA.

Rank	Log(rank)	Size	Log(size)
1	0	110	2.041393
2	0.30103	96	1.982271
3	0.477121	91	1.959041
4	0.60206	48	1.681241
5	0.69897	34	1.531479
6.5	0.812913	33	1.518514
6.5	0.812913	33	1.518514
8	0.90309	32	1.50515
9	0.954243	31	1.491362
10.5	1.021189	27	1.431364
10.5	1.021189	27	1.431364
12.5	1.09691	25	1.39794
12.5	1.09691	25	1.39794

trend suggest that the hierarchy of retail centers in Virginia Beach can be well anticipated with Zipf's Law. There are many more small retail clusters than large ones. This relationship holds in all cities—the sizes of retail clusters are always exponentially distributed, with few relatively large retail clusters but many small agglomerations.[14]

There is thus a remarkable consistency in the organization of retail establishments in cities. Not only do metropolitan areas have a predictable number of stores, which can be derived from their population, but the way in which these stores are arranged into hierarchical cluster sizes is also astoundingly regular. Instead of distributing around equally sized centers or single mega-centers, retail, food, and service establishments sort themselves into predictable hierarchical constellations, just like cities within countries or words within languages.

Uniqueness of Retail Clusters at the Micro Scale

Every once in a while, I go on a trip with my family to discover new towns in America. This mostly means getting in a car in Boston and driving out to some new place in Vermont, New Hampshire, Rhode Island, or western Massachusetts. We usually go on day trips where we walk around a town, step into a museum or park, and grab a meal at a local restaurant or diner. Sometimes, I fly to a further destination—Los Angeles, Chicago, Savannah, Seattle, New Orleans—and tack a few extra days onto a conference trip. Like many other newcomers to this country, these trips help me discover how vast and varied the United States really is.

Whenever I get to a new place, one of the first things I do is look up where the main amenity clusters are. In a small town, I look up where the main street

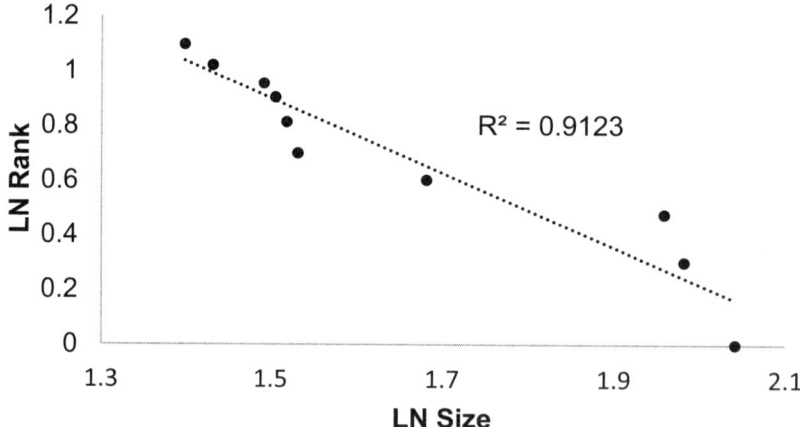

Figure 11. Scatter plot comparing the rank-size distribution of retail clusters in Virginia Beach to the linear relationship predicted by Zipf's Law.

or the downtown areas are on Google Maps. In a bigger city, I might read up on the character of different neighborhoods from travel blogs, contact friends who are more knowledgeable about the place, or talk to the front desk at the hotel. Personal recommendations usually end up being the best.

Every town is different, entirely unique at first glance—the buildings along main streets are never the same, businesses tend to have a distinctive character, and the streets, squares, and public spaces that glue the buildings and amenities together all boast local particularities. The triangular Main Street and town square in Keene, NH, feels so different from the T-shaped downtown of Concord, MA. The curved Dock Square and Ocean Avenue that trace the shape of a question mark in Kennebunkport, ME, stand apart from the grid of historic streets in Savannah, GA. Running errands in Los Angeles and New York couldn't feel more different. And Pike Place market in downtown Seattle, WA, feels surprisingly more European than many East Coast centers. How do we explain this, having just encountered that retail patterns across cities are actually quite predictable?

The macro scale regularities of street commerce we encountered above represent trends—correlations between metropolitan populations and the number of amenities they contain, and linear relationships between the logs of ranks and the logs of sizes of retail centers across cities. But it is important not to mistake trends with particularities found in individual cities. While the overall pattern of retail clusters in a city exhibits regular rank-size properties, there is considerable variation among particular places. At the micro scale—a perspective we get when walking along streets and experiencing retail clusters firsthand—unique characteristics are everywhere, not only in architecture, public space, shop-front design, and visitors' characteristics, but also the same rank-size relationships, cluster location patterns, and overall numbers of stores we encountered above.

While a custom fitted trend-line equation for each city confirmed that the rank-size distribution of retail centers is exponential as Zipf's Law predicts (Figure 11), applying the average trend line within each population tier to predict cluster sizes in specific cities produces an over- or under-prediction of 68%, on average.[15] This is because the slope and y-intercept of Zipf's trend line we encountered in Virginia Beach, VA (Figure 11), are not the same in Keene, NH, or Savannah, GA. I explain some of the idiosyncrasies of Zipf's Law in different U.S. cities in greater detail in the Appendix. But what we see here in a nutshell is that cities differ and the way in which their cluster sizes conform to Zipf's Law also differ. Some cities have more street commerce than their population would predict, some less. And even though almost all cities have a hierarchical system of retail clusters with few big ones and lots of small ones, the exact balance of this hierarchy, which the Zipf's trend lines describe, varies widely among individual cases.

Despite the impressive "average" fit between metropolitan populations and the number of commercial amenities we saw in Figure 1, a closer examination of even that trend with actual population and establishment numbers reveals considerable scatter around the trend line. Figure 12 shows the same average trend line as Figure 1 but presents the same axes with anti-logged population and retail numbers in core based statistical areas (CBSAs) with populations between 250,000 and 500,000 residents. All MSAs in Figure 12 that fall above the trend line have more establishments than the national average trend would predict. Some of them a lot more. For instance, San Luis Obispo-Paso Robles CBSA in California has around 3,800 retail, food, and service establishments, while its population would only suggest around 2,500. Myrtle Beach CBSA in South Carolina has around 5,750 retail, food, and personal service amenities, while the trend line would predict 2,500— less than half of what is really there. Both towns have strong tourist economies, enabling their businesses to sell to a much larger clientele than their own populations would suggest. San Luis Obispo-Paso Robles is part of California's wine country, attracting hundreds of thousands of visitors each year. Myrtle Beach attracts hordes of tourists with its beautiful sandy shores.

But while both of these qualities have a lot to do with natural geography that has gifted these areas the climates to support grapes and sandy beaches, and human geography that has installed considerable amounts of wealthy populations nearby to visit them, conscious planning and development efforts have also capitalized upon these advantages in both metropolitan areas. Natural waterfronts and fertile soils are not enough to lure in tourism—a beach economy requires considerable investment to provide access to the beaches, infrastructure around beaches, and the lodging and amenities that make beach tourism attractive. Myrtle

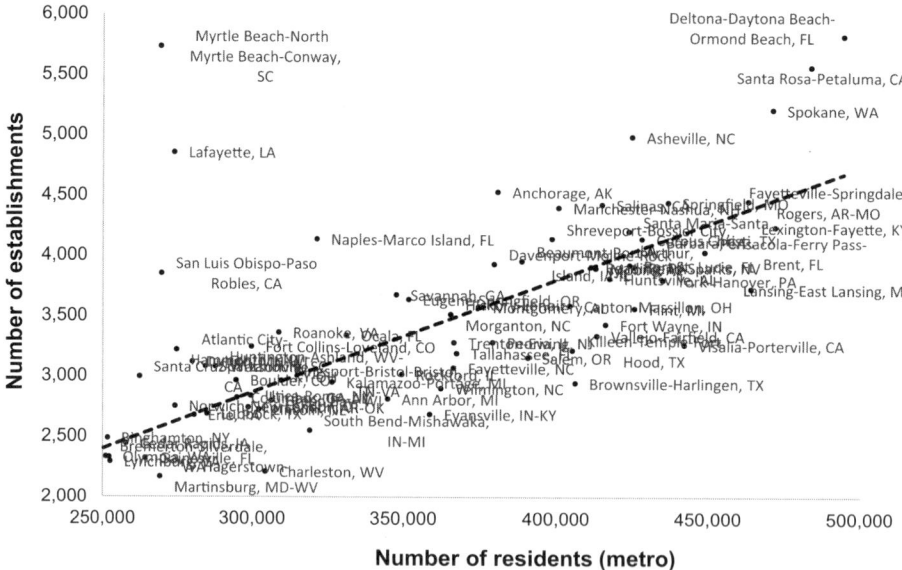

Figure 12. Relationship between the number of residents and the number of retail, food, and service amenities in US metropolitan statistical areas with populations between 250,000 and 500,000 inhabitants.

Beach has plenty of these—golf courses, amusement parks on the waterfront, charming main streets with ample sidewalks, and lots of hotels. Similarly, it took considerable effort to turn the fertile soils in California into wineries and to build the corresponding infrastructure and amenities that support a tourist economy around wine. In both cases, economic strategy, planning, and policy have played a key role in developing tourist economies, which in turn have led to generous provisions of street commerce that caters to populations much broader than are found within the MSA boundaries.

Denser cities tend to have proportionately larger downtown retail clusters, but urban density, too, is not a naturally occurring quality that results purely from the location and history of a town. Cities that actively promote higher-density developments through conscious zoning rules, growth-boundaries, or investments into public transit systems achieve higher densities of development and consequently end up having larger dominant retail clusters. Cities that promote public transport and active mobility on foot or by bike incentivize active streetfront commerce around transit stations and disincentivize dispersal of retail amenities into far-flung suburban malls.

Even though all cities and metropolitan regions are, to some extent, held captive to the regularities of retail distribution that scaling laws describe, conscious efforts have led some cities to develop more amenities than others, generate larger downtowns or subcenters than their mere population would predict, or make street commerce more accessible on foot and by public transit to a greater share of their population than others.

Cities can deploy an arsenal of strategies, policies, and tactics to make their retail patterns bigger, better, and more diverse than their population size, geography, and history would suggest. These opportunities are precisely what interest planners. But capitalizing on them is not necessarily up to the city governments and planners alone. Sometimes the initiative emerges from business owners, business associations, or the communities that care about street commerce. Yet opportunities to improve street commerce—to make it more inclusive, economically broad-based, beautiful, or walkable—are present in every town and community.

The chapters that follow examine the various factors that shape both the macroscopic pattern of retail landscapes we have encountered in this chapter, as well as the microscopic differences that result from geography, climate, place history, and conscious planning. They examine why and how planning, design, and policy really matter, producing benefits for not just store owners, but also the economic, environmental, and social well-being for everyone in a city.

If there is one good lesson from cities where street commerce has either been successfully introduced, bolstered, or reinvented, or where the forces of gentrification have been equitably balanced, it is that successful street commerce almost never emerges or survives as a result of pure market forces. Good street commerce usually represents the fruits of conscious planning choices. City streets do not get better via a laissez faire attitude, where planners, local governments, and regulators take a back seat and wait for the market to play out. Quite the opposite: good streets with diverse retail and service choices, run by diverse owners and serving diverse interests, require conscious planning and management. Sometimes the planning is done by forward-looking city governments, which coordinate policies and investments that recognize and support healthy commercial streets as central to community vitality. In other cases initiative stems from citizen groups and civil society organizations. Entrepreneurs and the business community also sometimes see a need for coordination and joint action and urge public officials to support street commerce via zoning, incentives, or capital investments. In each case, conscious policy, planning, and design play an essential role in transforming the quality of street life and the health of the local business community that lines those streets.

CHAPTER 2

The Survival of Individual Stores

There is a great independent bookstore in the Tiong Bahru neighborhood of Singapore called Books Actually. It was established in 2010 as the first shop on Yong Siak Street, across from a trendy café and a block away from the apartment I lived in while working in Singapore. The neighborhood was otherwise quiet, primarily residential, and known more for its older eateries and small hardware shops run by the area's elderly residents. Yong Siak Street had almost no foot traffic at the time, and Books Actually got a two-year lease for S$3,800 per month. That was a pretty good deal, but it also reflected the dormant character of the street.

Over the next couple of years, Books Actually became a favored weekend destination for young and highly educated Singaporeans, helping to energize the whole street. Other stores and coffee shops followed. Several design firms and two yoga studios set up shop. Younger and wealthier Singaporeans along with foreign expats discovered the neighborhood as an attractive place to live. But two years in, when the first lease was up, the bookstore's rent more than doubled to S$8,000 per month. Even though business was good, such a leap put the store in a difficult position. It wasn't generating enough sales to survive doubled rent. A landmark business that had helped redefine the street, and perhaps the entire Tiong Bahru area, seemed to be falling victim to the gentrification it helped create.

The owners started an online fundraising campaign, appealing to loyal customers—who were more of a fan base—to help keep the shop open. The campaign paid off. Not only did Books Actually generate enough immediate support from its fans to sign a new lease, the media outreach also increased its long-term customer draw, helping generate more visits and higher monthly revenues that could sustain the new rent for a while.

For any retail business to stay in business—whether it sells books, clothes, food, or furniture—it needs to bring in enough revenue to justify a continued existence. In order to survive, Books Actually, just like every other store out there, had to attract a sufficient number of customers to pay off its costs.

To understand how clusters of shops together constitute street commerce, it is necessary to first deconstruct their basic component—the individual store. This chapter explores retail microeconomics and discusses how fixed costs and revenues affect the sustainability of each store. To demonstrate how the inputs required to keep a store in business vary across store categories, I will compare two very different types of businesses—a coffee shop and a taxidermy store—to make a simple but important point: different types of businesses have different customer purchase frequencies and consequently require different-sized market areas to break even. "Market area" is the section of a city from which a shop draws most of its customers.

Using evidence from the 50 largest cities in the United States, this chapter presents the actual, observed ratios of local population per store to show how a complex set of inputs that affect the survival of each individual store produces an urban environment where some types of stores are much more numerous than others. From there, I will discuss two economic models—Central Place Theory and DiPasquale and Wheaton's one-dimensional retail density model—to explore how a number of different factors, working together, limit how many competing stores of the same kind a district can sustain. While these economic models offer a powerful set of predictors for retail density, they are deliberately simplified and idealized. They leave out factors such as price variation, marketing differences, and variable customer densities that also play a role in shaping retail patterns in cities. Many of these factors are impossible for planners and urban designers to alter. But two key factors—population density and transportation—do depend a great deal on the structure of the built environment, which planners and urban designers partially shape and regulate.

Market Areas for Frequently and Infrequently Purchased Goods

In order to stay in business, each store needs to make enough money to cover the costs of its operations.[1] The simple fact that revenues need to exceed costs for a business to stay viable is one of the foundational pillars of all business economics (that only some Silicon Valley tech unicorns seem to evade, though also not indefinitely). In the long run, unprofitable businesses vanish. Staying afloat between upturns and downturns can be a delicate act, especially for retail and service businesses, whose revenues literally depend on the number of people walking in the door but whose costs can constitute a complex structure, depending on the business type, size, and location, as well as a range of market forces that lie well beyond the store itself.

The costs of retail and service businesses can be divided into four parts. First, there are the costs of goods that a store must acquire before offering them to consumers. These costs are called *variable costs*, since they can vary month to month or year to year. Variable costs include furniture for furniture stores, groceries for grocery stores, or ingredients and drinks for restaurants. Store managers continuously submit new orders for supplies with variable costs.

Second are operating space costs. This may include rent, percentage rent—which charges a portion of revenue as rent for the landlord—or loan payments on the space that a business owns. Rent can constitute a significant share of total costs for a business, especially at highly coveted locations. Third are *utility costs* such as electricity, security, cleaning fees, and so on.[2] And fourth, there are *labor costs*—salaries and wages for workers, including a cut for the business owner.[3] Taken together rent, utilities, and wages are jointly known as *fixed costs*, since they typically do not vary from month to month and remain rather predictable throughout lease terms and employment contracts. It is really the balance between fixed costs and patronage that determines whether a shop is sustainable and how many competing shops can occupy a market area.

Let's look at an example of a coffee shop to see how these fixed costs stack up. At a good urban location, a typical coffee shop may pay around $8,000 a month in rent for its space and an additional $3,000 a month for utilities and cleaning. Let's say it hires 15 staff. Thirteen are baristas who are paid $12 an hour and work 20 hours a week, and 2 are managers who are paid a bit more—say $20 an hour while working 40 hours a week. This means that the monthly wage bill comes out at $6,400 for the 2 managers plus $12,480 for the 13 baristas. Adding the rent and utilities, the shop faces a total of $29,880 in fixed costs every month.

Customers come to the shop to purchase coffee or pastries at a certain price. Having acquired the pastries and coffee supplies from a distributor, the shop will then sell the products at a markup to cover the costs of the supplies and fixed costs, resulting (hopefully) in a profit. In our example coffee shop, then, the markup and the quantity of goods sold must be large enough to both pay for supplies and to offset the $29,880 in fixed costs from rent, utilities, and wages it faces each month. If the total purchase receipts are insufficient, the store cannot remain viable for long.

Arriving at the right markup price is key to moving the needle from loss to profitability—adding too little of a markup on coffees and pastries will leave the business in the red at the end of the year. Adding too much can chase customers away. Charging $10 for a coffee that costs 20¢ to make and $20 for a croissant will make even the most bougie customers balk and push stores in most neighborhoods to bankruptcy (perhaps some Silicon Valley neighborhoods aside). In order to break even, enough customers need to show up willing to pay the price.

Say a typical coffee shop customer is willing to spend $4.50 on a purchase and the shop, in turn, uses around 80% of its total proceeds on covering fixed costs.

Figure 13. Carluccio's Café in Hampstead Heath, London, UK. Photo by author.

This means that for every 4.5 dollars that come in, 80%, or $3.60, is used to cover fixed costs. The remainder covers the variable costs of goods themselves. Knowing the amount from a typical purchase that can be directed to covering fixed costs shows us how many purchases are needed to offset the $29,880 in fixed costs every month. The coffee shop needs 29,880/3.60, or 8,300 purchases a month, or around 277 a day, to break even.

Attracting 277 customers a day requires a considerable market area. Among the potential patrons living, working, or passing by the store, there are people who don't drink coffee at all, some that come once in a while, and others who might be regulars. Competing stores around the area may attract some of these customers away. If, say, only 1 in 20 people in the area patronize the coffee shop every day, then it takes a minimum market area of 277×20, or 5,540 people, to keep the shop in business. This is not a terribly large number—a typical subway stop in Boston serves around 20,000 passengers a day, and there may be tens of thousands of residents and jobs within a 10-minute walk from the station.

The number of customers required to sustain a store varies for each type of business. Consider another example, a taxidermy store on Essex Road in London, which runs as an old family business. I used to walk by this store while living in London and each time I passed it, I couldn't help but wonder how large a market area a store selling lifelike mounted animals would need. The store owner already owns the space and so doesn't need to make monthly rent payments. Since there aren't that many customers for stuffed animals, the store can get by with only three employees, who are family members and take shifts. Each of them gets paid £2,000 a month. With utilities, taxes, and fees included, the total fixed costs to run the store come to around £8,000 a month.

Let us assume an average mounted animal costs the store £200 to make. The store owner marks it up to a customer price of £465 in order to recuperate the store's occupancy and labor costs. This means that on average, 57%, or £265, can be used from each receipt to cover salaries and other fixed costs. Now we can see how many customers the store needs to stay in business. In order to break even, it needs £8,000/£265, or 30 customers a month, or just 1 customer a day. That doesn't seem like much. But, then again, there are not a whole lot of people who buy mounted animals.

If only 1 in 10,000 Londoners buys a full-scale mounted animal, and each of them does so once in three years, then how big a market area does the taxidermy store need? Since 1 buyer goes to the store only once in three years, or 365×3, 1,095 days, it takes 1,095 buyers to get at least 1 customer to the store every day. And if 1 out of 10,000 Londoners is a potential buyer, it takes $1,095 \times 10,000$, or 10.95 million people. In other words, it takes the entire population of Greater London to support a taxidermy store, give or take some tourists who might also make an occasional purchase. Even though the taxidermy store needs a lot fewer customers each day than a coffee shop, it requires a much greater market area to stay in business, because people's purchase frequency for stuffed animals is much lower than their purchase frequency for coffee. Following a similar logic, it becomes easy to see why different types of stores require vastly different market areas to stay in business.

A convenient shortcut to approximating how big a market area different types of stores need is to count how many businesses of each type are found in each city, juxtaposing that number with the city's population. This doesn't tell us how many people actually visit the business, but it gives us a rough estimate of population thresholds needed by various trades. Caution should be used in cases where the residential population doesn't reflect the actual potential customer population—in some cities, for instance, the daytime working population is much greater than the city's residential population because a large proportion of workers travel to their jobs from outlying towns. Some cities also attract significant numbers of tourists and visitors, which census data will omit. The opposite can also occur—towns that serve as commuter suburbs around larger cities have populations who spend much of their disposable income outside their own town. But on average, comparing the number of stores in each category with the town's population can give us a reasonable approximation of necessary market areas.

Figure 14. "Get Stuffed" taxidermy store on Essex Road in the Islington borough, London, UK. Photo by author.

Using data from a 2010 national business database,[4] Figure 15 matches retail and service businesses with the corresponding 2010 city population according to the US federal census. The resulting ratio shows the median number of residents per business establishment among the 50 most populous US cities in 2010.

Businesses that require the fewest residents are found at the bottom of the table. Restaurants and other eating places constitute the most common components of urban commerce in US cities—one establishment is typically found per every 445 residents. If you look around the city you live in, you will probably encounter restaurants, coffee shops and bars, convenience stores, and grocery stores most often. They might be called different names in different countries—a *toko* or *warung* in Indonesia, a *marché* or *brasserie* in France, a *bodega* or a *diner* in the United States—but we find them in cities of any size because food and drinks are some of the most frequently obtained goods and services out there. Most of us eat three meals a day, and even if we don't do it at restaurants or coffee shops often, an urban population collectively generates a lot of demand for food-related businesses.

But you are probably not going to run into many taxidermy stores, furniture stores, or art dealerships, unless you happen to live next to one of their rare clusters—a phenomenon I will come back to in the next chapter. Most of us don't buy mounted zebras, couches, or paintings very often. We certainly do so much

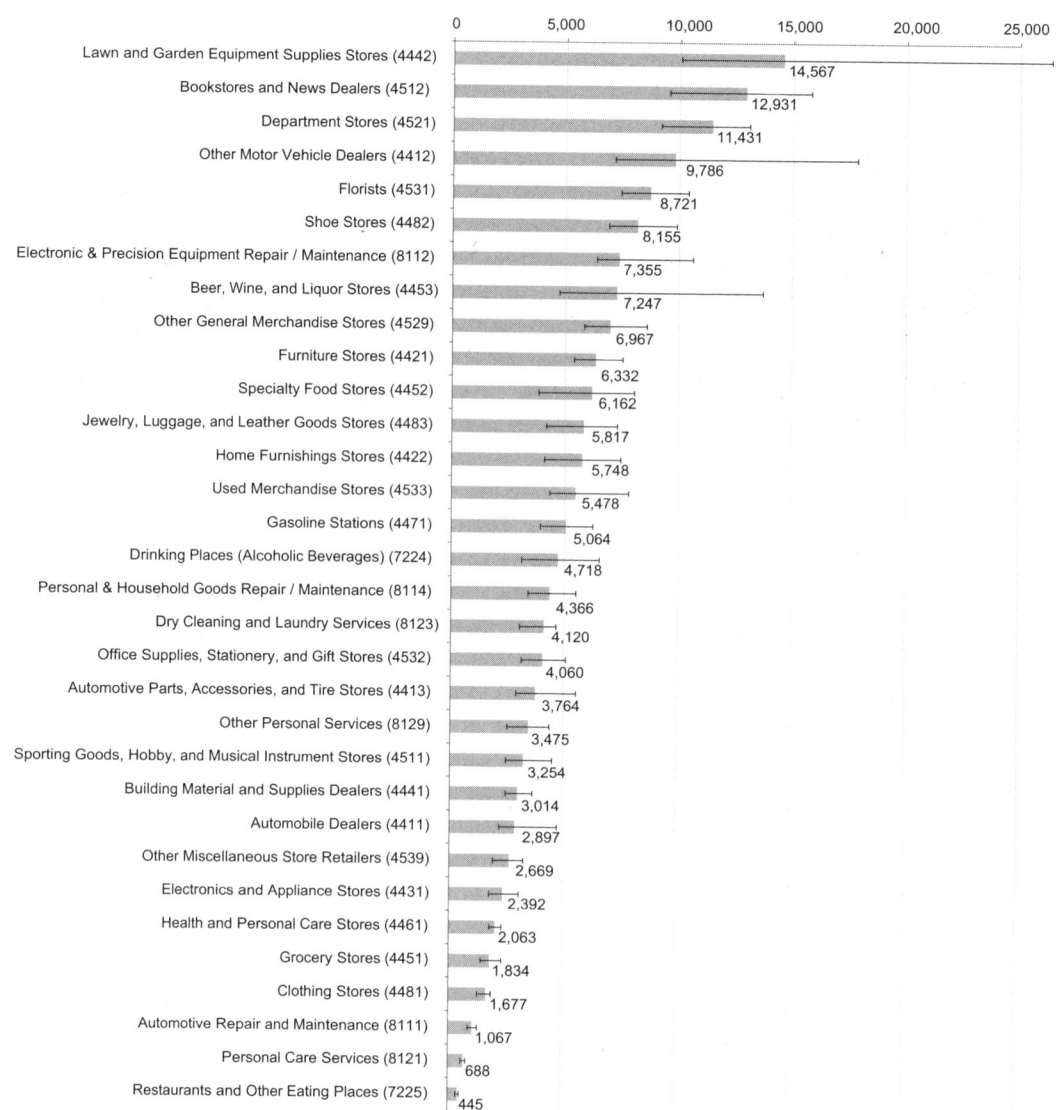

Figure 15. Median number of residents per store among the 50 most populous US cities in 2010. Numbers in brackets after each business category correspond to NAICS codes. Data Sources: Infogroup 2010 Business Listings, provided as part of ESRI Business Analyst software; US Census 2010.

less frequently than we buy coffee or go out to eat at restaurants. Consequently, in a typical American city, there are around 14 times more food service establishments than furniture stores.[5]

The top of the chart shows businesses that need the most residents to break even. These include lawn and garden equipment supply stores (one per every 14,567 residents) and department stores (one per every 11,431 residents). Such establishments are either infrequently patronized or, in the case of department stores, face high fixed costs. Sadly, even bookstores and news dealers are increasingly rare in American cities—there is only one per 12,911 residents on average.[6]

Error bars in the chart indicate variability in the median values across cities, showing the 25th and 75th percentile values. A large deviation suggests that the minimum number of residents to support a store varies widely among different cities. This variation can have two sources. First, it depicts real differences in the offerings of goods and services across the 50 largest cities in the United States. Some cities have more furniture stores per capita, others fewer; some punch above their weight when it comes to restaurants, others when it comes to automobile dealers. And second, since the data only show the number of stores in each city without accounting for store sizes, the variation is also partly attributable to differences in shop typologies and floor areas. Cities where more commerce is housed in big-box structures may have fewer retail establishments but not necessarily less retail floor area than cities where stores come in smaller sizes.

Retail trades with the most variability across American cities include lawn and garden equipment stores, automobile and auto parts dealers, gas stations, alcohol stores, and department stores. Differences in the number of gardening stores are likely to be related to climate—cities with dry desert climates or harsh winters and densely populated cities where more families live in apartments have less need for such stores. Variability in car-related businesses reflects differences between cites built before and after the advent of the automobile. Pre-automobile cities tend to be denser and more public transit oriented, generating less demand for cars and related products.

The fact that every business needs enough customers to break even ultimately limits how many stores a city can sustain. If there were no costs involved with operating a business, we could have a café, a taxidermy store, and any other type of business on every city block. But costs are real, and how many customers a store manages to attract matters a great deal. Market areas determine not only whether stores break even and stay in business, as discussed above, but also how many stores of a particular kind can coexist and how closely they might be spaced with respect to their competitors.

Central Place Theory and the Spatial Distribution of Competing Stores

Walter Christaller and August Lösch, a geographer and an economist, first worked out the schematic theory of retail market areas, calling it Central Place Theory, in the 1930s and '40s. They named specialty shops like taxidermy stores "higher order" goods.[7] Higher-order goods and services are rarely obtained because they are either rarely needed or because they are so expensive that only a few can afford them. They consequently require larger market areas to remain viable, and we find fewer of them around.

While purchase frequency is a critical determinant of store density—the number of stores per unit area of land—how frequently people go to stores, in turn, depends on the transportation costs customers face. Going shopping does not come at a zero cost. It takes time to walk to a store, and time has value. Gasoline, maintenance, leasing fees, and car insurance impose costs for those who drive, and metro or bus tickets tax those who take transit. Transportation costs can be perceived differently by different people, but they inevitably affect us all.

Central Place Theory refers to purchase frequency and transportation costs as *thresholds*—the minimum number of patrons a store needs to stay viable, and *ranges*—the maximum distance people are willing to travel to a store. Christaller proposed a schematic that illustrates how a combination of range and threshold leads to a regular hexagonal pattern of minimum market areas and distances between competing stores. Hexagon size is determined by the maximum range of customers and the minimum threshold of a store. Identical stores divide market areas evenly; each store is equidistant from its neighbors, as shown in Figure 16.

Similar stores have similar market areas, but stores with lower purchasing frequency need larger market areas. Bread, for instance, is bought frequently and a relatively small market area will generate enough demand for a bakery to remain viable. If you walk around Paris, where more baguettes are consumed each day than perhaps in any other city in the world, you will indeed find a relatively dense pattern of boulangeries and pâtisseries throughout the city. Kitchen supplies, on the other hand, are bought less frequently and kitchen supply stores require correspondingly larger market areas. You will find many fewer kitchen supply stores in Paris than bakeries.

Christaller demonstrated how market areas of higher-order goods reach across market areas of lower-order goods with an overlapping pattern of hexagons, illustrated in Figure 17. Higher-order centers tend to combine a wider variety of stores, while lower-order centers tend to offer convenience goods that can be supported by a smaller clientele. Part of the genius behind Chiristaller's pattern of overlapping hexagons was to produce a hierarchical distribution of center sizes—few large ones and an exponentially longer list of small ones—similar to Zipf's Law, which came to describe the rank-versus-frequency rule in language a dozen or so years later.

Commercial streets also tend to offer lots of smaller, lower-order retail clusters that serve a neighborhood clientele, alongside a few higher-order centers that serve a regional clientele (Figure 18). And different types of stores require different market areas. A convenience store can get by on customers from a radius of

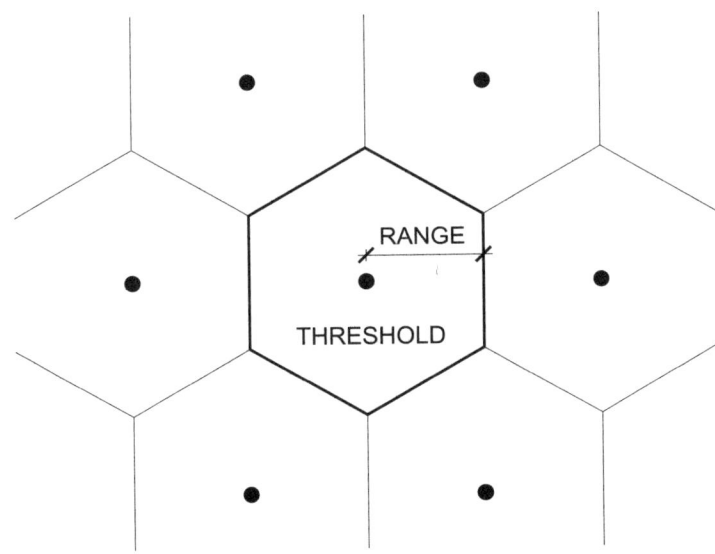

Figure 16. Market areas of identical stores in Central Place Theory.

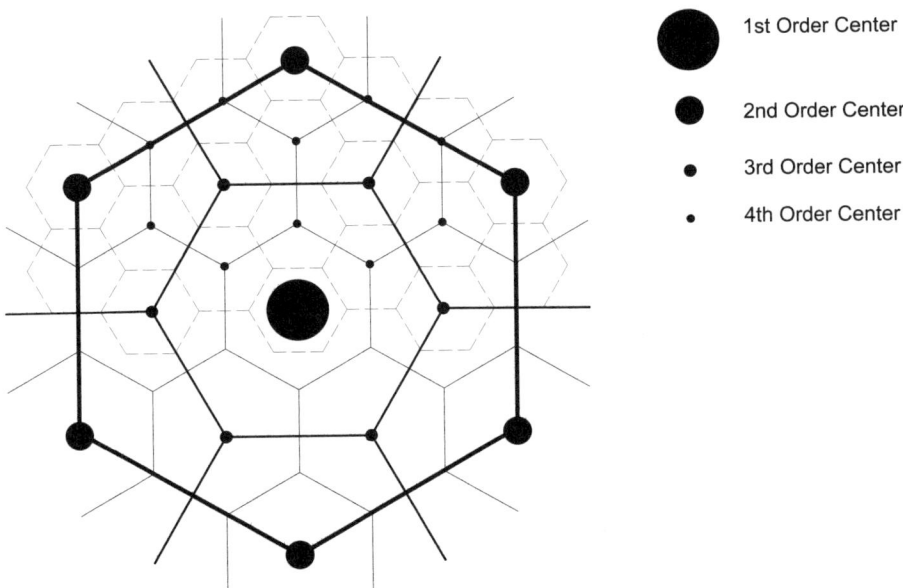

Figure 17. Overlapping market areas of hierarchical centers in Central Place Theory.

a few blocks, while a clothing store may need to attract shoppers from the whole city to cover its costs. A specialty rug store has an even greater market area and may need visitors from the entire metropolitan area to stay in business.

Central Place Theory has inspired a great deal of empirical research. Christaller produced the first assessment of Central Places in southern Germany in his original publication.[8] Similar findings were contemporaneously produced in Estonia by

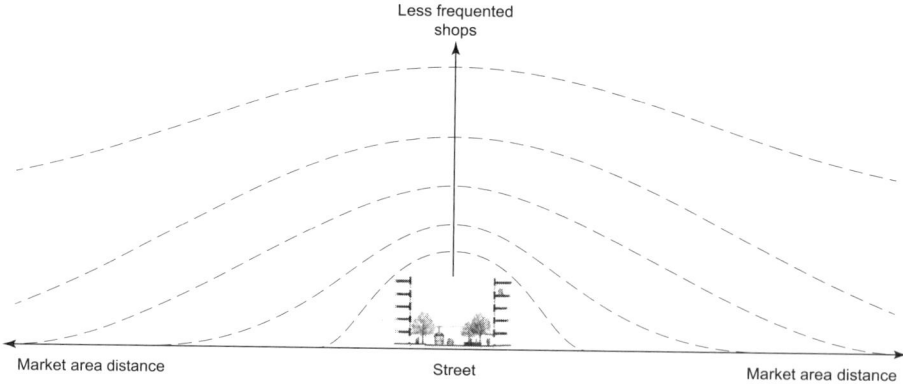

Figure 18. Different stores on a commercial street require different market areas—some extending only a few blocks away, and others covering a whole metropolitan area.

Edgar Kant.[9] Evidence of Central Places in the United States is given by Brian Berry, a University of Chicago geographer, who used data from rural Iowa and urban Chicago.[10] But Central Place Theory has also been criticized because it provides more of a schematic than a robust economic model to understand retail market areas. It didn't come with a clear mathematical formulation and it ignores several factors that the spatial distribution of retailers is known to depend on.

Incorporating Additional Factors

Denise DiPasquale and William C. Wheaton have produced an elegant synthesis of additional variables affecting the density of competitive retailers.[11] Whereas Christaller's model determined the density of stores on a two-dimensional land area of hierarchical hexagons, DiPasquale and Wheaton's model focuses on the linear density of stores along a single street. Their model assumes that customers are uniformly distributed along the street, as shown in Figure 19, and that competing retailers offer identical products at identical prices.

The model starts with the point of view of consumers. Just as stores have the fixed and variable costs we encountered above, consumers also face costs—not only the prices they pay for goods, but also transportation costs incurred in physically going to stores and inventory costs of storing merchandise at home. The model views shopping frequency as a cost-minimization problem, where consumers are thought to adjust their shopping intervals to minimize both transportation and storage costs.[12]

Costs of storing merchandise at home are proportional to purchase frequencies—when they increase, purchase frequency also increases, all else being equal. For bulky items such as toilet paper, which is costlier to store, people go to the store

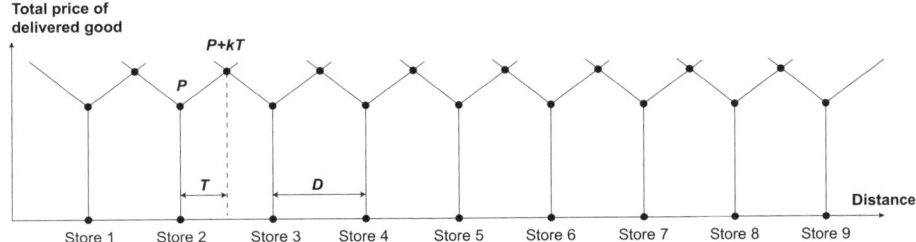

Figure 19. Retail market areas of nine stores along a line in DiPasquale and Wheaton's model.

more frequently than for smaller items, such as toothpaste. Likewise, perishable goods such as dairy products have higher inventory costs than nonperishable items, such as salt or flour. People consequently buy dairy products more often than grains. And shopping frequency is also proportional to annual consumption—the more we consume something per year, the more frequently we buy it, even if storage costs are constant. Most of us go the market more often to buy seafood than French macarons, because we eat fish more frequently than macarons, even though both take up roughly the same amount of shelf space and go bad in two to three days.

Transportation costs work in the opposite direction—the higher they are, the less frequently people go to stores. If you happen to live right next to a supermarket, chances are that you go there much more frequently than folks who have to drive a few miles. By balancing consumption needs, storage costs, and transportation costs, DiPasquale and Wheaton's model arrives at an optimal purchase frequency for any particular good.[14] Consumers are expected to shop at this frequency at the retailer whose total delivered price for the good is lowest—that is, the store that is closest to them.[13]

The most interesting part of the model describes how we arrive at the typical distance between any two competing stores—D in Figure 19.[14] This distance between stores is found as a function of four inputs: frequency of purchase trips, transportation costs, fixed cost for running a retail store, and the density of customers along the street. Without even getting into any arithmetic, the model allows us to see in which direction the distance between stores is bound to move when any of the inputs are changed. This consequently tells us how each factor affects the density of competing stores we encounter in a city.

Purchase Frequency

We already saw how purchase frequency works out with boulangeries and pâtisseries versus kitchen supply stores in Paris—given that most people visit bakeries much more frequently, there are a whole lot more of the former than the latter in

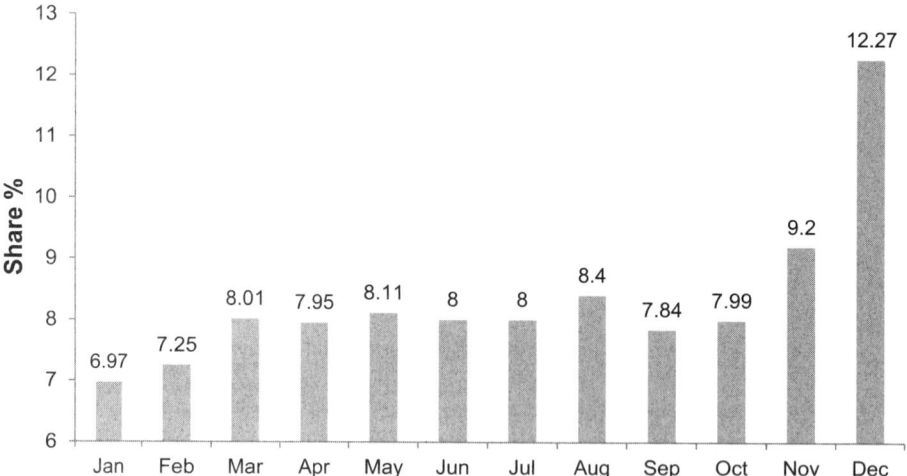

Figure 20. 2011 US monthly retail sales as a percentage of annual sales. Retail sales are defined as general merchandise, apparel, furniture/electronics, and other similar stores. Data source: Niemira, M. P., & Connolly, J. (2012). *Office-worker retail spending in a digital age*. Retrieved from https://www.icsc.com/uploads/t07-subpage/ICSC-Spending-in-Digital-Age.pdf.

the city. Distance between competing boulangeries is consequently smaller. Similarly, there are many more restaurants than art galleries, haircutters than fortunetellers, and newspaper kiosks than rare-books stores.

Demand also varies by time of year. Retail patronage in the United States is strongly affected by holidays, vacations, and even weather. Figure 20 illustrates monthly retail sales in the United States as a percentage of total annual sales. January and February at the start of the year are the least busy shopping months. The US tax year ends in December and people's taxes are due by mid-March. Looming tax payments and the start of a new year contribute to a visible dip in retail sales in the first two months of the year.

December, with over 12% of total annual sales, is the busiest month of the year for shopping. For an average retailer, sales in December are around twice the sales in January. End-of-the-year proceeds are important milestones for covering annual costs and paying off credit lines for many stores. November is the second most important month, partly propelled by the Black Friday sales after the Thanksgiving holiday, when retailers offer steep discounts. A lot of people save their larger purchases for this sale, whether it is for a new winter coat, a flat-screen TV, or a patio grill.

Seasonality of shopping behavior drives many shops to enlarge their inventories for the holiday season and prompts shopping centers and main street associations to organize temporary events and festivals, where the number of stores is temporarily increased with mobile vendors, food kiosks, and pop-ups. This illustrates the principle that higher shopping frequency increases the density of stores.

People's purchase frequencies for specific types of goods are generally very difficult to change, and when they do change, it is rarely a result of actions taken by planners. Purchase frequency depends on cultural habits and marketing dollars, over which planners, urban designers, and policy makers have little influence. However, the remaining three factors in DiPasquale and Wheaton's model—fixed costs of running a store, transportation costs, and buyer density—depend a great deal on policies, plans, and public sector regulations. Because of their importance to planners, I will examine fixed costs, transportation costs, and buyer density at greater length.

Fixed Costs of Running a Business

Fixed costs—the monthly rent, wage, and utility bills—are proportional to the distance between stores, and thus inversely proportional to store density. When it is less expensive to run a store, more stores appear.

In Indonesia, where 72% of employment was in the informal sector in 2015,[15] many food vendors operated out of mobile carts attached to bicycles, called *gerobaks*. A single person can usually run the whole operation alone—cook the food on a portable gas stove attached to the cart, serve drinks, collect payments, and clean the dishes in a bucket on the ground. The fixed costs for a gerobak business are very low compared to those for more permanent indoor shops—there is no rent to pay, utility bills only amount to the cost of cooking gas, and there is only one salary to draw.

Gerobak food vendors go to the city's vegetable markets in the early hours of the day to stock up on vegetables and spices. It is common practice to mark up meal prices around 100% over the cost of raw ingredients. Given that other fixed costs are very low, most of the markup can be used as salary for the operator. This might seem like a large share compared to restaurants in the Global North, where rents and utilities absorb a large part of the markup, but gerobak food prices are also low. A typical meal costs about $1.50 and a single operator might only serve around 30–40 meals a day because competition is high. If fewer than 30 customers a day show up, the business operator doesn't sink into debt over unpaid rent or utility bills; instead, his or her salary suffers. And if daily food supplies are left over, they can usually be used for family back home. This makes gerobak businesses agile and resilient—there is little risk to bear beyond one's own time and salary. The costs of market entry are low, and many who don't have better paying permanent jobs or who have recently migrated to cities in search of opportunity try street vending.

Figure 21. *Gerobak* businesses on wheels and *Pejak* bike taxis in Indonesia. Photo by author.

Just like the one-dimensional model predicts, the low fixed costs of running a food cart have increased their density on Indonesian streets. A 2014 survey of street commerce I conducted with students in Solo, Indonesia, revealed that only 22% of all vendors we encountered in the city center reported paying rent on their space. The remaining 78% either operated a mobile cart or ran their business from a residential structure they lived in or owned. Some of the operators were regulars, who came out daily and occupied a fixed location. Others were irregulars and sold food on streets during evenings, weekends, or on the few days a month when competition looked weak to supplement their regular income from day jobs. This created a vibrant scene with streets and alleys lined with food sellers on almost every city center corner. Central Solo has one commercial establishment per 29 inhabitants—a notably higher retail presence than the more developed setting of Cambridge, MA, for instance, where we find one retail or food establishment per every 90 residents. Residents in Solo have become accustomed to the convenience; they never need to walk more than a block or two to find the nearest food cart, laundry service, or mobile phone crediting service. And the city authorities have come up with a clever way of collecting taxes from nonpermanent street vendors—they send out tax collectors on scooters every day. These mobile tax collectors charge each *gerobak* vendor they encounter about one dollar a

Figure 22. Bleecker Street in New York City. Photo by author.

day. It is an agile taxation model for an agile business—if you are not selling that day, you don't get taxed either.

To support small-scale vendors, Mayor Jokowi, who was later elected president of Indonesia, invested heavily in renovating existing and creating new open-air markets. In an important concession to small-scale market vendors, Jokowi's administration banned the construction of modern retail stores and shopping centers within 500 meters of markets housing traditional vendors (of which there are over 49 in the city) and subsequently passed an act to preserve and protect traditional markets, acknowledging their contribution to the cultural heritage and character of Solo.[16]

At the other end of the fixed-cost spectrum lie high-end retail clusters in the superstar cities[17] of the world. Bleecker Street in Manhattan's famous SoHo neighborhood, for instance, is known as one of New York City's most fashionable shopping streets, sometimes compared to the posh Rodeo Drive in Beverly Hills (Figure 22). Unlike *gerobaks* in Indonesia, businesses on Bleecker Street face very high fixed costs.

Bleecker Street catapulted to world fame in 2000, after the popular TV series *Sex and the City* featured the street's Magnolia's Bakery as part of the fashionable environment where the city's elite women go for cupcakes and coffee. Marc Jacobs opened a clothing boutique on Bleecker and other brands followed—Comtoir des Cotonniers, Maison Margiela, Juicy Couture, Mulberry, Ralph Lauren, etc. Tourist buses started bringing shoppers to the area, and retail rents doubled, tripled, and then quadrupled. Bleecker Street now commands rents around $800 per square foot per year, close to triple the cost of Boston's Harvard Square.

But the rising costs of running a business on Bleecker Street have recently produced an unexpected outcome: high-end blight.[18] Running a store on Bleecker has become too expensive for even big international brands. Without the foot traffic of Fifth Avenue, a series of high-end stores have shut down on the street. Many of them didn't make a profit while they were running anyway; in fact, they lost money. Owners justified running a shop on Bleecker as advertisement value. But the recent wave of retail closures demonstrates that advertisement value has limits—even global brands have decided it is simply not worth it at present asking rents. Most independent stores left long ago—they did not have the deep pockets for advertising. At the same time, landlords appear unwilling to lower their rates, hoping to find new tenants that are willing to meet what they ask. Bleecker Street's astronomical retail leases illustrate what a late-stage gentrification bubble can do—make the fixed costs of running a business too high, and you will end up with no businesses at all.

Policy Innovations to Counter High Fixed Costs

Bleecker Street is not alone in its struggle with commercial upscaling. Rising space unaffordability and an increasing takeover of local businesses by higher-end brands or chain stores does not only affect affluent neighborhoods and historic retail clusters—commercial gentrification is indeed a widespread challenge. Among New York City's five boroughs, the Bronx has the lowest median household income, but it has witnessed the largest increase in evictions of small businesses[19] and the largest percentage increase in the number of chain stores.[20] Commercial gentrification is a topic much less discussed than residential gentrification, but it affects communities in an equally important manner.

Community-oriented independent businesses most commonly close because they cannot afford to pay rent. They are typically replaced with higher-cost stores. Lower-income residents consequently end up traveling to further destinations for cheaper convenience goods, spending a disproportionate share of their income on transportation.

Many cities around the world have implemented inclusionary housing programs to counter the effects of residential gentrification and displacement, and to make sure that inhabitants of all incomes can live in newly constructed buildings. A typical American policy requires that developers of new housing projects set aside 10–20% of units for households whose incomes fall to a level below the area median income (AMI). Affordable rental rates are set so that tenants pay up to 30% of their income on rent. Affordable sales prices are set such that the resulting mortgage and insurance payments do not exceed 30% of the owners' monthly income. Affordable units are only available to households whose income is, for instance, 65% or lower than the AMI. In the United States, the definition of "area" in the calculation is set at the federal level by the US Department of Housing and Urban Development (HUD), which typically uses an area larger than a city (e.g., county) to determine AMI because people often search for housing across municipal boundaries.

Analogous to inclusionary housing programs, we need inclusionary retail programs that support the creation of retail space that serves community interests. Aside from a number of failed attempts in American cities to implement retail rent controls, I am not aware of any city that has implemented such a policy, but I suspect that this lack does not reflect the absence of need but rather the complexity of a potential inclusionary retail policy and its implementation mechanisms. Without discounting significant complexities or claiming to provide a silver bullet, we can nevertheless speculate on the considerations an inclusionary retail policy ought to accommodate.

New developments or conversions of retail space could require that 20–30% of total retail floor area be only rented or sold to qualified shops and services whose rent is limited to a predetermined affordable level. Commercial real estate brokers typically cite 8% as a sustainable occupancy cost ratio—the percentage of total sales revenue spent on occupancy costs—which enables retailers to stay in businesses. In expensive real estate environments, such as New York or San Francisco, businesses often pay 10–20% occupancy costs. Such space costs are rarely sustained in the long run, producing rapid bankruptcies and frequent vacancies among stores.

Just like sustainable housing costs depend on both household income and family size (larger families have more people to feed and are thus expected to afford a lower share of their income on rent), inclusionary retail space costs need to come in a range, depending on the type and profitability of the store. Grocery and other relatively high turnover stores usually generate the lowest margins.[21] Retailers that sell more expensive goods or provide a higher level of customer service command higher margins and are able to pay a larger share of their revenue on occupancy costs.[22] This is why some of the most expensive shopping streets in the world—Fifth Avenue in New York, Brompton Road in the Knightsbridge area of London, and Rue du Faubourg Saint-Honoré in Paris—are lined only with luxury boutiques.

How should it be decided which stores qualify for inclusionary rents and which do not? There are specialty grocers who generate much higher margins than typical convenience grocers, designer hair salons that are much more profitable that a typical hair cutter. One option is to set up an inclusionary business registry, analogous to San Francisco's legacy business registry[23] (see Chapter 4). Entry to the registry could be based on the previous year's business tax documents, which would need to demonstrate the gross margins of the business. Higher-margin businesses can pay a higher percentage on occupancy costs. The list of businesses in the inclusionary registry could be annually reviewed and adjusted. A year or two after profits exceed the limits set by the policy, subsidies should be adjusted.

A further analogy is to "linkage funds" in affordable housing policies, which allow cities to collect slightly higher contributions from housing developers that do not agree to place affordable housing units on site along with market-rate units. Cities could establish linkage funds for affordable retail space. Commercial developers, who do not agree to place affordable retail spaces in newly developed properties, could instead pay a fee to a fund used to construct new inclusionary retail spaces at other locations. Linkage funds should be set at a higher cost to developers than on-site inclusionary space in order to discourage systemic avoidance of affordable retail spaces on site. In addition, linkage funds could be used to subsidize occupancy costs for retail businesses in existing commercial spaces whose construction predates the policy.

Evaluating the performance of such a policy—how successful it is—is tricky. On the one hand, it would be reasonable to set affordability—prices, relative to similar goods and services in town—as a key criterion. The purpose of the policy, after all, is to generate affordable retail and service options for communities.

It is not clear, however, how to guarantee that admitted businesses do indeed deliver relatively affordable goods and services, since prices can be meaningfully assessed only in conjunction with the quality of products and services offered. An affordable organic produce shop is inevitably going to be more expensive than a vendor that sells about-to-expire produce at rock-bottom prices. And a healthy restaurant using regionally grown produce cannot compete on price with unhealthy fast food. Despite higher cost, healthier offerings might be better for a community.

One option would be to have a community board evaluate the "community benefit" of each business in the inclusionary retail registry on an annual basis. Such an evaluation could require on-site visits and potentially rely on public opinion generated by rating platforms such as Yelp.com. But arriving at a fair community benefit rating is likely to be difficult—committee preferences could differ from community preferences.

Another option would be to consider the annual transaction count in the stores. If a store receives more visitors, then it benefits more constituents. Community benefit could be determined by patrons voting with their wallets. An upmarket specialty grocer is not likely to attract a lot of visits in a low-income community, just like a designer hair salon is not likely to attract as many customers as a regular hair salon. Transaction count evidence could be submitted as part of annual accounting to the registry. A comparison to the citywide transactions for similar businesses could be used to gauge if a business is attracting a healthy number of customers or instead providing a luxury service that few desire.

Yet, even transaction counts cannot prove who actually visits the store—at popular locations that draw groups of tourists, most transactions could belong to visitors rather than surrounding residents or workers. Should all visits count equally, or should local residents' and workers' preferences outweigh those of visitors? Worse yet, overall popularity could overshadow smaller but nevertheless critical businesses that serve minority populations who cannot compete on volume—pharmacies are critical to elderly residents, ethnic grocers to ethnic communities, multilingual tax accountants to folks that face language and technological access barriers to online tax filing.

More policy innovation is needed to come up with a feasible inclusionary retail strategy. Cambridge, MA, is currently exploring a policy along these lines. Other cities probably are too. Whichever city government can get a fair and reasonable inclusionary retail strategy in place is likely to establish a highly prized tool for maintaining retail affordability and supporting community interests in street commerce.

Transportation Costs

Transportation costs are inversely proportional to the distance between stores in DiPasquale and Wheaton's model. This means that all else being equal, the higher the transportation costs, the smaller the distances between stores and the higher the store density.

What is included in transportation costs varies by mode—travel in cars is affected by gasoline, insurance, parking, sunk costs involved in purchasing a vehicle, and vehicle taxes; Uber, Lyft, or taxi rides include fees and city taxes; trips on public transit include ticket costs and walking to and from transit stations; and pedestrian trips mostly cost time. Time is, in fact, a major cost item in any urban transportation mode, affecting driving, public transit, walking, and biking alike. Because of time, getting around on foot in low-density cities such as Phoenix, AZ, where trip origins and destinations are far apart, is typically much more expensive than driving—covering five miles on foot takes hours, whereas cars on a highway can breeze through the same distance in minutes.

While it may be rational to own a car in Phoenix, travel costs per mile are not always cheaper—transportation cost on different modes also depend on trip distances. For very short trips (e.g., half a kilometer), walking is usually the most economic option. This is shown in Figure 23, where the most economic travel

52   Chapter 2

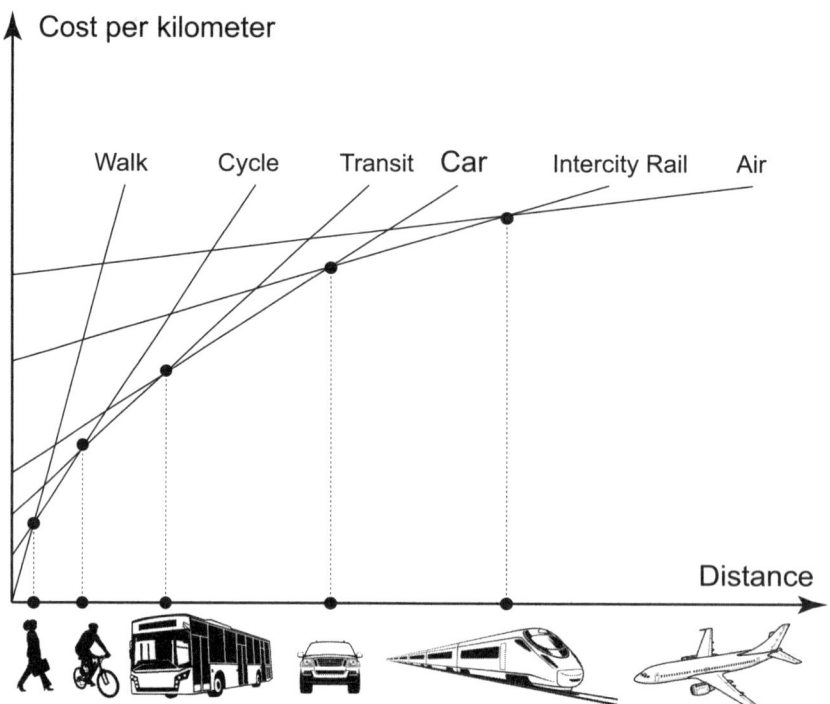

Figure 23. The most economical travel mode at different trip distances.

mode is highlighted on the horizontal axis under different distance intervals. For slightly longer trips, cycling and public transit become more cost efficient per mile (assuming their infrastructure is in place). At even longer distances, driving by car becomes more economical, until it is overtaken by intercity rail or air travel on even lengthier trips.

Given that mode choice for individual trips depends on distance, Figure 23 also suggests that a city's *transportation mode share*—the total percentage of home-work-home trips (or sometimes measured for all trips) taken on different transportation modes—depends on typical distances imposed by the structure of a city. The further apart homes are from jobs and amenities the more likely people are to resort to car-based commutes. These distances, in turn, depend on a city's urban form and land use pattern.

The three-way relationship between urban density, transportation mode share, and retail density is visualized in Figure 24. The left-hand side of the diagram depicts how dense urban form, highly mixed land use patterns, and multimodal mobility systems encourage shorter trips and a higher pedestrian and public transit mode share. A larger share of pedestrian and transit trips, in turn, helps generate higher retail density, where more stores can be accessed on foot and by public transportation.

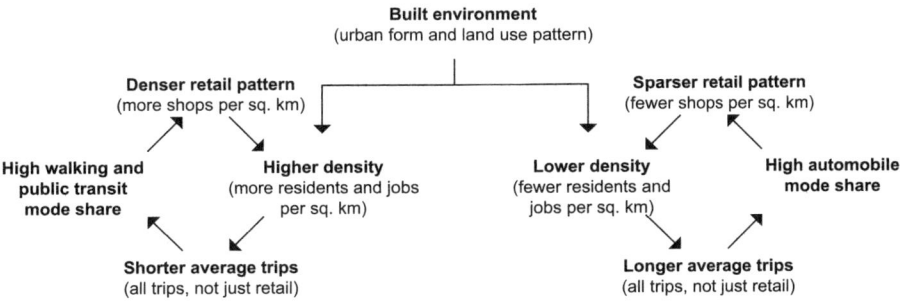

Figure 24. Relationship between urban density, transportation, and retail density.

The right-hand side depicts how in lower-density cities, where trip origins and destinations are spread far apart and transportation infrastructure encourages driving, average trip distances are longer and the automobile mode share is higher. Cities that follow the right-hand side cycle produce lower retail densities, with more shops concentrated in car-oriented shopping malls.

For the majority of residents to choose to walk, bike, or ride on public transit, two fundamental prerequisites have to be in place. First, urban density has to be fairly high so that average commuting distances are short. And second, quality infrastructure for pedestrians, bikes, and public transit needs to be in place. Transportation supply often induces demand—if a city offers high-quality public transportation that connects places faster and cheaper than a car, then people are willing to ride it. Similarly, when a city has lots of destinations close by and offers high-quality sidewalks, bicycle lanes, and road crossings to connect them, people are willing to walk and bike.

Cities such as New York, San Francisco, London, Paris, Tokyo, and Zurich demonstrate that with both of these prerequisites in place, not only do people who cannot afford a car walk or ride transit, but everyone does, including the wealthy and the privileged. Among workers who live and work in Manhattan, for instance, 53% get to work on foot, bicycle, or taxi,[24] 35% take the subway, 7% take the bus, and only 5% drive.[25] A high pedestrian mode share has little to do with income—close to half of all Manhattanites, whose area median income is a staggering $93,000 a year, walk to work. And Manhattan is not an outlier. In a number of other high-density mixed-use cities, where all modes are comfortably offered, the majority of trips are short and take place on foot, with slightly longer trips using public transit or bike. Cars are reserved for long and otherwise cumbersome journeys that may involve carrying bulky items.

On the other hand, in Los Angeles, which is a sprawling city with a far lower density than New York, 80% of workers drive a car to work, 10% take transit, 3% walk, and the rest take cabs, motorcycles, or work at home.[26] The density of retail establishments is consequently also much lower in Los Angeles—26 establishments per square kilometer—than in New York City, where we find 142 retail and service establishments per square kilometer.[27] A heavier reliance on car-based travel decreases retail densities and spreads everything in cities out—housing, jobs, land values—and shops are no exception. Yet even Angelenos are presently investing unprecedented sums into public transportation and walkability improvements in an effort to shift Los Angeles County's mode-share toward higher public transit ridership.[28]

To see how a change in urban infrastructure can lead to a change in transportation mode share, which in turn leads to a change in a city's retail landscape, consider the example of Tallinn, the capital city of Estonia, which I visit a few times a year to see my family.

In the early 1980s, while still under Soviet occupation, Estonians had 85 cars per 1,000 inhabitants. Car ownership was strictly limited through a centrally planned economy, and the vast majority of trips took place on foot and by transit. Retail activity in Tallinn was concentrated in the city center along radiating arterial streets and transit hubs. Stores were generally small and distributed among numerous neighborhood centers. The only shopping center was a five-story department store in the city center, surrounded by public transit options.

With the collapse of the Soviet Union in 1991, the country regained its independence and adopted a capitalist market structure. As access to wealth and opportunities expanded, people started buying more cars. A lot more cars. At the same time, the state and city governments started investing much of their transportation budgets into new road infrastructure, leaving trains and buses behind. For a while, during the mid-1990s, informal jitneys (minibuses or station wagons carrying 5–12 passengers) popped up, filling the void in supply created by a failing public transit system. I remember jitney rides to school, where you had to pay a couple of crowns cash to the driver to enter. The price changed month to month and there were no prepaid passes.

Tallinn had a rich legacy of light- and heavy-rail transit systems. The city's light-rail network was over 110 years old in the early '90s. Heavy-rail lines connected a number of southern and eastern suburbs to the main train station—Baltic Station—while light-rail lines fanned out of the city center in four directions. Both systems fell into decay during the transitional 1990s. Light rail, which passed through the denser areas of the city center, never stopped operating, even though its rolling stock and tracks were out of date and in desperate need of repair. Inspired by Thatcherian policies in the UK, heavy rail was privatized, leading to little or no new investment in trains. For a period during the city's most rapid expansion, suburban rail lines were entirely decommissioned.

Survival of Individual Stores 55

Figure 25. Rocca al Mare shopping center in Tallinn, Estonia. Photo by Andres Haabu, Äripäev.

Meanwhile, Estonia's car ownership rate increased sixfold in 25 years compared to 1980 levels. By 2015 there were over 520 cars per 1,000 people in Estonia, more than the EU average. This must be one of the fastest leaps in car ownership Europe has ever encountered. Tallinn city government favored suburban growth and even built suburban roads and utilities on its own dime to incentivize private developers to erect new single-family housing on fields that formerly surrounded the city. Unlike the nearby Scandinavian cities Stockholm and Copenhagen,[29] Tallinn's urban expansion resulting from rapid economic growth was not concentrated along rail corridors leading out of the historic core. On the contrary, new growth was entirely dictated by automotive infrastructure. More than 50% of all trips now take place in private cars, including both driver and passenger trips, and a large portion of residents have moved to outlying suburbs, taking long trips to and from workplaces or schools, which still largely remain in the center.[30]

Such a drastic modal shift in only two decades left a significant imprint on the city's retail landscape (Figure 25). Former small-scale commerce in the center has given way to large, car-oriented shopping centers on the periphery and along major arterial intersections. Storefronts and basement shops in the center have largely vanished, except for souvenir shops and restaurants that primarily cater to tourists in the Old Town. As of 2016, Tallinn had the highest amount of shopping center space per capita (1.35 square meters per person) of any European city.[31] While a number of different socioeconomic trends, foreign investments, and policy choices also contributed to this outcome, the development of car-based transportation infrastructure and a relatively sudden increase in trip distances have played a key role in dispersing the city's commerce.

Tallinn has only recently come to a point where additional car-oriented infrastructure investments are starting to receive widespread public criticism. But an auto-dominated urban development trajectory is hard to change. It not only requires a change in thinking among thought leaders, politicians, and city managers, but also a reversal of institutional culture and business-as-usual behavior at all levels of municipal government. The good news is that several other cities have been at this juncture before and have demonstrated that a reversal of car-oriented transportation development is not only possible but can lead to a number of social, economic, and environmental benefits in the long run. Copenhagen, Stockholm, Zurich, Melbourne, and Munich are but a few examples, where a deliberate shift to a more pedestrian- and public transit–oriented city brought along robust improvements in all of these areas, including greatly expanded commerce throughout their street networks. Robert Cervero's book *The Transit Metropolis* traces some of these precedents in detail.[32]

In Melbourne, Australia, for example, over 70% of all shopping trips take place on foot or transit.[33] This remarkable achievement did not happen by itself. Both the city of Melbourne and the State of Victoria have been promoting collective transportation and active transportation that requires physical exertion for decades, which has gradually shifted automobile commuters toward higher use of public transit, walking, and biking. This, in turn, led to shorter trips and more foot traffic—both prerequisites for street commerce.

In the 1970s, downtown Melbourne, too, was clogged by cars. Residents and jobs alike had started migrating out of the congested city center; the downtown economy and retail streets were hurting. In order to remove unwanted traffic, the city decided to turn Swanston and Bourke Street Mall into pedestrian-only streets, prohibiting vehicles from a key downtown crossing. The city established an identifiable, pedestrian-oriented "core." It adjusted trams to share public space with pedestrians and improved tram frequencies and routes to provide a viable means of arriving downtown without a car. It developed park-and-ride garages near peripheral tram and regional rail stations, while introducing new restrictions for parking in the city center.

As a result of "transit-first" policies, the proportion of all traffic in the city center that drove through without stopping dropped from 52% of all cars in 1964 to only 8% in 1986.[34] A series of urban design improvements, inspired by Danish urbanist Jan Gehl, added footbridges over rail yards, pedestrianized waterfronts, implemented building height guidelines that ensured that streets get sunlight, protected historic facades, and installed new landscaping features all around downtown. These projects and policies were all based on a belief that public transit, public amenities, and good urban design would jointly lure in new private capital to the city center and bring commercial and civic life back to downtown streets.

The initiatives were highly successful. Southbank, along the Yarra River attracted new housing, retail, and office developments, connected by a generous pedestrian waterfront promenade. Zoning gave preference to new full-time residences and new retail instead of high-end investment homes that would have stayed half empty. This helped bring more residents back to the center, whose purchasing power, in turn, bolstered retailers. Over 40% of all downtown workers now take transit to work. Many additional downtown residents walk or bike to work. And downtown streets gradually filled with shops and services. Even the historic back lanes, originally designed as service alleys to cut through the network of city blocks, are now largely populated with small-scale commercial establishments, ranging from cafés, restaurants, and shops to beauty salons and art galleries. Along with vibrant street life and an enviously high public transit and pedestrian mode share, the *Economist* has ranked Melbourne as the most livable city in the world several years in a row.

There are many other examples around the world where transportation policy and investments that favor public transit, walking, and biking have bolstered street life and street commerce. Similar transformations to Melbourne's have occurred in Zurich, Copenhagen, Munich, and Curitiba. Positive examples are not limited to historic cities but can also be found in newer built environments such as Medellin, Singapore, and Perth. Since public transit supports density, mixed-use development, and walking, a high public transit mode share generally correlates with strong street commerce. The impact is greatest if public transit investments are combined with fewer parking spaces, higher building density and use mixing around stations, zoning that supports ground-floor commerce, and pedestrian-friendly urban design on sidewalks. City governments can nudge this process along by facilitating the legal processes involved in land use conversion and streamlining the approval processes with shorter waiting times. And planners, commercial tenants, and civic organizations can rally to organize shop owners along key streets to harmonize opening hours and organize outdoor activities—food festivals, holiday events, car-free Sundays, music events, and so on—that benefit all stores alike.

The examples from Tallinn and Melbourne illustrate how transportation planning and policy are closely linked with a city's retail landscape. Once you start prioritizing vehicular infrastructure, you increase the demand for car-based travel and decrease the density of stores, encouraging car-oriented malls. Prioritizing walking and public transit infrastructure instead can create a positive feedback cycle for street commerce—better sidewalks and transit connections lead to more pedestrians on city streets, which in turn lead to more stores on these streets, which in turn attract more pedestrians to come out on foot.

Customer Density

The third variable affecting the density of competing stores that is closely intertwined with spatial planning is customer density—the number of people per unit length in DiPasquale and Wheaton's model, or the number of people per acre or square kilometer in Central Place Theory and actual built environments. Customer density is also inversely proportional to the distance between stores—when it increases, distances between stores tend to decrease and retail densities increase.

The density of customers in different areas of the city is a particularly important element for urban planners and policy makers since it can be affected, albeit slowly, via planning, zoning, and real estate development. Customer density can be affected by two related factors—how much floor area there is for residents, jobs, or other human activities, and how intensively this floor area is utilized. When built floor area in a district increases, either due to higher structures, larger floorplans, or more densely spaced building footprints, customer density typically goes up. Customer density also goes up when more people cram into existing buildings.

Hong Kong, for instance, has a much higher population density than Singapore. It also boasts a much higher density of shops. In fact, one of the most densely populated neighborhoods of Hong Kong, Mong Kok, has a district-wide population density that easily exceeds 100,000 people per square kilometer. For comparison, the average population density of Singapore is only 7,500 people per square kilometer and the average population density of the Manhattan borough of New York City is around 28,000 people per square kilometer. Mong Kok is one of the densest districts in the world and its retail landscape doesn't disappoint. Not only are street-facing ground floors packed with businesses, commercial space also continues upward to the 2nd, 3rd, 4th, and even higher floors (Figure 26). It is not unusual in Mong Kok to find signs on the street that invite customers to take stairs or elevators up to the 10th floor.

Mong Kok might be an extreme example, but higher-density built environments tend to have correspondingly higher retail densities in all cities. Figure 27 shows the densities of retail establishments in American cities by population density. The relationship is very clear—the higher a city's population density, the higher its retail density as well. I have also added Singapore and central Solo to the chart for comparison.[35] Cities that are above the line exceed the overall trend—Miami, FL, San Francisco, CA, and Cambridge, MA, have a higher retail density than their respective population densities would predict. This may be due to

Figure 26. Mong Kok district of Hong Kong. Photo by author.

several characteristics of these cities—more people walk rather than drive, they have higher than average disposable income per capita, they get more outside visitors and tourists, and they all have grandfathered patterns of commerce that were well-developed before the automobile. Note that the data on retail distribution from cities across the United States in the previous chapter showed that cities with higher population densities also tend to have a larger dominant retail cluster, a proportionately larger downtown, which is not shown on this chart.

The example of Mong Kok demonstrates that built density can, in fact, impact retail density in two related ways. First, higher surrounding built densities with mixed land uses put more potential customers in buildings around a location, which produces more trips to stores and results in a higher store density. This is the more obvious and direct benefit of surrounding residential or job density on retail density. But second, urban density can also produce a higher propensity for walking to other types of destinations in the area—transit stops, meeting venues, parks, and so on—resulting in a multiplier effect for stores. Stores not only get access to more people from nearby offices, homes, and institutions who undertake planned purchase trips, but the occupants of such buildings are also more likely to pass these stores on foot on their other outings, making unplanned impulse purchases more common.

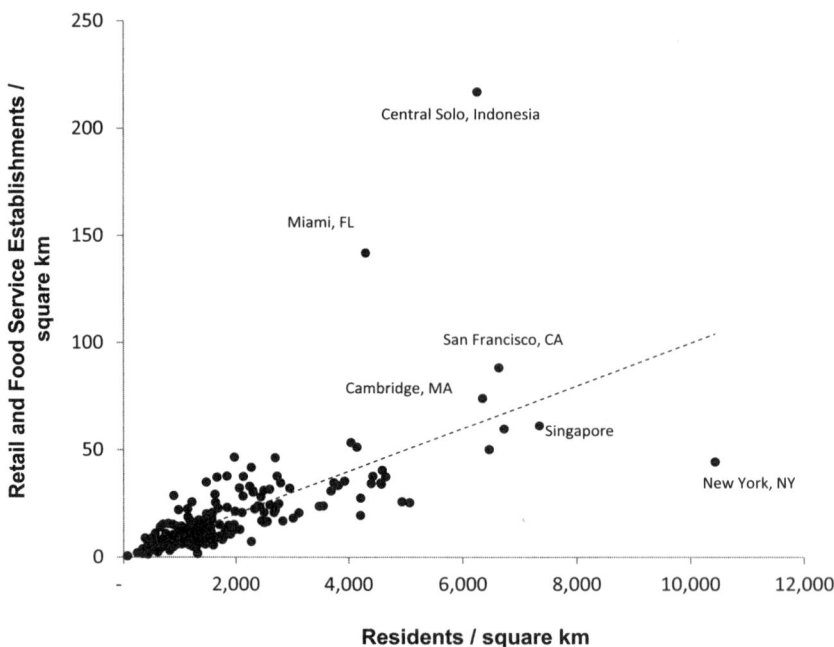

Figure 27. Relationship between retail density and population density in US cities. Solo, Indonesia, and Singapore are added for comparison.

This happens because dense places like Mong Kok don't only generate retail trips, they also make other, non-retail trips more likely on foot. With schools, parks, public institutions, or transit stations nearby, many people are willing to forgo the car and simply walk to these destinations. This is evidenced by crowded sidewalks in dense built environments, such as Manhattan, Brooklyn, Boston, Washington, or the downtowns of San Francisco, Seattle, Denver, and Los Angeles, as well as dense European or Asian city centers. Streets with higher overall pedestrian activity generate further unplanned or "impulse" purchases for stores situated along them. A 2012 survey of office workers' shopping habits conducted by the International Council of Shopping Centers, a global trade association of the shopping center industry, showed that workers in denser environments with a wider variety of retail offerings spent three times more on food and shopping than workers who had limited nearby retail options.[36] The more shops we walk by, the more likely we are to spend at one.

Most people who walk to shops come from homes, workplaces, or transit stops close by—typically from a 10-minute walkshed or less. The likelihood of visiting a shop drops exponentially as walking distance increases. This suggests that having a higher development density—of residents, jobs, institutions, transit stops and recreational amenities—around retail clusters will benefit stores most when the density is close by, within a couple of hundred meters. The more that new residents, jobs, and transit stops are channeled closer to retail and food-service businesses via economic development plans, land use plans, or area renewal schemes, the better the business clusters do.

The connection between density and walkability can seem counterintuitive for transportation engineers. Travel-demand models typically assume that as transportation demand increases—that is, the density of employees and residents in an area increases—transportation infrastructure, particularly the need for vehicular lanes, parking spaces, and garages, must also increase. Higher-density areas of the city, as the logic goes, therefore need wider roads and bigger parking lots to accommodate the increased traffic.

This logic seems intuitive if you start out with an area where people mostly drive and envision what happens to transportation demand when the area slightly grows and densifies. But the logic contains a fallacy. Lower-density environments produce a lot of vehicular trips largely because such densities do not offer diverse trip destinations nearby that you could reach without a car. People need to drive to further areas of the city to find places to eat, shop, meet colleagues over coffee, or visit them at their workplaces. Denser mixed-use districts, on the other hand, not only place more residents and workers near each other, but also generate more shops, services, restaurants, and cafés on their ground floors. And because of this, transportation demand for lunchers, shoppers, and those running errands or traveling to meetings in other offices changes from driving to simply walking to these destinations. When higher density and mixed land uses are developed around public transit, then the area's workers and residents also tend to walk the first or last half mile to and from their public transport stop on their routine home-work-home trips instead of driving. As a result, the per capita need for larger parking lots and wider roads actually *decreases*, rather than increasing or staying constant with higher development densities. Instead of wider roads and parking lots, higher-density districts actually need wider sidewalks, quality public spaces, and activity-generating ground floors.

When residents of a community want a new grocery store in their neighborhood, it is important to think of both effects of density to understand whether the environment can support the desired grocer. A recognized supermarket, such as Trader Joe's, typically occupies 10,000–15,000 square feet of net leasable area and will require about 1,500 customers a day. Getting 1,500 customers a day to the store in a low-density, suburban setting would necessitate a market area of about 20,000 people.[37] Without this catchment, the store is unlikely to survive. A community that cannot support a grocery store the size of Trader Joe's would benefit from knowing these factors and could instead explore a smaller, perhaps independent grocery store, which does not need as large a market area to remain in business.

But in higher-density urban areas, the same Trader Joe's can get by with only half as many residents in the market area. On the one hand, density puts more residents closer to the store, reducing their transportation costs and enabling them to go to the store more frequently. At the same time, people might also walk by the store on other outings—on their way to the playground or subway—producing additional unplanned visits to the store. And third, higher-density mixed-use environments also attract other trips to the area—workers, visitors who come for meetings, or shoppers attracted to a wider choice of stores—which add customers to the Trader Joe's, enabling the store to rely less on the local residents and more on passersby.

These differences between low- and high-density neighborhoods within the same city are further illustrated in Figure 28, which depicts the average distance to the nearest cluster of at least 25 stores in Los Angeles by population density.[38] In the least dense census tracts of Los Angeles (20th percentile), where population density remains below 1,586 people per square kilometer, the average distance from residential buildings to the nearest street commerce cluster is around 20 kilometers. In areas with average population density (2,793–3,843 people/km2), the nearest street commerce cluster is within 3.41 kilometers from an average home, and in the top 20th percentile densest neighborhoods within 2.11 kilometers. Variations in residential and commercial density go hand in hand even within a city. But higher-density areas of Los Angeles not only have more residents close to stores, these residents also encounter the stores more frequently on foot and the stores near their homes get a lot more outside visitors than similar stores in the city's suburbs.[39]

What Else Influences Retail Density?

While the four key factors DiPasquale and Wheaton's model I have discussed so far—purchase frequency, fixed costs, transportation costs, and customer density—play a crucial role in real-world retail distributions, there are a number of additional factors missing from both Central Place Theory and DiPasquale and Wheaton's one-dimensional model. Unequal spatial accessibility to customers, regulatory policies, branding, and cultural and technological trends all play a role in shaping urban retail landscapes too. The following pages will briefly review these factors, emphasizing the point that the retail pattern of a city is really an example of organized complexity, as Jane Jacobs would call it.[40] The pattern is shaped by a set of complex forces, some of which planners can affect and others which are beyond anyone's conscious control.

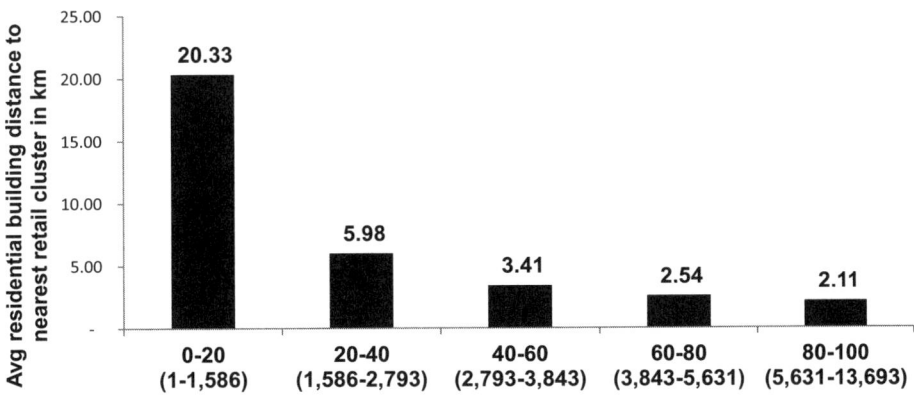

Figure 28. Proximity to retail clusters in Los Angeles, CA. Data Source: Infogroup 2010 Business Listings, provided as part of ESRI Business Analyst software.

Both the one-dimensional retail location model and the two-dimensional Central Place Theory assume a spatial environment with no streets, subway lines, or variation in customer access. This is typical of most spatial-economic models. Quoting William Alonso, "The city is viewed as if it were located on a featureless plain, on which all land is of equal quality, ready for use without further improvements, and freely bought and sold."[41] This assumption allows the distribution of centers to become perfectly uniform across space in the model. Stores selling the same goods divide customers evenly, with each store obtaining an identical market area, located at an equal distance from competing stores (see Figure 17 and Figure 19).

The assumption of a homogenous environment is, of course, a coarse simplification that clarifies the analysis and produces a more parsimonious model. It eliminates the role of uneven transportation networks and urban form from the analysis and allows retail location patterns to emerge in response to market forces that can flow freely across space. But the reality of built environments is more complex. The geometric configuration of the street network and transit system generate an uneven level of accessibility throughout a city, limiting access to customers in some places while favoring others. These variations can exert an important influence on the spatial distribution of urban commerce.

Wheaton and DiPasquale's one-dimensional model of competing retailers assumes stores will locate at equal distances from each other (Figure 19). If one store were to move right or left, closer to its next competitor in order to grab a larger market area, it would trigger similar moves by other stores. The moving

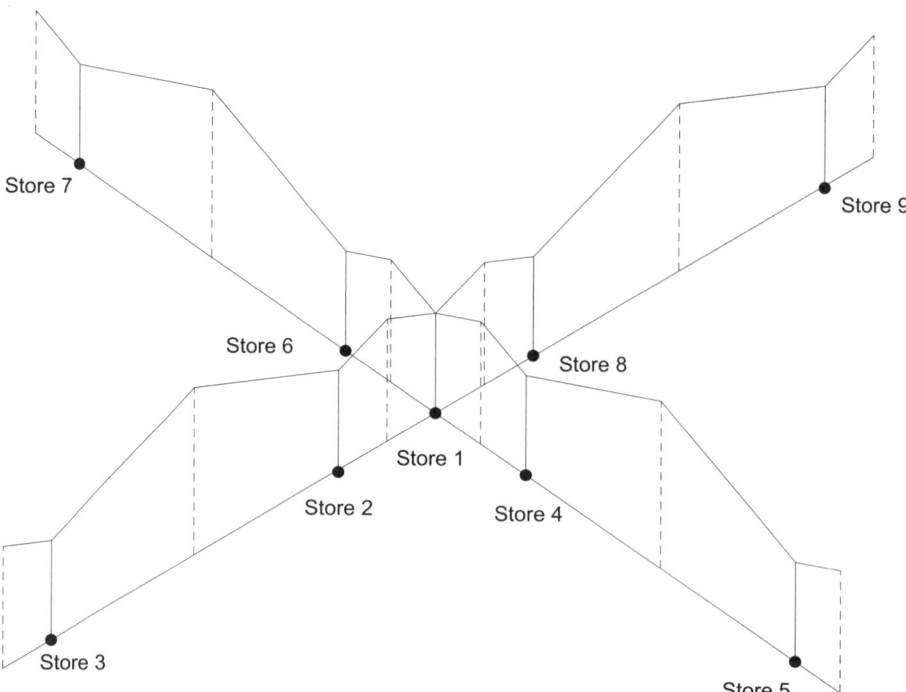

Figure 29. Equal-size retail market areas of nine stores on a cruciform linear network.

would continue until an equilibrium is reestablished and each store has an equal-sized market area.

But consider an analogous model with a different spatial configuration, where stores are no longer arranged on a straight line. If we rearranged the nine stores from Figure 19 around a four-way intersection, for instance, keeping the total linear length of streets the same, then different locations along the network face different levels of accessibility to customers (Figure 29). Assuming that customers can still only travel along the lines that form the cross (city streets) and that customer density is still uniform along all streets, a store at the center would now reach four times as many customers within a given walkshed as stores at the far ends of the network. This is because the central location can be approached from four intersecting streets, whereas the end points of the network only reach customers from one side. An equilibrium, where all stores' market areas are equal, would require that distances between stores be shorter around the center—the most accessible location in the layout. Higher spatial accessibility generates a higher density of stores.

This crossroads example is not simply hypothetical. Places of heightened accessibility to customers are found in every city and every neighborhood, and increased levels of accessibility often result from an intersection of numerous streets. Some of the most iconic public spaces and retail clusters of the world—Campo di

Figure 30. Times Square, New York City. Photo by author.

Siena in Italy, Times Square in New York City, or the Shibuya crossing in Tokyo—are places of exceptionally high accessibility within their respective urban contexts. Campo di Siena is entered from 12 streets around it. It is by far the most accessible place in the historic town of Siena. Times Square lies at an exceptional location within the regular street grid of Manhattan (Figure 30). It is not only marked by regular four-way intersections like most street corners in Manhattan, but also by the diagonal Broadway. Its location in midtown makes access convenient from lower and upper Manhattan as well as the east and west sides of the city. Furthermore, the eight subway lines below Times Square form the busiest MTA station in the city. Add to that the Port Authority bus terminal, which is just a block away, and the sky-high buildings around the area, and you'll find few places in the world with a level of accessibility that matches Times Square's.

Both Central Place Theory and DiPasquale and Wheaton's model also assume that customer density is constant and uniform across space. This is a simplification that makes the models elegant and useful as deductive tools. But customer density in actual built environments of course varies, and these variations can exert a strong influence on the store densities we encounter from one neighborhood to another.

Figure 31 maps accessibility to residents within a 15-minute walking radius in New York City. Far from a homogenous environment, different locations in the city provide notably different levels of access to the city's residents. At peak locations (95th percentile)—the Upper East Side, East Village, Upper West Side, and parts of the Bronx—you can reach over 60,000 residents within a 15-minute walk (the maximum is over 110,000 between First and Second Avenues around 83rd and 94th Streets). While the citywide mean is around 24,000, the sites in the lower 5th percentile reach only a fraction of that—2,242 people.

Population density itself depends on number of factors: building sizes, building heights, how far buildings are spaced from one another, and how densely the buildings are inhabited. At locations with peak population densities, all these qualities tend to be highest. While some of these variables are fairly constant throughout Manhattan (building forms and building spacing don't vary that much), inhabitation density—the amount of floor space per inhabitant—has considerable variation through the borough. For instance, Figure 31 shows that access to residents is higher in Chinatown than in Lincoln Square, even though both neighborhoods have largely similar built form and street networks. A typical corner store in Chinatown reaches 60,000 residents in a 15-minute walkshed, while around Lincoln Square the same store would reach 20% fewer, or 50,000 customers. This difference results partly from unequal inhabitation densities between the two areas. The average household in Chinatown is occupied by 2.4 people. In Lincoln Square, a typical household size is 1.5 people. This higher population density is reflected in the higher retail density in Chinatown, where we find 4.8 establishments per acre as opposed to 2.5 establishments per acre in Lincoln Square. In addition to population densities, this almost twofold difference in retail densities between the two neighborhoods may also result from a higher number of visiting and passing patrons in Chinatown, where three major bridges enter Manhattan—the Williamsburg Bridge, the Manhattan Bridge, and the Brooklyn Bridge. Such links to the broader New York metro area are missing at Lincoln Square.

Even in smaller cities, street commerce is usually distributed around locations where a higher than normal number of streets intersect, where transit hubs are found, or where a denser built fabric provides access to more customers. In the absence of regulatory forces holding back development, additional retailers join these locations until profits resulting from advantageous accessibility are dampened through competition. A cluster stops growing when enough retailers have entered to lower profits to the same level as the next best alternative location.

Regulations

The regulatory environment that controls the retail market also varies across cities. Even though Singapore's population density is considerably higher than that of most American cities, its retail density falls below the trend line in Figure 27.

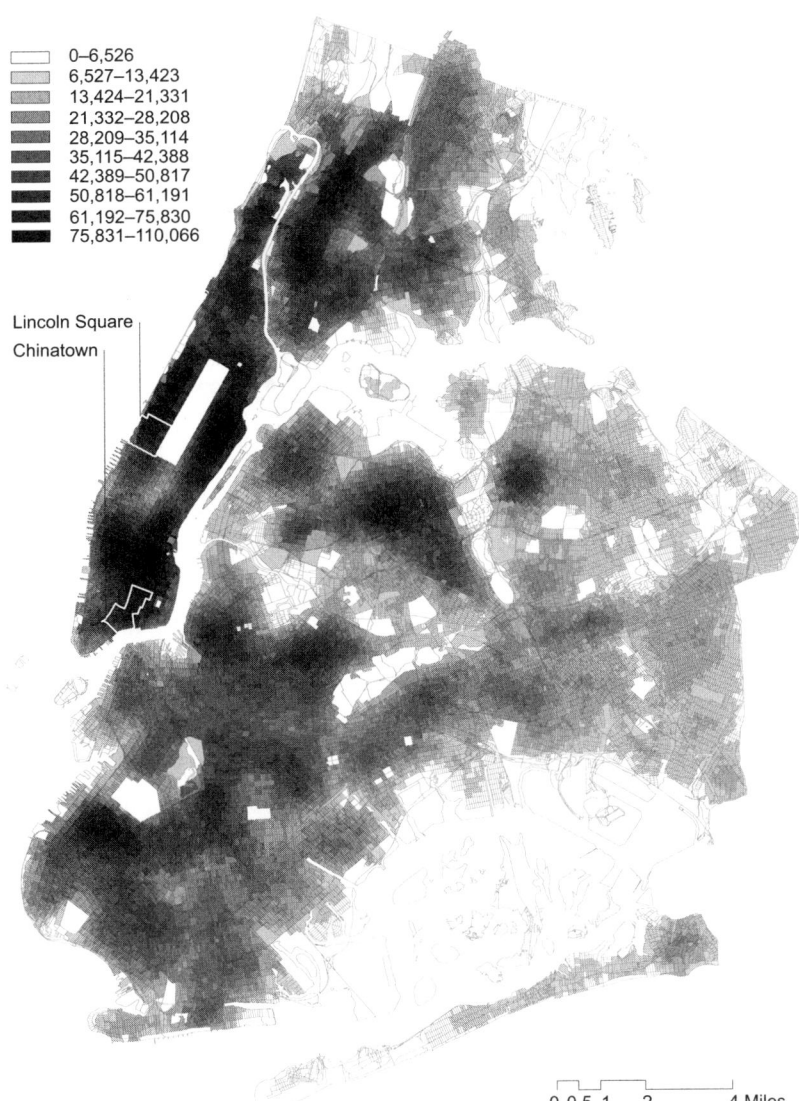

Figure 31. Access to residents in a 15-minute walkshed in New York City.

Singapore had a total of 47.2 million square feet of retail space per 5.54 million inhabitants in 2015.[42] This makes 8.52 square feet of retail space per inhabitant. The greater Los Angeles area, including Los Angeles County, Orange County, and Inland Empire, by contrast, had 469.7 million square feet of multi-tenant shopping centers and single-tenant properties in 2015—the largest retail market in the United States.[43] This makes 25 square feet of retail space per inhabitant, far ahead of Singapore (and still ahead of the 1.35 square meters or 14 square feet

Figure 32. A food court underneath Housing Development Board housing project in Dover, Singapore. Photo by author.

per capita encountered in Tallinn!). Singapore has a population density that is more than an order of magnitude greater than the Los Angeles metro area's, but it has almost three times less retail space per capita. The economic models I discussed above do not explain this discrepancy.[44]

Most of Singapore's urban fabric was built in the last five decades. Aside from the historic city center, which dates to the 1800s, over 80% of residents live in relatively recent high-rise public housing towns built by the Housing Development Board (HDB). About 65% of the population travels to work by public transit. According to the model, both the high population density and high public transit mode share suggest that the city should have a high retail density.

It is possible that Singapore's relatively low per capita retail density is attributable to the young age of the urbanized island state compared to older American or European cities. Given that most of its built environment was constructed post-1965, after it split off from Malaysia, maybe Singapore's retail densities haven't had enough time to mature? That may be part of the story, but the country's top-down development model and strict regulatory policies have also played a role.

Large swaths of public housing throughout the heartland of the island-state have been planned, developed, and remain closely regulated by the government of Singapore. These housing towns are perfect examples of modernist principles of city building as laid out in the Athens Charter of 1933.[45] Almost exclusively envisioned for residential purposes, they embody the separation of land uses: their building typologies are primarily tower blocks surrounded by large open spaces, and most tower blocks are lifted off the ground on *pilotis* over empty ground-floor spaces, known as *void-decks* in Singapore. These void-decks are reserved for open-air community activities. The spatial arrangement of the built fabric and the architectural typologies of residential blocks here are largely unfit for retail development. Buildings are set far back from sidewalks that channel pedestrian flow. To enter a ground-floor store would require walking 20 yards away from the sidewalk. This distance is long enough to make it difficult to even see what is being displayed in the store windows. I will have more to say about the influence of building types on street commerce in Chapter 6.

Singapore's retail landscape is also shaped by regulatory constraints of various kinds—zoning of allowable uses, city regulations of sidewalks, building occupancy guidelines, neighborhood committee decisions, etc. Singapore is one of the most regulated cities in the world. It not only is known for its extensive protocols concerning the use of urban space, but violations are closely enforced through an elaborate system of permits and fines.

HDB towns are predominantly zoned for residential use. Commercial zoning is confined to a few designated sites—mostly town, neighborhood, and precinct centers. As a public landlord, the HDB regulates what specific types of shops and services are allowable within each of the commercial centers. It exclusively designates many commercial spaces for a particular use—a convenience store, an eatery, health-service provider, etc. Commercial spaces around bus stops, for instance, typically invite bids from eating houses and convenience stores. It is forbidden, by contrast, to run eating establishments, beverage services, entertainment facilities, or retail stores (other than those selling small convenience goods) underneath most residential void-decks. Even the store mix in multistory shopping structures can be regulated by the HDB, with a certain portion of spaces bid out for desired categories of shops. While the strong government hand has helped ensure that basic goods and services are always available to residents within a short walk, overregulation has also held back a market-led evolution of retail environments, contributing to a lower retail density around the island than we would expect from its population density.

Most American cities also use zoning regulations to restrict retail space to specific streets and parcels—a legacy of 20th-century modernist planning that promoted a spatial separation of land uses. These regulations often prohibit commercial land uses on residential streets and vice versa. They often cluster workplaces in a part of town where even offices and retailers are found in different

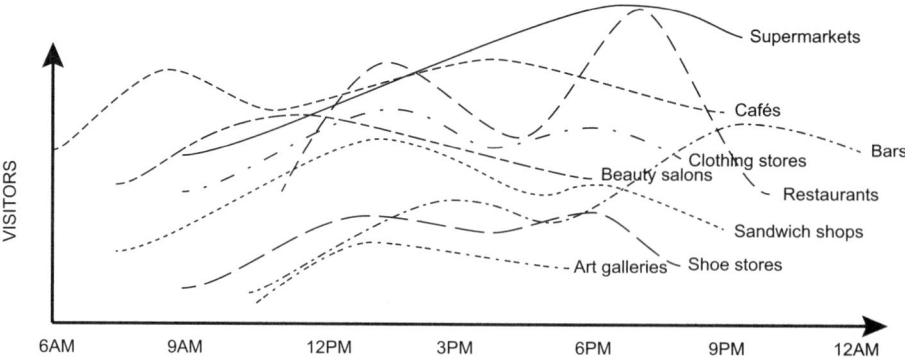

Figure 33. Typical visits throughout a day for different types of businesses. Based on Google Places Data, a machine-readable interface for establishments listed on Google Maps.

buildings. This might make for an easier accounting of land, but it doesn't help foster street commerce.

Districts that only house office space and neighborhoods that are strictly residential are occupied at limited hours of the day. The workday usually starts at 8 a.m. and runs until 6 p.m. Residential buildings are used during the opposite hours. Parks, theaters, sporting facilities, and other recreational venues are mostly used in the evenings and on weekends. Monofunctional neighborhoods concentrate to-and-fro movement to specific hours, leaving streets and sidewalks empty during the rest of the day.

Healthy street commerce needs to operate all day long (Figure 33). Cafés tend to get started earliest, around 6 or 7 a.m., receiving breakfast-goers on their way to work. Some personal service providers, such as dry cleaners, tailors, and hair and beauty salons, also open shop in the morning to serve those who need work done before a morning meeting or to serve the retirees in a neighborhood who tend to start their errands early. Coffee shops receive most of their clients during breakfast and lunch, while restaurants do most of their business at lunch and dinner.

When workplaces and homes are spatially segregated, street commerce suffers. People leave residential areas in the morning peak hour and return after work, leaving stores with very few customers in between. Most retail visits in residential areas consequently occur during evening hours after work and on weekends.

Districts that mix both residents and jobs are preferable for shops. Strategically directing new public and affordable housing programs near Main Streets thus contributes to a more diverse selection of shops and services. The diversity of stores, in turn, generates vibrant public spaces where one can encounter folks from different income, race, and class backgrounds on the street. Even better is if schools, daycares, and recreational destinations are nearby too. Employees generate visits to restaurants, cafés, and shops throughout a day, starting as breakfasters before work and ending as shoppers, theatergoers, and diners at night. Workers produce a notable concentration of visits to eating and drinking places during lunch, which is sometimes followed by running personal errands or quick shop visits in the afternoon, if such amenities are available nearby. Young professionals without kids and those whose kids have already grown up also value opportunities to meet colleagues or friends over a meal or a drink at the end of a workday, generating another spike in visits after 5 or 6 p.m. Evening hours are also busy for grocery stores, clothing and apparel stores, and hobby shops, music shops, and bookstores, which catch customers on their way home. Mixed-use employment and residential districts both produce more visits overall and generate around-the-clock demand for local amenities.

A strict separation of land uses in a city's zoning code works directly against this. Small-scale street commerce does not generate enough of an attraction for people to make a trip to a separate location like a shopping mall does. Many small stores rely on passing foot traffic rather than designated trips by car. Segregating retailers out to designated shopping zones thus benefits big box stores and shopping centers, but not street commerce. The latter does much better in higher-density, mixed-use areas with good transit connections and walkable streets.

Branding and Marketing

Both Central Place Theory and the one-dimensional economic model also assume that all competing stores are identical, selling indistinguishable merchandise. We know, however, that quality, branding, and marketing can make a substantial difference to store revenues and patronage and affect store density.

If you have ever been to Lisbon, Portugal, you probably sampled some *Pastéis de Natas* or egg-custard tarts—a traditional Portuguese dessert that is also popular in parts of Southeast Asia and American Chinatowns due to a colonial history. In Lisbon, the most popular place to get egg-custard tarts is called Pastéis de Belém, located next to the historic Belém monastery. Pastéis de Belém attracts more buyers among locals and tourists alike than any other bakery in town. Its success has little to do with location or prices—the bakery is located more than four miles outside the historic city center and its *natas* come with a slightly above average price. Instead, it offers the most famous product. The slightly burned outer skin of the baked egg-yolk, a creamy paste underneath, and a perfectly crisp dough basket around it make Pastéis de Belém's *natas* perfect in the eyes of many Portuguese. You'll even find some packaged versions on sale at the Lisbon airport, but those won't be as fresh as the ones found in Belém.

Figure 34. Pastéis de Belém store in Lisbon, Portugal. Photo by Paul Barker Hemmings.

Pastéis de Belém, which has been around since 1837, has become a recognized brand in Lisbon.

It is rare for an independent store to achieve such brand recognition as Pastéis de Belém. It can take decades, even centuries, and requires consistent performance over time. Brand recognition is achieved more frequently by chains that run many stores nationally or internationally, and due to their economies of scale, can spend significant resources on advertising. No single Subway sandwich shop is as popular or famous as Pastéis de Belém, but Subway as a franchise attracts many more customers through its tens of thousands of outlets around the world. The sandwich restaurant invests over $500 million a year on advertising in the United States alone. People do not recognize its shops for their individual qualities and specialty cooking methods. But everyone knows that Subway stands out from other sandwich stores for their predictably fresh produce and customized sandwiches that can be found in any Subway outlet around the world.[46] Branding helps assure that customers seek out particular shops even when competitors are more conveniently located.

Some stores and food-service businesses also develop a devoted following without any deep-pocketed marketing investments by offering products and services that speak to current cultural trends and aspirations. The so-called "cool factor" or "hipster" effect can bring in as many customers as costly advertising campaigns. Many fashionable coffee shops that boast tastefully designed interiors, meticulously perfected coffee, and service staff that seem to be in the "know," attract more millennials than Starbucks, Coffee Bean, or any other chain café. They are simply cooler than any chain out there. There is even a reincarnated "speakeasy" phenomenon among trendy bars, which claim to be so cool that they don't want you to find out they exist. Or they do, but they want you to discover them through word of mouth from a fashionable and knowledgeable friend. Just like the original speakeasies that emerged in the United States during the Prohibition era, there is no sign on the door and sometimes an actor-like concierge asks for a password, announced on a weekly basis to a small group of Facebook contacts who then spread the word.

One such establishment, called the Library Bar, is located on the trendy Keong Saik Road in Singapore. From the street, the place looks like a small designer bookstore. But when you step in, something doesn't gel. A small showroom space, clad in red light, has books on the shelves—but if you ask about prices, you will hear from the person staffing the store that they are not for sale. If you instead tell the person the code word of the week, she will skillfully flip one of the bookshelves around its axis to unveil a secret door that leads to a bar. The bar is bustling with trendy customers and offers a pretty amazing list of craft cocktails whose names are as extravagant as the spectacle of their preparation.

Eschewing traditional marketing, these "speakeasies" achieve a sizable following precisely because they don't spend a dime on marketing—instead they endow their visitors with a sense that they are in on something trendy and secretive. Secrecy can be a form of marketing, just like better quality *natas* or well-publicized Subway sandwiches, helping stores attract more customers and higher revenues than their competitors.

Prices

The model also assumed identical prices in competing stores. But lower than usual prices can motivate customers to travel longer distances in search of bargains.

In the 1990s, a new shopping-center model—the discount outlet center—emerged on this principle. Generally located in exurban areas where land is cheap, outlet centers sell overstock brand items and merchandise from passed seasons at steeply discounted prices. One of the most popular outlet centers around Los Angeles, for instance, is Desert Hill Premium Outlets. It is located close to Palm Springs, 90 miles east of downtown Los Angeles, and getting there takes most visitors past several other well-known shopping centers. With significant cost incentives, people are willing to drive longer distances, even when other shopping centers are closer. But as I will discuss in Chapter 7, this model is presently under serious threat from e-commerce, which offers both affordable prices and very low transportation costs.

Social, Cultural, and Technological Shifts

Beyond the role of building types, regulatory policies, branding, and pricing, retail location patterns are also affected by social, cultural, and technological trends that no store, planner, or city government can directly control. Consider another example, the rapid increase of specialty coffee shops in the United States in the last two decades. Specialty coffee is distinguished from commercial coffee by the fact that it is made of whole beans that are ground right before brewing. Specialty coffee is typically also roasted in small stores or factories, using traditional methods as opposed to the mass roasting and packaging of commercial coffee. According to the Specialty Coffee Association of America, the number of specialty coffee shops in the United States in 1993 was 2,850.[47] By 2013, the number had risen to 29,300—a 928% increase over 20 years, or roughly 12.5% annual growth. In other words, the number of coffee shops in America exploded in the period, contributing a great deal to street commerce across the country. Why? A classical retail location model doesn't seem to explain it. Neither do prices or regulations.

On the one hand, people's tastes changed. In the 1980s, most people brewed their coffee at home, using electric drip coffee makers. Only around 3% of US adults went out daily to buy specialty coffee in coffee shops. Since then, the demand for specialty coffee has rapidly risen. Now, around 18% of US adults drink specialty coffee daily. It is impossible to pinpoint a single factor that caused this rapid shift in preference for joe. Perhaps it is partly the deep-pocketed marketing campaigns by the newly emerging national coffee chains like Starbucks, Coffee Bean, Dunkin Donuts, Pete's Tea and Coffee, and McCafé, which have made "cappuccino" a common household term in America.

But the rapid rise of specialty coffee shops is partly also due to notable changes in communication technology that has enabled American work schedules to become more flexible and mobile. In 1989, at the end of the Reagan era, 15% of American households had computers, none of which were connected to the Internet. By 2013, around 80% of households had a computer connected to the Internet. In 1988, fewer than 1% of Americans had a cell phone. By 2015, over 92% of adults had a cell phone and 68% of people had smartphones, complete with e-mail, apps, and all-purpose Internet access.[48]

The rapid adoption of Internet and mobile communication devices have enabled an increasing number of people to remain connected to work, even when

Figure 35. Broadsheet Coffee Roasters in Cambridge, MA. Photo by author.

physically absent from the office. I must confess that much of this book has also been written in coffee shops near my home and office. And since I see a lot of regulars around these coffee shops, I suspect I'm not alone in getting work done around a cup of coffee. For some, coffee shops have become de facto offices—not just a temporary escape from the personal cubicle, but the only work space available outside the living room at home. Laptop computers, Wi-Fi, and mobile internet connections make work accessible anywhere, while colleagues and clients remain only a cell-phone call away.

And for those who do have an office, wireless connectivity has not only enabled them to skip out to the café during a workday but has made overall work schedules more flexible. The National Household Travel Survey shows that non-routine home-work-home journeys have been on the rise, suggesting that people travel more during as well as after their workday. The share of work-related business trips, personal errand trips, and shopping trips have all increased since the 1990s.[49] Coffee shops benefit from a more mobile population. Moving throughout the day makes it easier for more people to pop into cafés along the way.

Economic retail density models thus only portray a limited set of factors that affect the viability of individual stores or densities of systems of stores. Though patronage frequency is important for every store, fixed costs, transportation options, and customer density play the most important roles for planners, whose work directly affects these factors via zoning policies, neighborhood plans, strategic plans, and urban design guidelines. From business owners' point of view, branding and pricing also play important roles, affecting the attractiveness of a store. All these forces together remind us that no democratic and market-oriented city can fully control its street commerce—there are simply too many factors involved in shaping the patterns of stores we encounter on our streets.

Not only does each shop's ability to remain in business depend on a number of different factors, but a similar shops' health can also vary from one city to another and even one month to another. Every store that survives another year on a street illustrates a triumph of survival in an evolutionary competition for the fittest. The types and patterns of shops that we see today reflect traces of the complex interactions between patrons' shopping behavior and store owners' operational choices, which need to leave both sides satisfied enough to keep going. Every store is subject to change when people's preferences for goods and services change or when the cost of doing business changes. Each of the inputs required to keep a store in business—people's purchasing frequency, transportation costs, prices, wages, rents, access to customers, as well as government regulations or urban form—change over time. As a result, the pattern of stores we see on city streets is in constant flux, adjusting from year to year.

CHAPTER 3

How Stores Cluster

Both Central Place Theory and the one-dimensional retail density model describe competing stores and do not suggest any reasons for shops to locate in clusters. Instead, they show competing shops locating at even distances from each other, each dominating an equal market area in equilibrium. Christaller's two-dimensional Central Place Theory implicitly suggests that lower- and higher-order centers could form where multiple shops collocate but does not explain why this should occur. There is nothing in the threshold and range definitions of his schematic to suggest that stores would have anything to benefit from agglomeration.

We have already seen how agglomerations can start from advantageous accessibility—in Times Square, Campo di Siena, or just around a local subway station. Places that reach more customers attract more stores until profits are equalized with stores at other locations. This type of clustering is caused by *exogenous* environmental factors—highly accessible locations near major intersections, thoroughfares, or transit stations that generate better access to customers. But retail agglomerations can also arise from *endogenous* factors—relationships between stores that make it inherently beneficial for them to locate in proximity to each other.

Around Rue St. Michel on the left bank of the Seine in Paris, close to the Sorbonne, there is an astonishing density of booksellers. You can find everything ranging from the most recent paperback novels to hardcover classics, from highly specialized mathematical texts to large-format architectural lithographs. There are multistory bookstores attracting a wide range of visitors, and specialized language stores that only carry texts in English, German, or Latin. On weekends, an open-air book market on one of the streets even sells books by weight.

A short walk away, on Rue Saint-Séverin, you'll find a restaurant cluster bustling with tourists at lunch or dinner time. There are hundreds of restaurants lining the streets, offering bites for backpackers and fine diners alike—a Greek gyro restaurant next to a traditional brasserie, an Italian restaurant next to a

Figure 36. Gilbert Jeune bookstore on Rue St. Michel in Paris. Photo by Pascal Gobbi.

Lebanese one. Given that many of the customers are tourists, restaurants assign a garçon to the door who will walk with you, menu in hand, trying to lure you in with conversation.

Across the Seine on the right bank, Le Marais is home to hundreds of clothing and apparel boutiques. People who go shopping for fashion in Paris are likely to start in Le Marais. There are no department stores (except for a BHV selling home appliances on Rue de Rivoli) and the dense network of pre-Haussmann streets is dotted by small clothing shops and bars. Most of the establishments are not part of brands or chains we are used to seeing in shopping malls, but rather small, independent French or European designer stores. You can find pricy designer T-shirts, handmade fall coats, Japanese wooden sandals, bags made of recycled fire hoses, and meticulously crafted jewelry of various sorts. Dress stores and shoe stores stand side by side, seemingly engaged in a fierce competition over buyers. Similar competitive retail clusters are found in cities around the world.

Already in 1937, geographer Malcolm J. Proudfoot categorized the principal spatial patterns of stores in early 20th-century American cities into five types of clusters: (1) the central business district; (2) the outlying business center; (3) the principal business thoroughfare; (4) the neighborhood business street; and (5) the isolated store cluster.[1] These five types of retail clusters continue to this day, with a few additions. Over the course of the 20th century, the car-oriented shopping mall, which is somewhat analogous to Proudfoot's outlying business center, became one of the most important retail typologies of our time. Much of retail location literature has come to focus on this typology. The strip mall—which resembles Proudfoot's principal business thoroughfare, but which serves a predominantly vehicular clientele—might also be added to the list of prominent 20th-century retail cluster typologies.

Why do some stores prefer to collocate with other stores? What makes some gravitate toward competitors and others escape them? Why do clusters form in the first place? And why do some stores choose to locate in complete isolation? This chapter address these questions.

Multipurpose Shopping and the Clustering of Complementary Stores

Mapping retail clusters across American cities in Chapter 1, I showed that retail and service establishments often come in clusters, which can be as small as 25 stores each or as large as thousands of stores that form a continuous downtown retail cluster. And even though I generally refer to retail clusters as groups of stores that contain at least 25 establishments in this book (Figure 2), I refer to clustering in this chapter more broadly to describe colocation dynamics of 2 or more stores. The visible outcomes of these dynamics can range from the sizable shopping districts I described in Paris to much humbler street-corner clusters where only a handful of stores or restaurants site next to each other.

Neoclassical retail location literature refers to agglomerations of stores that offer a variety of products and services as *complementary* retail clusters, or multipurpose shopping clusters: an ice-cream kiosk next to a theater, a butcher next to a vegetable store, or a restaurant near a clothing store. Complementary retail clusters generally include restaurants and retailers. Some also offer a post office, repair services, banks and tax advisors, travel agencies, hair cutters, beauty salons, and so on.

Complementary retail clusters form for two key reasons. The first has to do with visitors' transportation and time costs. For someone who is going out to buy groceries, return an Amazon package at the post office, and then buy some flowers, heading to a cluster, where all of these errands can be completed side by side in a single trip, is a much more attractive prospect than traveling to three separate locations. Transportation savings that customers accrue by visiting complementary retail clusters is the primary catalyst that drives complementary stores to cluster. The larger variety of goods draw a larger pool of customers and create a positive feedback loop, incentivizing stores to bundle in even larger heterogeneous centers.[2]

Empirical surveys that have examined whether shopping trips are single or multipurpose have found that around 60% of all retail trips involve purchasing different types of goods.[3] Multipurpose shopping is slightly less prevalent in grocery shopping than non-grocery retail outings.[4] And multiple studies have shown that people do not necessarily choose the closest shopping venues to visit; instead they often shop at multiple stores at different venues on the same trip. One study in rural Iowa found that only 35% of the respondents shopped at the nearest center, illustrating that people were willing to travel further to access bigger complementary clusters.[5] Another study in New Zealand showed that nearest-center patronage, which Central Place Theory and the one-dimensional retail density models in the previous chapter assumed, becomes less tenable as the size of the destination center increases—a bigger destination compels visitors to forego closer options for the sake of greater choice.[6] Whereas 63–83% of trips to small shopping centers chose the nearest destinations, only half of the total number of trips going to larger centers chose the closest destination. The difference is explained by transportation savings achieved by multipurpose shopping at the larger destinations.

Retail location literature has suggested that complementary retail clusters also form due to a second, related phenomenon: customer spillovers that complementary stores can produce for one another. Given conveniently small distances between stores, customer traffic attracted to higher-order stores can increase traffic in lower-order stores. Unlike planned visits to *complementary* clusters, which enable customers to purchase a set of *planned* goods at lower total costs due to transportation and time savings, customer spillovers produce additional *unplanned* purchases in lower-order stores. A person visiting a clothing store on a main street, for instance, might pay a visit to a coffee shop on the same street, thus making a purchase that he or she would avoid if a separate trip to a bookstore were required. This is what my wife and I did on London's Upper Street, where we bought coffee after we had finished our shopping that Sunday morning, as described in the beginning of this book. We did not head to Upper Street for coffee but decided to grab a cup from a conveniently located shop after completing other errands.

Customer spillovers are generally described as flowing in one direction—from more popular to less popular stores, or from anchor stores to non-anchor stores. Smaller, non-anchor stores are therefore thought to benefit most from complementary clustering. Whereas a large supermarket may attract customers regardless of whether it is found in a cluster with other stores or not, many small specialty stores around it may completely depend on the customer spillovers that a neighboring grocery store generates for them. However, a cluster of numerous small stores can also produce customer spillovers in the other direction—toward

Figure 37. A cluster of stores along Broadway in Bushwick, Brooklyn, New York City. The adjacent stores include both complementary and competitive establishments: a Brazilian café, a karaoke gastropub, a 99-cent store, and a Chinese takeout restaurant. Photo by author.

higher-order anchors, such as department stores. A department store that locates near a busy cluster of independent businesses not only brings new customers to the area, but also benefits from existing patrons of the cluster.

Customer spillovers are a familiar topic to shopping center managers, who try to orchestrate such benefits. A purposeful manipulation of spillover effects in a shopping center can maximize the center's overall revenues. The theory goes as follows: The sales volume of a particular store located within a cluster of stores depends on the variety of goods that the store offers.[7] When the store expands its choice of merchandise, its sales are expected to rise. But in the presence of complementary spillovers, sales can also depend on the variety of goods or services offered at other, nearby stores in the cluster. If a nearby store generates positive customer spillovers, then the first store's sales can increase as the neighboring store increases its sales through a better choice of offerings. But if no spillovers exist between the two stores, then the increased sales at the neighboring store have no effect at all on the first. If the cluster contains multiple stores of the same kind, however, then competition between such stores might reverse the customer spillover benefits. For instance, if there are two shoe stores, then

82   Chapter 3

Figure 38. Arkády Pankrác shopping mall in Prague. Photo by Martin Vorel.

increased sales at a neighboring store could mean reduced sales at the first store because of competition and vice versa.

Following this logic, and equipped with detailed data about actual customer spillovers between each type of store, a purposeful, coordinated manipulation of store types and store floor areas can lead mall owners to maximize profits for the center as a whole. Indeed, positioning stores inside shopping malls in ways that capture the greatest amount of unplanned spillovers, leading to a higher total amount of spending, has become a science of its own in the mall industry.

This practice is not only common in centrally managed shopping centers but is one of the key reasons behind the profitability of shopping centers as compared to uncoordinated street commerce, which lacks central management. The owner of the mall can select tenants that maximize positive inter-store externalities and increase profits for the entire mall. The joint ownership of space gives mall owners the opportunity to pick and place their tenants in purposeful ways. Unwanted entry by competition can be avoided at the owner's discretion and desired complementary stores can be lured in with subsidies.

A large body of empirical research has studied customer spillovers in shopping malls. Some studies have examined the degree of spillovers, or "retail compatibility" across different types of non-anchor stores.[8] Others have explored the scale of the benefits that customer spillovers produce. One study that focused on the degree of retail compatibility for a sample of stores in 54 regional shopping centers in the United States found that centers with greater quantities of space devoted to anchor tenants have higher non-anchor tenant sales for eight out of nine merchandise types.[9]

Theories on profitable mixing of tenants in planned shopping malls have also led numerous researchers to look for implicit evidence of customer spillovers embodied in tenants' rent contracts. In a widely popular practice, mall owners charge stores rent based upon their expected impact on the revenues of the mall as a whole.[10] Stores that constitute the primary motivation for customers' trips to the center (i.e., department stores), generally pay low rent per square foot, while odd specialty stores that are not on many shoppers' lists pay high rent per square foot since most of their foot traffic comes from other stores. This difference in rents is seen as implicit evidence of customer spillovers that anchor stores generate for non-anchor stores.[11] Large anchors, such as department stores, also tend to spend significantly on advertising, which not only benefits them but all the stores located around them.[12]

So complementary agglomerations, both in malls and main streets, are explained by two related phenomena: customer savings in transportation costs and customer spillovers between stores. However, as we saw with Parisian bookstores, clothing stores, and restaurants, competitive retailers sometimes also cluster, selling very similar goods. Competitive clustering is commonplace among bookstores, restaurants, clothing stores, accessory stores, and occasionally even competitors whose merchandise is virtually identical, as in the case of gasoline stations.

According to Central Place Theory and the one-dimensional retail density model we encountered in the previous chapter, competitive sellers should locate as far apart as possible, producing even distances between each other. Why then would competing stores decide to colocate? And why is clustering with competitors common among some types of stores and not others?

Clustering of Competing Stores

I already discussed how advantageous accessibility can lead to higher concentrations of competitive stores around cities' most accessible locations. Better access to customers is *exogenously* responsible for competitive clustering at locations that boast enough customers for more than one business around the same location. But there are also *endogenous* reasons that lead competing stores to cluster. These have to do with (1) risks of competitors' moves, (2) transportation costs involved in comparing similar products, and (3) lower prices found in competitive clusters.

One of the earliest explanations for competitive clustering was given by Harold Hotelling in his 1929 paper, "Stability in Competition."[13] Hotelling provided an example of two ice-cream sellers on a beach, facing perfectly inelastic demand,[14] and demonstrated how competitive price and location games between sellers can produce an equilibrium where both sellers are spatially clustered.

The example goes as follows: Imagine a situation where two ice-cream carts operate on the same beach. Customers are uniformly spread throughout the beach and both kiosks sell almost identical ice cream. If one vendor locates at the point one-quarter of the way between the center and one end of the beach and the second vendor at the same point on the other side, then both vendors are closest to the same number of customers and earn the same revenues. This constitutes a socially optimal equilibrium situation for both kiosks and all the ice-cream buyers on the beach, whereby the least possible amount of walking is required from customers. That means there is no better position for the two ice-cream kiosks to reduce transportation costs for all beachgoers collectively.

But what if one of the vendors moves its kiosk closer to the other, as shown in Figure 39? Doing so would increase the market area for the first vendor, since its new location is now closer to more beachgoers. The increase comes at the cost of the second vendor, who now has fewer customers.

Seeing how the first kiosk is benefiting from more customers gives the second kiosk an incentive to also move. By moving closer to the middle of the beach, the second kiosk also can attract more customers. Thus both kiosks could continue moving tit for tat. At one point they will end up locating shoulder to shoulder in the middle of the beach and discover that in this situation, they split the proceeds equally—neither of the kiosks benefits from more customers. In fact, any time a kiosk moves away from the center, it loses customers to the other vendor. The center of the beach is the only point where the risk of competitor's moves vanishes—a kiosk at the center cannot lose revenue, no matter where the other vendor moves. Consequently, neither seller has an incentive to move away from the center because a move would only cause a decrease in sales. This situation is called a Nash equilibrium, named after the famed Princeton mathematician John Nash, who was awarded a Nobel Prize for generalizing this outcome. In a Nash equilibrium, each seller sees the other's moves and neither has an incentive to change its situation without suffering negative consequences.

But what about customers? If both kiosks are located in the middle of the beach, then customers who come from the far ends of the beach need to walk longer distances than before. When the kiosks were at the one-quarter and three-quarter points where we started, they required visitors to walk the shortest possible time while still guaranteeing that both ice-cream kiosks have the same number of customers. In this case, from a social perspective, the Nash equilibrium

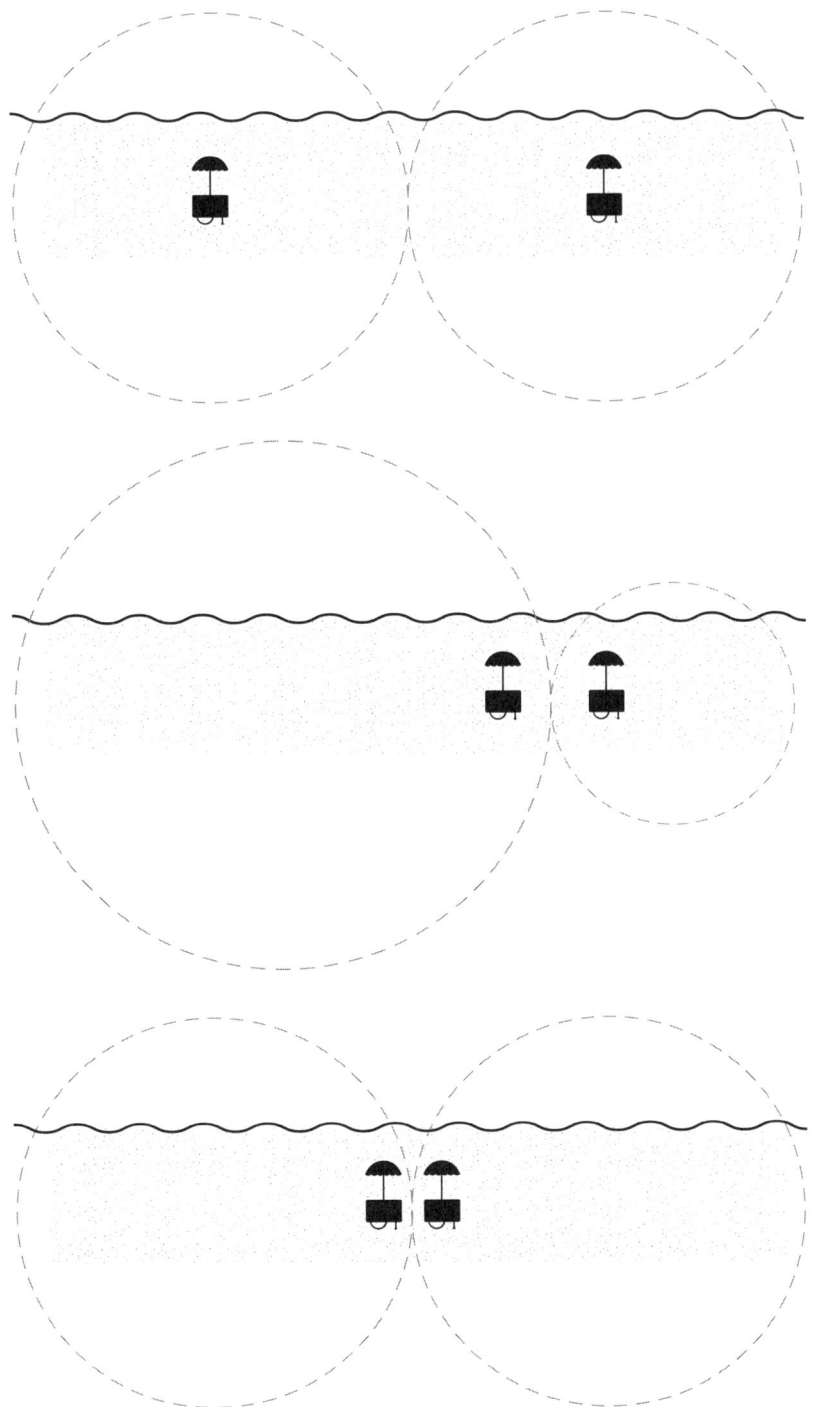

Figure 39. Hotelling's example of two competing vendors on a street. Top: socially optimal solution. Middle: competitive movements between vendors. Bottom: Nash equilibrium with clustering at the center of the beach.

with both stores in the middle of the beach is worse. But uncertainty about competitors' moves creates a clear incentive for the kiosks to cluster together.

Hotelling's example of competitive clustering might work with ice-cream kiosks that are mobile and face very low moving costs. But moving costs in actual commercial real estate markets are not negligible. In fact, for stores in brick-and-mortar structures, moving costs can be very substantial. Retailers can have leases that are locked in for 5-to-10-year periods, with significant penalties if the lease is broken. Even if shops own their space, exchanging it for an alternative location can be equally cumbersome. In addition to direct moving costs, store locations that have existed for a long time may have developed a certain degree of popular recognition—patrons might now associate a particular location with a particular retailer. Revenue could diminish, especially in the short run, if the store moved, even if by other standards the new location was as good as the old one. A move could also be taxing on a firm's employees, whose travel schedules would need to change due to a different commuting pattern. Inconveniencing existing workers could mean search costs for new staff, new salary negotiations, and so on. And finally, there is also uncertainty involved with a new location. Store owners know how many customers they get and how much revenue they make at their present location. A move to a new location would put their numbers in question—would customers still come, would the store still be able to break even? If it turns out that a store loses a good portion of its customers due to the move, then the costs are sunk with no way to recover them. All these considerations make relocations in urban environments less likely than Hotelling's ice-cream kiosks portray.

Hotelling's model also assumes equal revenue for stores both at the socially optimal one-quarter and three-quarter locations and the socially wasteful middle location. But this does not take into account the price elasticity of demand for ice cream. The price elasticity of demand for a product describes how changes in the price of a product affect the quantity of the product sold. For inelastic goods, a given percentage increase in prices results in a smaller percentage decrease in quantity sold. For instance, a 10% increase in electricity prices is likely to reduce electricity use a bit, but not quite the same 10%, because electricity has relatively inelastic demand—it is difficult to substitute another form of energy. Hotelling's model assumed that beachgoers have inelastic demand for ice cream—that increasing the total costs of obtaining ice cream, including the transportation costs involved with longer walks, didn't reduce the quantity of ice cream sold. This is why competitive vendors who cluster in the middle of the beach are still able to generate the same revenues as in the case where they were located at socially optimal locations, which required shorter travel times from their customers. In reality, however, ice cream does not face inelastic demand. As a nonessential product, it has reasonable substitutes—people can resort to cold sodas instead of ice cream—and an increase in transportation costs to obtain ice cream can bring about a decrease in the quantity of ice cream sold. With reasonably elastic demand, rather than being beneficial, locating in the middle of the beach could instead reduce sales and penalize all vendors.

In a similar vein, it is both costly to move real shops in a city, and the demand for most retail, food, and personal service establishments is not quite inelastic. Increases in costs, including transportation costs to obtain these goods, do bring about a decrease in the quantity sold. It is therefore both more profitable for stores, and less wasteful for people, not to have all shops clustered in a single location in the city. Instead, retailers distribute in multiple clusters of various sizes as I showed in Chapter 1.

Second, retail location literature suggests that another endogenous reason, one indicative of people's shopping behavior, is responsible for competitive clustering. Clustering of competitive stores selling similar merchandise can offer time and transportation cost savings to patrons whose purchase decisions are led by a desire to compare prices and products.[15] Whereas Hotelling regarded competitive clustering as socially "wasteful," clustering is in fact useful for consumers because it saves them search costs that would otherwise accrue from visiting multiple competitive stores at disparate locations. But unlike customer spillovers, which we saw running from anchor stores to non-anchor stores, producing mainly one-way benefits (in favor of non-anchor stores), the demand increase that results from comparison shopping generally benefits both stores.

Though potentially useful for customers who like to compare prices and products, for stores, competitive clustering can cause two significant problems. First, if competing shops locate near each other, they will have to split customers between them. If available market area can only support a certain number of customers, enough to keep only one store in business, then the addition of another similar store can lead to the ruin of both, producing a strong disincentive to cluster.

Second, competition over customers between similar shops will also reduce revenues by forcing stores to engage in a competition that lowers prices. Isolated retailers always possess a certain degree of monopoly power over their market area. When shops are spatially dispersed, then reasonable markups in prices can increase profits without chasing away customers whose next best alternative is inconveniently far away. Isolated retailers can theoretically increase their prices to a point where total price, including transportation costs, remains just below the total price at the next best alternative.

On the Massachusetts Institute of Technology campus, there is a supermarket called LaVerde's. Located inside the Student Center, it is the only supermarket

Figure 40. Competing gas stations sell identical products with minor price differences. Photo by author.

on campus and the closest one to the undergraduate dormitories along the Charles River. The next supermarket is located close to Central Square, about half a mile, or a ten-minute walk, up Massachusetts Avenue. If you asked MIT students, most of them would agree that LaVerde's is slightly overpriced compared to other markets selling similar groceries in town. For example, a gallon of milk at LaVerde's costs $4.89, while the same milk up the road costs $3.99.[16] Yet, LaVerde's remains popular among students who don't want to undertake the walk to the further alternative. If MIT students value their time at roughly the State of Massachusetts's minimum wage of $11 an hour, then a 20-minute walk (2×10 minutes each way) is equivalent to a third of an hour, or $3.67. As long as a bill at LaVerde's isn't more than $3.67 over the other market, it still provides a more economical alternative to the students.[17] It is enough of an incentive to keep trips that involve small purchases on campus. But the transportation savings that LaVerde's closer location offers disappear for students who buy a larger bundle of goods—with bigger purchases, price savings at the more remote market make a longer walk worthwhile.

Monopoly power that comes with an isolated location disappears when retailers face direct competitors next door. Two competitive retailers can potentially engage in a duopoly, both raising prices according to their perception that doing so makes both stores better off—but such understandings between competitors are fragile. The chances of inflated oligopoly prices sharply decrease as more shops are added. Research has shown that competitive clusters generally offer lower prices to customers.[18]

These lower prices, as well as customers' ability to compare goods from one store to another, can attract more visitors to competitive clusters than the sum of isolated stores together would otherwise suggest. Competing stores are thus expected to cluster if the increased customer flow that results from clustering with rivals exceeds the loss of customers due to competition. If the number of consumers who show up at a bookstore cluster, shoe store cluster, restaurant cluster, or clothing store cluster is large enough for every store to generate more sales than they would alone, then each of them has an incentive to side with competitors. The bookstores on the Rive Gouche in Paris, the clothing boutiques in the Marais, the restaurants in Cambridge, and the flower vendors in downtown Los Angeles colocate next to their competition because doing so brings in more customers than locating alone.

However, not all stores are equally likely to value competitive clusters. Competitive clustering is common among *search goods* for which price and product comparison is important and practically feasible only by visiting retailers in person, not via remote communication channels such as telephone or Internet. Already in 1952, the Hungarian-born American economist Tibor Scitovsky observed that "when the majority of buyers are experts, who insist on inspecting and comparing alternative offers before every purchase, then it is in the sellers' interest to facilitate such comparisons. For example, if a buyer has to choose among five alternatives of which four are easily comparable but the fifth is not, he will concentrate on comparing and choosing among the four and may ignore the fifth altogether. Hence the desire of every seller who faces expert buyers to be near his competitors and render his wares easily comparable to theirs."[19]

Sellers of *convenience goods*, on the other hand, are unlikely to cluster with competitors because a tactile comparison of their merchandise offers little added value. At liquor stores, for instance, a tactile comparison of one merchant's bottles with the same bottles in another merchant's store has little effect on purchasing decisions—the merchandise is basically the same in every store. But trying on shoes at a shoe store or smelling flower bouquets in person can be an important step before spending. This difference explains why shoe and flower stores are expected to cluster, but liquor stores are not.

The role of comparison shopping in influencing competitive clustering has been validated by ample empirical evidence. Research has found that the variety of retail merchandise for comparison shopping is a strong predictor of shopping center sales.[20] More options to compare search goods brings in more customers.

Another study concluded that the number of competitive retailers at a shopping center is significantly correlated with the center's income.[21] The variety in similar merchandise can be one of the strongest predictors of customers' shopping destination choice, corroborating the hypothesis that competitive clusters attract more consumers than the same number of competing stores located in isolation.[22] A survey of 1,200 individuals in six malls in the United States found that visits without specific shopping lists and visits to look at goods that might be bought in the future constituted 62% of all trips.[23] Around two-thirds of all mall visitors were there without immediate shopping plans, eyeing and comparing goods they might buy in the future.

Much of what we know about competitive clustering comes from shopping center research, not urban street commerce. Empirical attempts to analyze competitive clustering on main streets have been hampered by the lack of data and the difficulty of controlling for the endogenous and exogenous factors that affect clustering. Do shoe stores cluster along the streets of Hong Kong's Mong Kok district because of endogenous attraction to each other, or for exogenous reasons, such as surrounding density or accessibility that provide enough visits to each store despite competition (Figure 41)?

In a recent study of urban retail clusters in Cambridge and Somerville, MA, I estimated the tendencies of different types of retailers to cluster with their competitors, accounting for both exogenous effects of location and endogenous effects of clustering with similar stores.[24] Table 6 shows clustering coefficients (Rho) for six retail categories that had a large enough sample size. Higher coefficients mean that a store category is more likely to cluster with its competitors. These coefficients are controlled in the presence of other covariates, meaning that they pick up on the likelihood of businesses to cluster after accounting for the influence of other location factors, such as access to jobs, residents, public transit, or foot traffic in the area. For each group, I drew an equal-size random sample of 90 stores to make the estimation consistent across categories, regardless of how many such stores there are in the city.[25]

Stores selling sporting goods, hobby supplies, music, and books were most likely to cluster with competitors (Rho = 0.82). These stores sell classic comparison goods that patrons tend to browse from one store to another. People enjoy browsing books on physical shelves and neighboring bookstores usually offer a slightly different selection. Around Harvard Square, for example, there are eight different bookstores—a cooperative university book store, a long-standing independent bookstore, a poetry shop, a used bookstore, three comic bookstores, and a children's bookstore—each with a unique selection and feel.

Restaurants and bars follow second. Restaurants are almost perfect competitors—people choose only one for dinner even if multiple are available for

Figure 41. A cluster of competing shoe stores in Hong Kong. Photo by author.

comparison. Yet, despite competition, restaurants appear to attract more customers as a group than they would by locating apart. Inman Square and Davis Square are examples of competitive food clusters in Cambridge and Somerville—over a third of all retail, food, and service establishments around both squares are devoted to food and drink.[26]

Going out to eat is typically a social affair—few customers go to restaurants and bars for lunch or dinner alone. Having more choices makes social dining easier. Maybe a dinner companion doesn't feel like seafood today and wants to get Indian buffet instead. Perhaps one restaurant has too long of a line. Or perhaps everybody feels like having an ice-cream cone or a night cap after dinner. Competitive restaurants clusters that offer these options side by side attract more customers.

This study also showed competitive clustering among electronics stores and clothing and apparel stores. Harvard Square has 33 clothing and clothing accessory stores within minutes of each other. On weekends, you can observe shoppers wander from one clothing store to another looking for new ideas, better prices, or complementary garments that neighboring shops offer—a pair of shoes to go with new jeans, a bracelet to match a dress, or a pair of gloves to go with a winter coat. Just like restaurants, hobby shops, and bookstores, clothing stores that locate near competitors draw more customers.

Table 6. Clustering coefficients for six categories of retail and food businesses.

Store category	NAICS code	Rho	z-statistic
Sporting goods, hobby, book, and music stores	451 (n=90)	0.82	*** (6.50)
Food services & drinking places	722 (n=90)	0.56	** (2.44)
Electronics & appliance stores	443 (n=90)	0.42	* (1.86)
Clothing & clothing accessories stores	448 (n=90)	0.33	** (2.06)
Miscellaneous store retailers	453 (n=90)	0.25	~ (1.64)
Food & beverage stores	445 (n=90)	0.10	(0.70)

Significance level ~p<0.25, *p<0.1, **p<0.05, ***p<0.01

The two last categories in Table 6 represent *convenience* goods—grocery and beverage stores and miscellaneous retailers (e.g., CVS, Walgreens). In complete agreement with competitive clustering theory, clustering coefficients for these groups of stores were smallest and in fact statistically insignificant, as shown by the z-statistics in the last column. There is little benefit to having two or more supermarkets next to each other. Supermarkets tend to sell similar groceries. Even if their prices vary, consumers usually know these variations up front and rarely waste time browsing through breads or vegetables in one grocery store after another. Rather, grocery stores tend to cluster with complementary produce stores—fishmongers next to vegetable stores, ice-cream kiosks next to restaurants. Convenience stores, such as 7-Eleven or Walgreens, also tend to sell standardized merchandise that differs little from store to store, creating little incentive for comparison shopping. We consequently rarely find them sited next to competitors.

Like hydrogen bonds that hold water molecules together, retailers are held together by agglomeration forces between stores. Yet hydrogen bonds cannot hold all the water in a landscape in one large body—instead water bodies of various sizes scatter themselves into droplets, puddles, ponds, lakes, and rivers, settling in natural bowls, canyons, and valleys, where the Earth's gravitational force pulls them. Clustering effects are similarly not strong enough to hold all the retailers of a town together in one big agglomeration. Instead, as we saw Zipf's Law describe in Chapter 1, clusters divide into hierarchical constellations, gravitating toward advantageous locations in each city.[27] These location forces and the site characteristics that draw both groups and individual stores alike is the subject of Chapter 5.

But first, there is another form of grouping among stores that we need to discuss. This form of clustering has less to do with inter-store externalities and explicit preferences to locate next to specific complements or competitors and more to do with the well-being and resourcefulness of the cluster as a whole.

CHAPTER 4

Coordinated Clustering: Business Improvement Districts, Co-ops, and Malls

In the early 1990s, downtown Los Angeles was not the highly sought-out place to live, work, and play that it is today. In 1992, Los Angeles witnessed extensive street riots. Economically marginalized and underserved inner-city residents of color clashed with police and business owners. The riots were sparked by the acquittal of four white Los Angeles police officers in the beating of black motorist Rodney King in 1991. Rioters looted hundreds of businesses and set cars on fire, and 50 people died. Two years later, a 6.7 Richter scale earthquake shook Los Angeles, killing 57 people and producing tens of billions of dollars in property damage. Both events worsened the already dire state of the downtown.[1] Few people who didn't live or work downtown would choose to shop, eat, or walk around there.

In 1995, a year after the earthquake, a group of property owners in downtown came together to form the city's first property-based business improvement district (BID). Close to 60% of the property owners in the 56-block Garment District signed a petition to form a BID, with all signers agreeing to pay an additional fee on top of their property taxes to form an association that would enable them to invest into the management and improvement of the streets on which their businesses were located. The BID placed privately hired security patrols on streets, hired teams to remove graffiti from the walls, collected trash, and started marketing the area as the Los Angeles Fashion District. BID members were also successful in lobbying the city to pass an adaptive-reuse ordinance that would allow developers to convert former manufacturing and office buildings into residential lofts.

New businesses started coming in, public confidence in the safety of downtown streets gradually improved, and tourists started noticing the area. Developers transformed formerly vacant multistory industrial structures into fashionable residences with large windows framed by a grid of iron mullions and square glass tiles. Each day, privately hired workers descended on downtown in bright-colored shirts, providing security, collecting trash, scrubbing graffiti, power-washing sidewalks, and keeping downtown tidy for the expanding crowd of visitors from all parts of the city.

Other BIDs formed nearby. The Arts District established a BID, along with Downtown Center, South Park, Little Tokyo, and Chinatown. There were 9 BIDs in downtown Los Angeles and 41 in the city as a whole in 2018, covering almost every square foot of downtown with private place-management services.

Many in Los Angeles credit BIDs with helping turn around the once-desolate downtown by using aggressive maintenance and security services that the city could not afford. Others have been more critical of the BIDs and have cautioned the public against the private management of public space. Some contend that BIDs had their place in the early revival of the downtown but have now become catalysts of unwanted gentrification and suggest that BIDs primarily benefit already big and successful firms and place unnecessary burdens on small, local stores. But few would say that BIDs have played no role in restoring street commerce along otherwise ailing downtown Los Angeles streets.

BIDs provide coordinated upkeep, marketing, and place-making services in selected areas of the city, making up for some of the disadvantages that otherwise uncoordinated street-based retail and service clusters face in comparison to highly orchestrated shopping centers. In several cases, BIDs have helped make street commerce work where it hadn't previously, due to failing city services, poor inter-store coordination, or lack of organized action. But as organizations that include and favor some members while excluding others, BIDs have also been subject to criticism and debate.

Business Improvement Districts

Business improvement districts are quasi-governmental organizations (i.e., public-private partnerships) that provide a group of businesses and property owners collective financing for services that are underdelivered by the city and that enhance the attractiveness, competitiveness, or general welfare of their members.[2] The International Downtown Association, a networking body based in Washington, DC, that represents the interests of BIDs nationally and internationally, has set three basic conditions for defining a BID.

First, BIDs are publicly authorized districts—publicly approved nonprofit entities in a well-defined spatial territory that include two or more businesses. The sizes of BIDs vary widely and tend to be larger in large cities. In New York City, a typical BID includes 343 retailers and around 1,180 business altogether. Within most BID

Figure 42. Santee Alley, Fashion District BID in Los Angeles, CA. Photo by author.

district in the United States, a mandatory fee is levied on all the properties or businesses. Charges are typically levied by the local government on behalf of the BID, although there are a few BIDs that have authority to charge levies directly. BID levies are applied as additional taxes on top of regular municipal property taxes using the same payment mechanisms as property tax collection. All owners within BID boundaries are legally responsible for paying charges, regardless of their support for the formation of the BID. Many BIDs also use additional funding sources, including grants, in-kind contributions, and fundraising revenues.[3]

Unlike voluntary business associations, which are also popular in American downtowns, BIDs are formally incorporated by a municipal government, which enforces participation by collecting taxes that fund the BID. In voluntary business associations, there is a free-rider incentive, since individual businesses can benefit from the association services without becoming members or paying dues. Benefits resulting from street cleaning, security, and public space improvements cannot be easily excluded from individual stores that haven't joined the pool. In BIDs, however, once established, financial participation is mandatory and enforced by the local municipality.

Second, BIDs are administered by a nonprofit body with substantial independent policy-setting authority. Even though BID funds are generally raised by a local government, they are administered by an elected BID board, which usually consists of business owners as well as municipal representatives. BIDs are therefore not just receivers of grants from government like most traditional nonprofits but instead have substantial authority to decide what the level of funding will be, how funds will be expended and levels of service. Such authority must operate within laws or contracts that govern BIDs in each state or municipality.

And third, BIDs engage in certain types of activities, including street cleaning, security, and marketing, in the interest of all member businesses. Some also engage in attracting new tenants and providing grants for façade improvements, and almost all act as policy advocates with local municipalities. Services and activities are delivered only within the spatial boundaries of a BID. For instance, in New York City, one can distinguish the spatial boundaries of the Flatiron 23rd Street Partnership BID by following the black iron trash bins with BID logos that dot the streets within the limits of the BID.

The first BID was established in Toronto, Canada, in 1970 at the initiative of local business owners. By 1974, BIDs had entered the United States, starting in New Orleans. By 2011 there were more than 1,200 BIDs across the United States.[4] Other countries that have established BIDs include the UK, New Zealand, Australia, South Africa, Jamaica, Serbia, Albania, Germany, Ireland, and the Netherlands. A strong focus on the maintenance of public space suggests that BIDs are more likely to form in environments where property owners feel that municipal governments are not providing enough public space management, cleaning, and security services to benefit businesses. Business districts happy with security and cleanliness typically do not form BIDs. Harvard Square in Cambridge. MA, for instance, is a premiere cluster of largely independent stores in the Boston area that does not have a BID. It does have a business association with voluntary participation fees, which delivers some services that resemble BID offerings—attractive street plantings, extra cleaning during busy periods, and, most notably, organization of numerous public events, markets, and festivals that help raise revenues for the association. But city services providing street sweeping, graffiti removal, security, infrastructure, and public transportation are robust enough so that a private counterpart is not warranted. Other cities with similar high-quality municipal services have also found no need for BIDs.

How Effective Are BIDs?

It is unclear about how successful and beneficial BIDs actually are. Most evaluations of BID performance have been compiled by BIDs themselves, which poses a potential conflict of interest and credibility issue.[5] BIDs typically do not provide specific assessments on a regular basis, nor are they legally required to do so.[6] Second, it is difficult to demonstrate definitive positive changes within a BID that are directly caused by the BID itself. If the property values or revenues within a BID's boundaries visibly improved during a period of evaluation, it is difficult to disentangle the effects of the services rendered by the BID from the spatial, policy, or socioeconomic trends that affected the district along with the rest of the urban context around it. For this, proper econometric research methods are needed, which remain beyond the analytic capacity of most BIDs. And third, it is difficult to pick a single best success indicator for BIDs. The positive effects of BIDs can include an increase in business revenues, reduction in storefront vacancies, reduction in crime, increase in property values, or increase in visits of all kinds to an area.

An extensive study carried out by the Rand Corporation in Los Angeles concluded that the introduction of BIDs did have a marginal positive effect on crime reduction.[7] A longitudinal analysis of crime reports within the chosen BIDs and comparable control areas in downtown Los Angeles showed that the rates of interpersonal violent crime, in particular robbery, declined after the establishment of BIDs. Though statistically significant, the BID effect was small—robberies in BIDs dropped by 7% compared to a 5.7% reduction in non-BID control areas during the same 1994–2005 evaluation period.[8] As expected, BIDs that spent more resources on security also witnessed a larger reduction in violent crime. Other types of crime, such as property-related crime, by contrast, exhibited no difference between BIDs and non-BID control districts.

Stacey Sutton from Columbia University studied the effects of BID formation on retail sales and employment in New York City between 2000 and 2008.[9] Using longitudinal information from the National Establishment Time-Series (NETS) database, she evaluated economic outcomes in three different types of BIDs—large, corporate ones such as the Times Square and Flatiron 23rd Street Partnership; medium-scale destination BIDs along retail corridors, such as 125th Street in Manhattan and Jamaica Avenue in Queens; and small community BIDs, which tend to operate in weaker economic markets with higher rates of retail vacancy and less foot traffic. Evaluating BID districts alongside comparable non-BID retail clusters in the city, Sutton found that the effect of BIDs on retail sales and employment differed significantly across the three types. While in large corporate BIDs, both retail sales and employment tended to increase as a result of BID formation compared to control areas, the opposite was true in community BIDs. The latter, in fact, witnessed a decrease in sales and retail employment after a BID was formed. Sutton suggests that this troubling finding is partly explained by the fact that community BIDs have smaller budgets and mainly focus on business retention and street upkeep, while larger BIDs spend more resources on marketing, events, and business recruitment. But small community BIDs also include a higher proportion of independent businesses owned by local members of the community. Given that community BIDs are most numerous in New York City, Sutton cautions that "rather than serving as a buffer against economic decline for independent retailers, it seems that Community BIDs are a hindrance to sales and employment growth, relative to comparable areas."[10] When all BIDs were taken together as group, irrespective of size, there was no statistically significant effect on either retail sales or employment relative to similar areas of the city that never adopted BIDs. This was surprising, given widespread claims about the positive economic effects of BIDs.

Another study that examined BID formation in California concluded that BIDs do have positive effects on property values compared to non-BID areas, but these effects were unevenly distributed between small and large properties.[11] Large property owners and big anchor tenants tend to be most supportive of BID formation and also experience the largest increases in property values as a result of implementing a BID.[12] Both the New York and Los Angeles studies suggest that BIDs tend to be more favorable toward chain businesses and large commercial operators. The evidence for positive BID benefits on small, independent businesses is sparse. The *New Republic* magazine has even gone so far as to claim that "Business Improvement Districts are a favored neoliberal practice that transforms mixed-income neighborhoods into the same chain stores one can find at any outlet mall across the country."[13]

In Figure 43, I compare the cross-sectional annual sales volume per employee in three types of businesses—retail, food services and drinking places, and personal service establishments—in both BID and non-BID retail clusters in Los Angeles. The chart shows that sales per employee are not significantly higher in BIDs compared to non-BID retail clusters. Sales are similar across all three establishment categories, suggesting that from a retailer point of view, the benefits of BIDs appear to be less pronounced than often claimed in BIDs' self-reports. This is consistent with Sutton's results in New York, where BIDs did not benefit independent neighborhood retailers in small community BIDs.

Coordinating the Store Mix

Aside from their contested advantages over independent and fragmented retail clusters, another common reason for BIDs to formulate is to strengthen retail clusters' capacity to compete with shopping malls. Like malls, some BIDs do not just wait for desirable stores to join their organizations, but they go after them with marketing strategies and incentive packages. Many BIDs engage in marketing

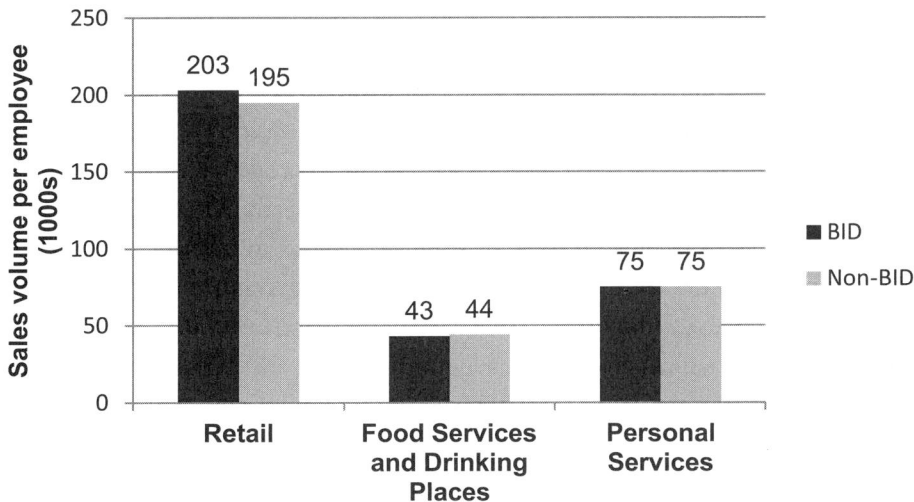

Figure 43. Comparison of sales volume per employee in three commercial establishment categories in BID and non-BID retail clusters in Los Angeles. Data Source: Infogroup 2010 Business Listings, provided as part of ESRI Business Analyst software.

activities to recruit desirable types of businesses when vacancies emerge among their storefronts. This soft form of coordination involves reaching out to commercial brokers about the BID needs and advertising space vacancies using various media channels. The International Downtown Association (IDA), a Washington DC based organization that represents BID interest nationally and internationally, estimates that roughly 82% of all BIDs in the United States engage in either in-house or outsourced marketing activities, and 62% engage in outright business recruiting.[14]

But the key difference between shopping centers and BIDs lies in financial lease coordination among participating businesses. As we saw in the previous chapter, in shopping centers of all sizes it is common for center owners to offer different tenants different percentage rent contracts, depending on their expected customer draw and financial impact on the center as a whole. This is a key advantage, which enables malls to financially orchestrate a profitable store mix. Discriminatory lease practices are especially valuable in attracting large anchor stores, whose fixed costs for locating on city streets can be significantly higher without subsidies. If pedestrian flows are equal in a mall and on a downtown street, there is considerably less incentive for a major-brand store to locate on an expensive Main Street and pay tens of thousands of dollars in rent every month when it can get the space for close to free inside a mall.

I have yet to find evidence of any BIDs engaging in a comparable level of business orchestration via monetary lease incentives as shopping centers. Doing this would require one property owner to be provided with a concrete, monetary incentive to take on a business at a lower lease value, a business that would then be expected to generate considerable spillovers to other nearby businesses whose extra proceeds collectively reimburse the loss to the first property owner.

On a spectrum of cooperation, BIDs therefore fall somewhere between independent and fragmented business clusters and shopping malls. Unlike independent and unorganized store clusters, BIDs do deliver a set of coordinated services that benefit all stores. Joint decision making through an elected board puts the common interests of all stores ahead of individual stores when it comes to using BID financing. But unlike malls, BIDs generally do not take cooperation to lease coordination between private property owners. Property owners in a BID are free to charge whatever rents they can get from businesses they rent to. Just like in fragmented retail clusters, there is an incentive for property owners to charge each tenant as much rent as they can. Any benevolent rent subsidies would not directly benefit the property owner but would instead accrue to neighboring businesses in the form of customer spillovers.

Still, it is increasingly common among BIDs to offer seed grants and one-time subsidies to attract desirable businesses to a cluster. For instance, the Westbury Village BID in the state of New York offers three tiers of incentive payments to commercial brokers who sign on a preferred tenant. A tier-one incentive of $7,500 is reserved for highly recognized national or regional chain stores or restaurants. A tier-two $5,500 subsidy is reserved for well-known brand stores, clothiers, regional/local chains, and other highly desirable business. A tier-three reward of $3,000 is reserved for brokers who sign on boutiques, artisan shops, specialty stores, or highly desirable start-ups.[15]

The Two Rivers Company in Clarksville, TN, on the other hand, provides lease incentives for a period limited to one year, with a potential six-month extension. The BID believes that "these early months are generally the months that businesses incur the greatest costs with the least amount of income."[16] During this period, the BID can help cover up to 60% of the business's monthly rent, or $600 per month, whichever is less. Applicants for this time-limited grant award must be businesses opening in a targeted, street-level vacant space on particular streets in downtown Clarksville. But the fact that this subsidy is limited to the first 12 months and is not directly tied to the expected positive externalities of the businesses makes it fundamentally different from a shopping mall lease-coordination model, which is perpetual and deliberately orchestrated to benefit the cluster as a whole.

Perhaps the most direct strategy for a BID to coordinate leases in a cluster is to own the spaces that it manages. Though it is rare for BIDs to own real estate directly, there is no legal reason why they can't. The Northeast Investment

Cooperative (NEIC) in northeastern Minneapolis, MN,[17] provides an interesting example. According to the organization, "NEIC was founded by a small group of community members who were tired of looking at poorly used property in their neighborhood and waiting for traditional developers to fix it. So they decided to do something about it. They envisioned a way for community members to become owners and investors in a real estate development cooperative that would buy and rehab properties in their community."[18] The cooperative was formed in 2011 by numerous members, each of whom committed $1,000 for a share in the co-op. Each shareholder is entitled to a vote as a board member and is eligible for dividend and capital account allocations. With the supprt of numerous local shareholders, NEIC purchased a commercial building on Central Avenue with a total of more than 175 member owners. It signed leases with two local businesses—Fair State Brewing Cooperative and Aki's Breadhaus—and the project opened in 2014. The co-op viewed a brewing company and a bread store as complementary, and the co-op's leadership can set the rents as it sees appropriate to keep both spaces leased at a profit. The proceeds from leasing accrue back to the co-op members.

Even though co-ops are common in the residential sector,[19] they are rare among retail businesses. I have found very few examples of co-ops where a group of members participate to run a set of retail and service businesses in a coordinated manner like NEIC. Cooperative grocery stores with multiple outlets are common, especially in Europe, but that is a very different model from a retail co-op that runs a cluster of different businesses from multiple adjacent buildings, akin to a shopping center but with a broader and democratic beneficiary structure. This is surprising, given that coordination could offer a number of benefits for BIDs.

While it might be legally complicated for individual property owners to enter coordinated ventures, due to antitrust laws that generally discourage cooperation between businesses, a separate legal body, such as a co-op or a limited liability corporation (LLC) jointly owned by a set of independent property owners and operated by a smaller group of executive members, makes cooperative retail clusters at least theoretically possible. These options could allow a cluster of independent stores to use lease coordination and incentive strategies much like a shopping center. Doing so would enable multiple individual property owners to engage in coordination rather than competition—a key strategy that benefits malls—and earn higher profits by doing so. Some properties would need to be rented out at discount prices in order to attract customer-generating brands or anchor businesses. These property owners must in turn be compensated for the loss by other properties that gain from the positive customer spillovers that the anchors generate.

If one building owner, for instance, rents out a space for free to bring in a popular grocery store—one of the most visited types of stores—then this will likely benefit all retail and service businesses in the vicinity. A cooperative agreement that pools revenues and profits together from multiple properties and redistributes them to landlords could enable the first property owner to be reimbursed for the loss by additional revenues generated at other stores. Unlike shopping malls, where the fruits of coordination are pooled into a single account—which, increasingly, is a remote real estate investment trust (REIT)—the gains here would be distributed back to numerous property owners or co-op members, producing direct benefits to the local community.

A municipal government can also act as the coordinator. London's Borough of Hackney, for instance, has actively bought up vacant retail spaces on its high streets, marketed them to desirable types of businesses, and leased them out at fair rates.[20] This does not amount to active lease coordination between anchor and non-anchor stores, but it does demonstrate that a proactive city government can act as an agent that works in the interests of Main Streets. Through ownership of retail spaces, a city government gains greater control over the store mix and an opportunity to reserve some of the space for more affordable stores with greater community benefits.

Does control over the tenant mix really make a difference in store performance between malls and urban retail clusters? It is hard to say precisely, since revenues are affected by myriad factors beyond tenant mix. But consider the data in Figure 44, which compares sales in stores that are located in shopping centers versus urban retail clusters in Los Angeles, CA.[21] Differences in sales volume are shown separately for retail, food and beverage, and service establishments.

The first three bars on the left describe the average sales volume for retail, food, and service establishments located inside shopping centers in Los Angeles. An average mall retailer sells $1.98 million worth of merchandise per year. A typical food-service establishment in a mall generates about half that amount—$0.91 million a year. And a typical service establishment, which includes repair and maintenance services as well as personal and laundry services, generates $0.74 million a year.

The second set of data bars to the right show the respective sales volume averages for businesses located in urban street clusters. Retail business that benefit from tenant optimization in malls attract considerably more revenue than uncoordinated urban retail clusters: businesses in shopping malls typically generate 65% higher sales than street retailers. The difference between mall and street retailers is equally large for service establishments, which sell 70% more, on average, in malls. For eating and drinking places, the gap is smaller—36%—though still sizable.

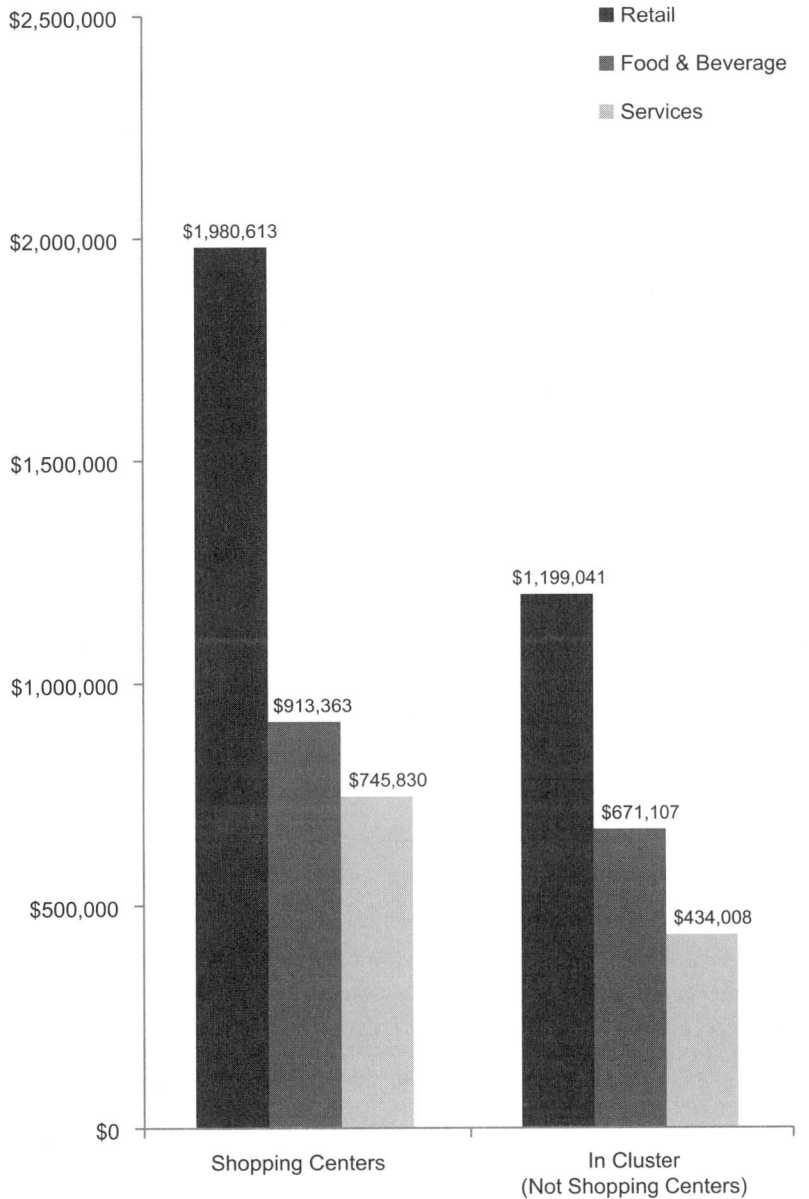

Figure 44. Average sales volume per business establishment in Los Angeles in 2010. Data Source: Infogroup 2010 Business Listings, provided as part of ESRI Business Analyst software.

But some caveats should be kept in mind. First, the types and sizes of stores in malls and urban clusters can differ—malls are more likely to attract clothing and apparel stores with larger floor areas than urban clusters, which may not have as much floor space. Second, malls also tend to work almost exclusively with recognized brand establishments, which devote considerable resources to marketing. Urban clusters, on the other hand, accommodate more independent shops that run smaller operations and lack large advertising budgets. Quality of the retail environment and public spaces is also likely to differ. These nuances may be responsible for part of the discrepancy in sales volume between mall and Main Street businesses, but there is reason to believe that benefits of tenant coordination are also at work.

Coordinated Retail Clusters Beyond the Mall

One of the most interesting examples of commercial clustering I have seen on the spectrum between coordinated malls and fragmented, independent Main Streets, is the Telliskivi or "Brick" Creative City in Tallinn, Estonia. Located in several large structures of a former railroad depot, Telliskivi has become one of the most popular cultural, retail, and dining venues in the city. This was not always the case.

Situated on a triangular site, surrounded by railways on all sides, Telliskivi stands behind Tallinn's main train station and is just a short walk from the city's historic Old Town. It occupies the former train factory structures that date back to the mid-19th century. Soon after the Soviet occupation of Tallinn at the dawn of the Second World War, the buildings were converted to house the Tallinn Electrical Engineering Factory. Just like with many Soviet-era electronics factories, which operated under a thick cloud of secrecy, it is not known what exactly was produced in the factory during the postwar years. According to at least one urban legend, parts of the Soviet Sputnik—the first orbital satellite in history—were produced at Telliskivi.

After the collapse of the Soviet Union, the factory fell into decay. A number of large buildings and warehouses were abandoned, and ongoing construction projects were left unfinished. A complex of buildings was accessed through one of two gates, completely unknown to the general public. In the mid-1990s, only adventure-seeking teenagers explored the crumbling factory structures covered in broken glass and rubble.

In the early 2000s, a REIT bought the complex. Its initial plan was to demolish all the structures to make room for new development. But cash-strapped and hit by a series of misfortunes, the REIT abandoned its plans, and one of the fund

Figure 45. Telliskivi Creative City in Tallinn, Estonia. Photo from the Telliskivi Creative City collection.

managers decided to piece together a new pool of investors and buy out the complex on his own. He had traveled around Europe and admired vibrant artist communities in Berlin—former hospitals, schools, and other institutional complexes taken over by artists, who established semi-legal studios, galleries, and shops, keeping doors open to the public. Couldn't something similar be done with Telliskivi, he and his business partner thought? But while the Berlin examples had received the real estate for free, and some of them were highly subsidized by the public sector, the conversion of Telliskivi would have to be purely commercial and financially self-sustainable. There would be no support from the city or national government.

The business partners came up with the Telliskivi Creative City concept in 2009, which envisioned a cluster of creative workspaces, retailers, restaurants, and entertainment venues. At first, they had difficulty getting buy-in from tenants, most of whom knew nothing about the area or its history. The first restaurant lease was signed in the former F-Building by owners who decided to name the restaurant after the building. A trailblazer in new Estonian cuisine and offering a family-friendly atmosphere in a grand former industrial space, F-Building quickly developed a following. Seeing that businesses could indeed prosper at a relatively unknown site encouraged new tenants to sign up. Designer stores moved in around the ground-floor corridor of a former factory administration building that became known as the "shopping street." An open stage theater opened at the back end of the site, pulling visitors deeper into the complex. More restaurants and shops followed, and creative businesses rented several upstairs units for office and workshop use. A club and entertainment venue opened in the attic of a five-story brick walk-up building.

The owners worked carefully with each new tenant or group of tenants on preparing the space to meet their needs, usually renovating one unit at a time. The only important criterion for admitting new tenants was that they had to exhibit a creative mission and contribute to the creative atmosphere of the cluster. A craft bicycle shop followed, along with a bakery making traditional dark bread from Muhu Island, a print shop, some local clothing-design stores, and more restaurants serving craft beers and international cuisine. Telliskivi also hosts a Sunday flea market, and music festivals throughout the year draw locals and tourists alike.

Most of the small businesses that further the creative mission of the cluster receive favorable lease terms. But more established and profitable enterprises pay top dollar per square foot for the benefit of joining the cluster. Entertainment venues put on both subsidized and highly profitable shows. Telliskivi has also become a popular place among major companies to host special events. Today, more than 200 companies occupy the complex. And even though a great number of them are charged rents that are much below market rate, several major commercial tenants make up for the loss. Numerous small entrepreneurs with creative flair have contributed to an atmosphere that attracts profitable anchors that more than balance the budget for the cluster as a whole. According to the owners, Telliskivi is significantly more profitable than a commercial shopping center in the heart of the city that they also own.

Unlike the traditional shopping center model, where a few large commercial anchors generate customer draw and enjoy heavily subsidized lease terms in return, Telliskivi flipped the mall model upside down and instead subsidizes a series of small creative entrepreneurs, who generate little sales themselves but produce a creative atmosphere that draws in many visitors and attracts more profitable commercial tenants. The owners have demonstrated a mindful management style toward each tenant, often renovating rooms one at a time to suit their specific needs. A great number of properties are still unused and in the same state of decay as they were in the mid-1990s. But the unfinished and unpolished feel of the place has only contributed to the creative and authentic atmosphere of the complex.

Telliskivi Creative City offers an interesting hybrid between a highly coordinated shopping mall and a moderately coordinated BID. Most management decisions are discussed on a closed Facebook group, where all business owners participate. Individual shop fronts or interior designs are not dictated to store owners, opening hours are left up to each business, and shop owners do not pay rent based on a percentage of revenues. At least for now, Telliskivi management behaves partly as a benevolent landlord that values the well-being of the creative collective, and partly as diligent accountant who needs to make sure the whole complex remains financially sustainable and continues to grow.

Unlike a BID, Telliskivi management not only coordinates cleanups, security, parking, tenant recruitment, and marketing for the area, it also controls lease contracts like a shopping center. But unlike a shopping center, Telliskivi consciously provides beneficial lease terms to numerous small and creative businesses that it deems useful for its mission. This doesn't mean that Telliskivi is a money-losing operation. Quite the contrary: any losses are amply compensated by a series of commercial tenants, who also align with the creative mission of the cluster but are charged top rates to make up for other subsidies.

Most cities, unfortunately, cannot rely on benevolent developers like those at Telliskivi. But Telliskivi does offer two poignant lessons to both shopping centers and BIDs. First, to shopping centers it demonstrates that customer draw is not only generated with large-scale anchor stores. Instead, a group of small and not very profitable but highly creative and interesting entrepreneurs can collectively draw in more visitors than traditional anchor stores. And to BIDs, Telliskivi shows that not all members of a BID need to pay equal membership rates to be valuable to a cluster. It can be well worth lowering the rates for small, barely profitable members if they have something else than sales to offer the rest of the cluster—such as diversity, creativity, or inclusiveness—that expands the attractiveness of the cluster as a whole.

How Malls Are Becoming More Like Main Streets

While coordinated retail clusters between numerous independent landlords remain an idea, trends in shopping center development in the last decade have moved in a similar direction in terms of use mix and aesthetics. "A new breed of shopping center is integrating so seamlessly into its urban surroundings that it can be difficult to draw any line between city and mall whatsoever," pronounced a recent *Guardian* article.[22] This breed attempts to capitalize on the dislike for generic strip malls and a growing popular appreciation for urban retailing. It is called the *lifestyle center*.

Seph Lawless, an American photographer who has documented and written about abandoned malls, describes lifestyle centers as follow: "Lifestyle centers

Figure 46. Assembly Row "lifestyle" shopping center in Somerville, MA.

were touted as the mall of the customer who eschews malls. Loosely defined, they are single story open-air projects, generally in high-income areas, that mimic Main Streets of yore; pedestrian friendly sidewalks and roadways wind through them, allowing shoppers to identify their destination's locations as they wind past, if not park right in front."[23] Two new lifestyle centers are located right outside of Boston—Legacy Place in Dedham and Assembly Row in Somerville (Figure 46), both designed with densely packed street-front shops reminiscent of traditional Main Streets. Across the United States, the number of lifestyle centers has tripled since 2004, numbering around 412 by 2015. At the same time, not a single enclosed mall has opened since 2007. Instead, some shopping centers, such as Biltmore Square Mall in North Carolina, have taken off their roofs to "de-mall."

The greatest incarnations of lifestyle centers have, in fact, emerged outside of the United States, in the downtown settings of the roaring economies of China, Singapore, and Taiwan. The Xin Tian Di, for instance, which translates literally as "New Heaven and Earth," is a 7.4-acre retail development that occupies the retrofitted quarters of historic Shikumen stone gatehouses and narrow alleys in the heart of Shanghai, China. The car-free development, which mainly targets tourists and expats who believe they are experiencing a piece of 19th-century Chinese urban morphology, is connected through a series of outdoor walkways lined with high-end restaurants, coffee shops, boutiques, and bars. To the south of the retrofitted development lies a modern 250,000-square-foot leisure and entertainment complex, boasting a movie theater and a fitness center as well as a complex of luxurious serviced apartments. Though several preservation scholars have argued that the development represents a grave violation of the principles of historic preservation—nothing but the geometric configuration and decorative tiles of the original buildings were left intact—Xin Tiang Di has been tremendously lucrative to its developers. The popularity of the center has attracted a series of super-luxury residential developments by internationally renowned architects around its edges, which further solidifies the image of the place as a 21st-century urban mall dressed up in historic buildings that are seamlessly integrated into the 19th-century neighborhood structure of Shanghai.

Lifestyle centers typically boast outdoor circulation between stores, reminiscent of traditional Main Streets. Instead of air-conditioned indoor covered walkways, customers walk in front of diverse and independent-looking shop fronts, which are still centrally owned like in any traditional mall. One sees fewer parking lots in front of big-box stores than in conventional malls. Instead a dense cluster of small shop fronts, often double-sided around a pedestrian walkway, put many shops and restaurant entrances within close reach of visitors who park their cars parallel to the curb in front of the stores or leave them in a hidden multistory garage, which typically offers two to three hours of free parking.

Second, lifestyle centers tend to offer a more diverse mix of amenities than a traditional mall. Restaurants, often high-quality establishments with healthy or organic menus, dot the sidewalks and plazas and spill out onto outdoor tables in pleasant weather. There are also ample entertainment options—cinemas, children's playgrounds, bars, outdoor stages, and ice-skating rinks in the winter—drawing in family and recreational visitors who come as much for fun as for shopping.

This description might suggest that lifestyle centers are similar to good old Main Streets, with their diverse architecture and shop offerings. This is indeed their intention. But lifestyle centers also stand apart from Main Streets with their rather exclusive focus on high-income customers. While most Main Streets tend to offer genuinely diverse shops and eateries for different income levels, lifestyle centers are packed with upscale establishments, with little offered for low-income households. Most lifestyle centers have, in fact, emerged in relatively high-income suburban settings, close to the upper-middle-class families that can afford them. The Boston metropolitan area's Legacy Place in the suburb of Dedham is a case in point. Legacy Place offers brands such as Apple, J. Crew, Anthropologie, and L.L. Bean, and food options such as Shake Shack, Acquitaine, P. F. Chang's, and Whole Foods Market. The median household income in Dedham is over $85,000, well above the average of $54,000 in the neighboring city of Boston.

Even though visually situated in a set of detached structures with storefronts facing busy sidewalks, lifestyle centers are still centrally owned, coordinated, and managed. They employ the financial advantages of coordination by offering differential lease contracts to different stores, depending on their impact to the center as a whole. Anchor businesses in lifestyle centers still get favorable lease terms, while small and lesser-known stores that benefit from customer spillovers—jewelers, apparel stores, newsstands, or souvenir stores—pay top dollar per square foot. Leveraging the benefits of joint lease coordination, lifestyle centers are combining the new urban citizens' demand for street-based commerce with the financial efficiencies of malls. Their quality of public space, mixed-use character, and reliance on streets for access and circulation make lifestyle centers arguably better contributors to the urban environment than the enclosed and introverted malls that preceded them.

But from a community perspective, street commerce offers a number of advantages over centrally owned shopping centers, including the more urban lifestyle centers. For one, an agglomeration of multiple, independent commercial properties is more likely to remain resilient to economic downturns and market shifts than single-owner centers. Shopping centers, which now are increasingly operated by REITs, are often highly leveraged with significant monthly loan payments, requiring consistent revenue and operating income. When times are good, commercial loans enable developers to supercharge their returns, but the opposite also holds for when times are bad. Relatively small revenue decreases on highly leveraged developments can reverberate into large losses and an inability to service loans. This can lead to harsh decisions to cut the losses and shut down centers, as several American cities have witnessed in the past decade.[24] Some estimates suggest that by 2022, one out of four malls in the United States could be out of business.[25] The situation is exacerbated by the fact that REIT managers often track the performance of their assets from a distance, without directly interacting with the local tenants, customers, and communities who are affected. When malls leave communities, local jobs suffer most. Since 2002, department store closures around the country have led to a loss of 448,000 jobs. Locally owned businesses outside of malls are more likely to stay anchored to a place, generating long-term multiplier effects for a local economy.

Urban retail clusters also tend to foster more democratic public space between stores. Even though a great number of shopping centers do organize community events, celebrations, and gatherings, such activities are usually carefully planned and scheduled. Common space in shopping centers is ultimately private—governed by private regulations and enforced by private security. Public space between along commercial streets, on the other hand, is typically owned by a city. The use of such space is governed by public regulations that prohibit the exclusion of visitors based on their looks or beliefs, and that tend to be more permissive toward unplanned activities, such as performance, vending, loitering, public gathering, skateboarding, or bicycling.[26] By enabling anyone to use public space at any time, urban retail clusters benefit citizens in ways that go well beyond consumption.

Furthermore, the fragmented ownerships of properties in urban retail clusters also tends to produce a genuinely diverse built environment that is experientially more enriching than a coordinated shopping center. Shopping center developers often find individual quirks in shop fronts, signage, facades, and maintenance undesirable. But diversity and difference have benefits that go beyond sales. Quirks tell stories about a place, and a personalized touch from a store owner can make an environment attractive to people who would otherwise feel uninvited. Even the best efforts in holistically coordinated shopping centers to achieve diversity and authenticity cannot match the serendipity that multifaceted urban retail clusters can spontaneously produce. The genuine diversity that results from fragmented decision making is itself an asset that invites people to a place not only to shop, but also to experience surprise, difference, and chance encounters.

Yet, instead of supporting smaller, independent stores, it is still more common for city governments to hand malls, lifestyle centers, and other big-box stores notable financial subsidies to set up shop in the form of infrastructure, land, tax breaks, and other subventions. Good Jobs First, a national policy resource center promoting corporate accountability in economic development, estimates that Walmart has received over $1.2 billion in economic development subsidies over the last two decades and keeps receiving $70 million worth of subsidies annually from local and state governments in the form of tax breaks, cash grants, and infrastructure investments.[27] Over 90% of Walmart's 100 distribution centers around the country received economic development subsidies, reaching as high as $46 million each. A nonpartisan group, Americans for Tax Fairness, has claimed that if you add both direct and indirect employee subsidies, federal tax breaks, and other financial benefits to these local perks, then Walmart's total annual subsidies could be as high as $7.6 billion from American taxpayers.[28]

Walmart is hardly alone in this windfall; most big retail chains receive similar incentive packages. The five largest retail chains in the United States—Walmart, Costco, Kroger, Home Depot, and Target—have thousands of stores around the country, each of which employs hundreds, sometimes thousands, of staff. The top four grocery chains in America—Walmart, Kroger, Safeway, and Publix Supermarkets—accounted for 36% of the total grocery sales in 2013. Home Depot and Lowes control around 45% of the hardware and building supply market in the United States.[29] So great is their bargaining power that leaving a town can leave entire communities unemployed and devastated.[30]

The economic benefits that subsidizing these chains is supposed to achieve tend to be overstated. A study done by Civic Economics that analyzed the pros and cons of a Borders chain bookstore as opposed to a local independent bookstore in Austin, TX, found that out of every $100 spent at Borders, only $13 circulated back into the local economy in the form of profit to local owners, wages paid to local employees, the procurement of goods and services from other local firms, and charitable giving.[31] And $87 left the area. For two local bookstores, however—Waterloo and Book People—$45 out of $100 remained in the local economy. The economic multiplier for the town was three times higher with local businesses.

Bookstores are not exceptional in this regard. Most small-scale local retailers tend to hire local staff and pay them better wages and benefits than large corporate retailers. National and international chain retailers rely on consolidated suppliers and service companies around the country. McDonald's doesn't source its beef from the local butcher, its bread from a local baker, or its trucking from a local logistics company. McDonald's ships its beef and buns from its factories and distribution centers to restaurants around the world using its corporate shipping companies. Similarly, Walgreens doesn't order its freight transportation from a local trucking company, its advertising banners from a local print shop, or its shelves and decorations from local suppliers. From each dollar that comes in over the counter, little trickles down into the local economy.

Purchasing merchandise and services from nearby businesses can be a point of pride for locally owned stores. One coffee shop I visited in Concord, MA—a town with a revolutionary history that has only 17,000 residents—has a blackboard on the wall proudly displaying its vendors for bread, chocolate, dairy products, vegetables, etc. (Figure 47). Of 11 vendors, 9 are from neighboring towns in Massachusetts, demonstrating that sourcing local is possible in towns of any size.

And when hit by hard times, small, locally owned retailers are less likely to cut their losses and fire their staff. Due to their personal investment in their enterprises and their connection to the places in which they operate and the people who live there, local retailers are more likely to seek any financial assistance and credit lines they can before calling it quits.

But despite the benefits they bring to local economies, small retail and service businesses typically do not receive any of the subsidies that their corporate counterparts enjoy. Unlike Walmart, which might receive tens of millions of dollars' worth of incentives and infrastructure investments before opening a new hypercenter, tens of locally owned shops, restaurants, and personal service providers, who collectively hire as many people and generate a bigger economic multiplier effect for a town, must get by on their own and survive in the presence of competition from subsidized big-box operators. It seems that politicians and economic

Figure 47. Local vendors supplying Haute Coffee in Concord, MA. Photo by author.

development directors prefer to negotiate one huge deal with a large corporation, which will make front-page news, than tens of small deals with lesser-known shops that never make the headlines but do in fact benefit the local economy.

Banks, similarly, tend to hand out construction loans and development financing more readily when a developer lines up a series of well-known national or international brand stores than an equivalent number of local shops. Stores such as Subway, H&M, and Anthropologie receive "triple A" credit ratings, signaling to lenders their low probability of failure. This produces a direct incentive for any retail developer to prioritize chain stores.

The effects of these preferences and incentives can be seen across Main Streets and town centers in the United States, where the choice of businesses is virtually identical from place to place and where street commerce no longer reflects the local identity of a place—a Chevron gas station next to a McDonald's, followed by a CVS pharmacy, a Ralph's grocery store, a Panera Bread café, a Quizno's sandwich shop, a Starbucks, and a Bank of America branch office. A Main Street in Utah becomes hard to distinguish from one in New Hampshire.

In addition to their inferior economic multiplier effects, chain businesses are not the types of shops, restaurants, and service providers that contribute to the livability and charm of a town. The perceived quality and amenity value of retail offerings is instead almost entirely created by small, local-flavor businesses. People like the streets of Boston not because of the chain stores you can find in any other town in the country, but because of the quirky local stores, seafood restaurants, and cafés that you can't find anywhere else. Similarly, people like Phoenix, AZ, not for its Taco Bells and Home Depots, but for its unique restaurants, hardware stores, bookstores, and clothing shops.

I am not trying to argue that chain businesses are bad and that successful commercial streets should not welcome them. It is simply not possible to produce or sell a wide variety of products locally in each municipality or region. In fact, most of the products we buy are not even made here but are instead shipped in from a number of other countries where it is cheaper or faster to manufacture them. If all T-shirts and pants we buy were made locally, then we would end up paying many times more than most of us can afford each time we renew our stock. This is especially true for clothing, shoes, apparel, household goods, tools, electronics, books, games, health and personal care products, cars and car parts, etc. But it is also true of grocery stores and restaurants. Many chain grocers, such as Trader Joe's and Safeway, and chain restaurants, such as McDonald's and Subway, achieve low prices through economies of scale that locally owned businesses cannot match. We cannot and should not escape relying on national and international operators to deliver affordable products as part of street commerce.

I am simply suggesting that the financial subsidies that towns and states hand out to retail businesses should not favor national and international giants. They should instead provide a level playing field for all stores, including smaller and locally owned ones. Instead of committing to a 10-year tax break, new service road, and sewage system for a new big-box store on the edge of town, allocate an equivalent amount of subsidy to local businesses in the form of tax breaks, low-interest loans, guarantees, support grants, or street upgrading investments. Direct and indirect support for small local businesses will both produce larger multiplier effects for the local economy and help contribute to the unique image of a place that attracts more people to the town.

What Cities Can Do to Equalize the Playing Field

San Francisco recently enacted a financial policy—Measure J—that is explicitly focused on protecting and supporting local legacy businesses that have been around for decades and are listed on a Legacy Business Registry. According to the nonprofit organization SF Heritage, which helped introduce the measure, the registry is open to businesses and nonprofits that are 30 years old or older and which have been nominated by a member of the board of supervisors or mayor. The nominees must prove that they have made a significant impact on the history or culture of their neighborhood in a hearing before the Small Business Commission. Up to 300 businesses can be added to the registry annually and all applicants must agree to maintain the historic name and craft of their businesses. For accepted businesses, the city government provides a grant of $500 per employee per year to help offset their costs. To property owners who agree to extend 10-year leases to legacy business, the city offers an additional rent grant of $4.50 per square foot per year for up to 5,000 square feet. The policy is meant to offset staggering commercial rent hikes that keep pushing locally owned and historic business out of the city. Annual grants are capped at $50,000 per legacy business and $22,500 for building owners. San Francisco's Measure J is an example of a progressive and proactive financial instrument to support designated street commerce, and other cities are starting to follow.

But the policy could also be improved. First, its current focus on uniquely historic businesses is attributable to the fact that it came about through the efforts of SF Heritage. Similar support should be extended to other types of business that are shown to deliver an essential benefit to communities—grocery stores, affordable restaurants, laundromats, etc. And instead of a one-time entry to a registry, the registry could be updated in three- or five-year intervals, adding or removing stores as a representative body deems necessary. Moreover, the current subsidy of $4.50 per square foot per year might seem generous in a smaller town, but it constitutes a tiny amount in the context of commercial rents in San Francisco. At prime locations, where retailers pay $100–$300 per square foot, the subsidy only covers 1–4% of occupancy costs—not enough to keep businesses in place. But the fact that the city only offers the subsidy to landlords who agree to a 10-year lease extension is very positive. Locking in a 10-year lease, even if costly, provides shop owners with some certainty about the future and avoids short cycles of nerve-racking rent hikes that often destroy local businesses.

Redirect and Channel Public Sector Procurement

City governments and other publicly funded institutions can also direct their own departments to make procurements from local businesses. City governments are often the largest employers in town, with considerable annual procurement needs. If all the breakfast, lunch, and dinner orders made daily for various events, conferences, meetings, and workshops were placed with local restaurants, grocers, sandwich shops, and pizzerias, a great deal of catering investment would stay in town. The same goes for other procurement needs, such as office supplies, cleaning supplies, kitchen and bathroom supplies, etc.

An analogous move to shift the procurement of supplies and services to local businesses has taken place among large anchor institutions elsewhere with positive results. In Cleveland, for instance, University Circle's three largest anchor institutions—Case Western Reserve University, University Hospitals, and

Cleveland Clinic—started shifting their annual procurements to local businesses and communities in 2010.[32] The University Circle's procurements of goods and services total around $3 billion a year, which were largely flowing out of the community. As a result of a cooperative effort and pledge to sustainability and community development, the institutions came together in 2010 to start channeling their purchases to local producers, service providers, and shops. Several community-based companies were born out of this shift. For instance, the Evergreen Cooperative established Green City Growers to produce sustainable food for local orders, and Evergreen Cooperative Laundry to operate a large-scale laundry and dry cleaning service, both of which train and hire local workers from historically marginalized neighborhoods close to University Circle.

Encourage "Condoization" of Commercial Space

In order to mitigate the effect of unpredictable rent increases on shop owners, regulations for new real estate developments could incentivize ownership rather than leasing of retail space. Even though acquiring a retail property necessitates a significant down payment, with fixed-rate mortgages, monthly payments remain stable and business owners do not have to fear rent hikes when lease contracts are up. Especially in growth areas that are likely to undergo high appreciation rates, factoring the cost of commercial property into the initial business plan can prove a safer strategy than relying on lease contracts with uncertain rate hikes. Long-lasting legacy stores along city streets have often survived because they own their space and no landlord could push them out. This was the case with the taxidermy store on London's Essex Road that I described in Chapter 2. As property owners, store owners also become more vested in a place. City governments can support local businesses by requiring developers of new mixed-use and commercial buildings to turn ground-floor retail units into commercial condominiums that are sold rather than leased.

Facilitate the Sharing of Resources Between Stores

The public sector can also explore joint development through public-private partnerships (PPPs) to support local commerce, sharing costs and risks with private developers. This approach can be especially important when investing in infrastructure projects that are too large or expensive for the private sector to undertake alone, but whose presence could benefit Main Street businesses at large and be profitable when undertaken jointly.

In cities with a large private automobile mode share, PPPs can be used to develop multistory garages that are shared by the area's businesses. Municipalities can issue bonds to finance a structured lot, which are either backed by the community's general tax revenues or revenues from parking fees. Concentrating parking in designated multistory underground or aboveground structures reduces the amount of space devoted to parking compared to the conventional requirement that each store provide its own four to five parking spots per every 1000 square feet of floor area.

Space savings in coordinated lots are achieved through several efficiencies. First, since different businesses receive visits at different hours of the day, a shared lot enables the same parking lot to be reused throughout the day, leading to fewer overall space requirements and higher parking occupancy. Second, each separated lot requires ingress and egress lanes, which can be shared in larger multistory lots. And furthermore, since structured parking is chargeable through a payment gantry, it can double as nighttime parking for the area's residents or businesses. It is also a relatively safe investment to recuperate. Church Street in Burlington, VT, and the Third Street Promenade in Santa Monica, CA, offer examples of successful street commerce where parking is efficiently managed in multistory shared lots a block or two away from shops.

Offer Training and Support Grants to Stores

Cities can also support street commerce by offering training and support programs to potential future tenants. The economic development division of the city of Cambridge, MA, for instance, offers both matching grants to small businesses for physical improvements as well as entrepreneurial training and technical support.

The Storefront Improvement Program is part of a suite of programs and services offered by the city to help small and independent businesses prosper in the town. It is targeted at property owners or commercial tenants seeking to renovate or restore commercial building exteriors, and provides technical and financial assistance to remove architectural barriers at storefront entrances and to improve the physical appearance of businesses. The program helps small business owners overcome financial barriers to upgrading their space and thereby attracting a larger clientele.

The program provides matching grants paying 90% of the costs up to $20,000 for improvements that make shop entrances conform to Americans with Disability Act standards, including ramps, lifts, door hardware and automatic openers, accessible parking, and signage. The city also provides 50% matching grants for up to $15,000 for other facade improvements, including better windows, paneling, architectural details, and restoration of historic features. A third type of matching grant enables shops to cover 50% of the total cost, up to $2,500, on improvements made to signage, lighting, and awnings. An architectural consultant retained by the city is available to provide assistance to applicants through the conceptual design stage at no cost.

Local governments can also offer professional training for prospective business owners in areas such as accounting, business-plan development, or marketing, including meetings with experienced business owners from around town. Having a network of advisors who can help navigate unfamiliar business situations is as important to prospective retailers as it is for technology startups and other forms of entrepreneurship, where peer support is widely practiced. Training helps reduce the risk of business failure and helps unexperienced owners grow their businesses to more sustainable sizes.

Each of the strategies I have outlined so far—financial subsidies, small-business support programs, zoning, and public transit investment—can help cities bolster street commerce. But unfortunately, none of the existing approaches offer municipal government enough leverage to tackle commercial unaffordability and gentrification head on. For this, a new set of policy and planning tools are needed. I discussed in Chapter 2 what considerations an inclusionary retail policy should include. More policy innovation is needed in this space.

Zoning new commercial spaces to be small and more suitable for locally owned independent establishments and providing rent subsidies like San Francisco is doing for legacy businesses can help. But overly restrictive zoning can also crowd out all chain businesses, with their lower prices and sizeable marketing budgets, that are important for attracting a larger clientele. And rent subsidies, such as those included in Measure J in San Francisco, are hard to implement in cities that do not enjoy property taxes and budget surpluses like those seen in the wealthy knowledge economies of San Francisco, Boston, or New York. Ultimately, street commerce needs both chain businesses and local businesses—striking a balance is key.

BIDs also remain a viable option for cities and neighborhoods that struggle with municipal public space services or face fierce competition from coordinated shopping centers. But in order to be inclusive, BIDs should focus more on the interests of smaller, independent business owners. They should also focus less on private securitization of public space and more on the economic performance of the cluster as a whole.

Beyond the organizational structures and inter-store coordination mechanisms discussed in this chapter, the economic well-being of stores is also affected by the urban environment around stores. In fact, location constitutes one of the most important ingredients of successful commerce overall. This is what the next chapter will investigate in greater detail.

CHAPTER 5

Location, Location, Location: How Retailers Gravitate to Homes, Workplaces, and Pedestrians

There are 19 Dunkin Donuts stores in Cambridge, MA. One of them, located in the middle of Harvard Square, draws over 3,700 customers a day. Another one, nearby on Massachusetts Avenue, receives only around 1,200 customers a day. The stores are nearly identical—they offer the same selection of coffees and donuts and charge the same prices for their services. The Dunkin franchise provides both with the same signage and marketing exposure. Quality, branding, and pricing do not explain the more than threefold discrepancy in traffic between them.

The first store is located inside the Harvard subway station, next to the university campus. There are over 20 competing coffee shops around Harvard Square, many of them more known to the locals than Dunkin. But Dunkin's prominent location inside the station guarantees that the 20,000-some passengers who use the station daily cannot miss it on their way out. The Massachusetts Avenue store, on the other hand, is located next to a number of other eateries on the raised ground floor of a multistory building. There is significantly less foot traffic in front of this location than at the subway station, and office and retail densities are notably lower around it. Only half a mile apart, there certain is not a threefold difference in housing and office prices between these sites. But for retail, which depends on foot traffic, there is. The *location, location, location* mantra is truer of retail space than any other type of real estate out there.

For retailers to occupy a good location, they need to outbid other competing uses. Ground-floor spaces can be as attractive to offices, institutions, and, under the right circumstances, even residents. Landlords typically rent their space to the highest bidder from the allowable use categories set by zoning. If an office is

Figure 48. Shop front occupied by an architecture office. Renzo Piano Building Workshop in Paris. Photo by author.

willing to pay more for a storefront than a retailer, then the storefront will go to the office. It is not uncommon for ground-floor commercial space to be used by doctors, design firms, banks, accountants, and myriad other nonretail businesses. Figure 48, for example, shows the famous Renzo Piano architecture office in Paris occupying a traditional shop front in the Marais. But just like every other land-use category is drawn to specific types of places, unique location qualities are also particularly appealing to retail, food, and personal service businesses. These location qualities help shops attract enough customers and revenue to outbid other competing uses.

Back in 1916, the Chicago urban sociologist Robert Park noted: "There is now a class of experts whose sole occupation is to discover and locate, with something like scientific accuracy, taking account of the changes which present tendencies seem likely to bring about, restaurants, cigar stores, drug-stores, and other small retail business units whose success depends largely on location."[1] A typical retail location model postulates that store owners are expected to locate at points of maximal demand—as close as possible to consumers who demand their commodities and strategically with respect to other stores, who either compete or complement them in attracting the desired clientele.[2]

But what does it really mean to locate as closely as possible to consumers? Who might these consumers be and where are they coming from? How do we find the locations in a city that are closest to most consumers and have the greatest potential for commercial success? Location decisions also need to account for competition and balance the risk of lower revenues that results from clustering with competing businesses against the increased market area that results from locating apart from competitors or next to complementary stores. The choice of location thus directly affects retail revenues.

Measuring Spatial Accessibility to Customers

The proximity of a location to a single source of demand—to a customer's home location for instance—can be measured in a rather simple manner using straight-line distance or travel time between a store and a home. But identifying locations that are closest to as many customers as possible may no longer be feasible with a simple proximity measure—maximizing access can, at times, mean distancing from some customers while approaching others so that access is maximized on aggregate, not individually. To capture this aggregate benefit, researchers have come to use *accessibility* measures.

Accessibility has emerged as a central concept in planning, transportation, and economic geography to describe how different locations in a city are spatially linked to surrounding opportunities. There is generally a consensus that land use location choices are affected by accessibility. According to Richard Hurd, author of the now classic book *Principles of City Land Values*, "Since value depends on economic rent, and rent on location, and location on convenience, and convenience on nearness, we may eliminate the intermediate steps and say that value depends on nearness."[3] "The more accessible an area is to the various activities in a community," argued Walter Hansen, who first formulated the connection between land use and accessibility, "the greater its growth potential."[4] Retail location choices rely fundamentally on accessibility to customers.[5]

A large body of literature has developed on accessibility since the 1950s. Though writings on accessibility actually go back further,[6] it is often Hansen's classic paper of 1959, "How Accessibility Shapes Land Use," that is credited for paving the way for joint accessibility and land use studies.[7] Albeit considerable variation in definitions,[8] accessibility is most commonly defined as the ease of an individual to pursue an activity of a desired type, at a desired location, by a desired travel mode. We can, for instance, talk about accessibility from homes to healthy food markets on foot.

A range of different accessibility measures have been proposed to describe location qualities.[9] For analyzing retail locations, two types of accessibility indices are particularly useful: *gravity* accessibility measures and *betweenness* measures. Furthermore, the American geographer David Huff has proposed an elegant way of combining accessibility indices in what has become known as the Huff model of retail patronage. In the following, I will walk through these accessibility metrics and discuss how they are integrated in a Huff model to both explain which location factors affect store patterns and to predict how many patrons a store is likely to attract at a given site.

The Gravity Accessibility Index of a Location

The gravity index has obtained its name from a conceptual similarity with Newton's gravitational law, which states that the gravitational force between two objects is proportional to their weights and inversely proportional to the distance between them. This index can be used to gauge how readily businesses can be accessed from a variety of different places—from homes, workplaces, public transit stations, parks, or schools. For instance, we can discuss accessibility from a potential business location to people aged 25–35 within a 10-minute travel radius.[10] Its measurement is typically automated on a computer.[11]

Imagine that you place a set of rubber bands around a pencil that you are holding above a town map in your hand. The other ends of the rubber bands are attached to places on the map where people come from to access your business, such as home addresses. Each band pulls toward a home with a certain force. If you let the pencil go, it will wobble around for a while, but will eventually settle at an origin location of least tension—where the least amount of pull is exerted among all the rubber bands collectively attached to it. This is the location of maximum gravity accessibility to the set of places attached on the other ends.

While the rubber band pulls the pencil directly toward each home, in real urban environments it is useful to measure travel along street networks, the geometry of which imposes constraints on free movement. We usually cannot walk over private property or cut through buildings and city blocks. And because empirical studies have found that people's likelihood to visit amenities does not decrease linearly with distance but rather exponentially, travel costs in the index are often modeled in an exponential form. A person who is half a mile away is not just twice as likely to walk to a shop than a person who lives a mile away, but more than twice as likely.[12]

A careful reader might recall that I used a somewhat analogous index in Chapter 2 to measure how many residents could be accessed within a 15-minute walkshed in different parts of New York City. For instance, we saw that from a typical street corner in Chinatown, one can reach 60,000 residents within a

15-minute walkshed. The outcome dropped to 50,000 in Lincoln Square. But there is an important difference between the index that simply counts how many people can be reached within a given access radius and the gravity index. Whereas the former simply sums all residents so long as they fall within the given range (e.g., a 15-minute walk), the gravity index divides the number of residents at each household or census block that is reached by the travel cost of getting to it.[13] This makes the gravity index more accurate and reliable as a yardstick for accessibility.

The gravity index can increase as a result of three different conditions in the built environment. First, if more destinations of the same kind are found within the search area, then there are more rubber bands to pull and the resulting gravity index goes up. If a new metro stop opens near your house, your accessibility to public transit increases. Second, the result can also increase if the weights or characteristics of the destinations are more attractive, producing an increase in the numerator of the index. If we compare two buildings where both have a single metro stop within the same walking distance, but one metro stop serves three lines and the other just one, then the stop with three lines exerts stronger attractiveness and makes the houses close to that gain a higher accessibility result to public transit. And finally, the result can increase due to reductions in transportation costs in the denominator. If one building is closer to the metro, or it has better options to get there—a free shuttle bus, for instance—then the building with easier access to the subway obtains a higher accessibility result. The gravity index takes all three factors into account simultaneously.

Figure 49 illustrates gravity access to residents in a 10-minute walking radius from each building in Cambridge, MA.[14] A hypothetical 600-meter walkshed is traced along the street network around each building. For each household found within that walkshed, the number of residents is divided by the distance required to get to them. Locations that obtain higher results have better walking access to residents around them.

The map shows that access to residents is highest around sites where either bigger buildings, more buildings, or better connectivity are found. Values go up where residential densities are higher or households have higher occupancy. The darker structures toward the bottom edge of the map are close to the Harvard dormitories, where thousands of students live in relatively small spaces. But since travel costs play an important role in the index, residential access also tends to be higher at more connected locations—around street intersections and in areas where city blocks are smaller.[15]

A site's accessibility from surrounding residents can be an important criterion for locating a coffee shop, for example. Most people enjoy a cup of coffee; by and large, coffee shops value locations that maximize accessibility to everyone. Some

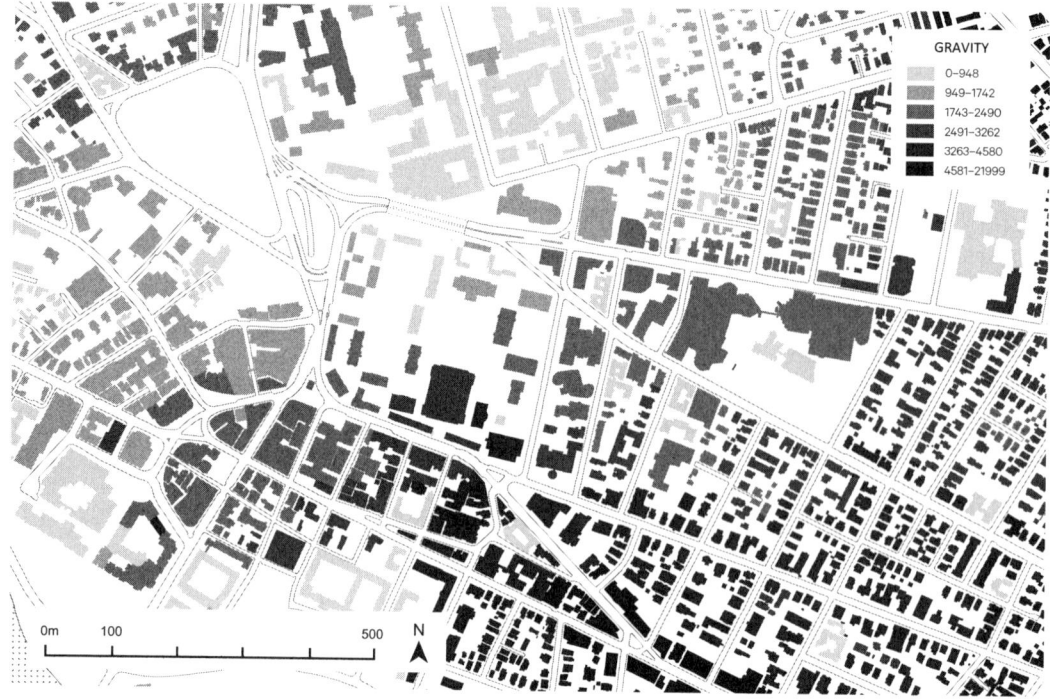

Figure 49. Gravity accessibility to residents from each building in a 10-minute walkshed in Cambridge, MA.

age groups may be slightly more likely to consume coffee than others—20- to 50-year-old working professionals and students, for instance—and we could weigh residents with such characteristics more strongly in the index in order to find locations where the target consumers are most readily accessed.

For a visitor looking to run an errand, accessibility depends on what location one is coming from and where one is headed to next, as well as how much time one has available. These limitations are known as time-space constraints, popularized by the Swedish geographer Torsten Hägerstrand.[16] Hägerstrand's time-space constraints are illustrated in Figure 50, where x and y coordinates represent space and the z coordinate denotes time. Time can only move in a single direction—from bottom to top—as a person's activities proceed throughout a day. The vertical cylinders in the diagram denote anchor points, such as homes, where individual trips start and end, and the lines between them show the trips people take. The diagram suggests that people can initiate trips to street commerce from either fixed locations or while moving between locations.

The map in Figure 51, for instance, captures access to households around a particular coffee shop—Darwin's in Cambridge, MA. The map shows homes

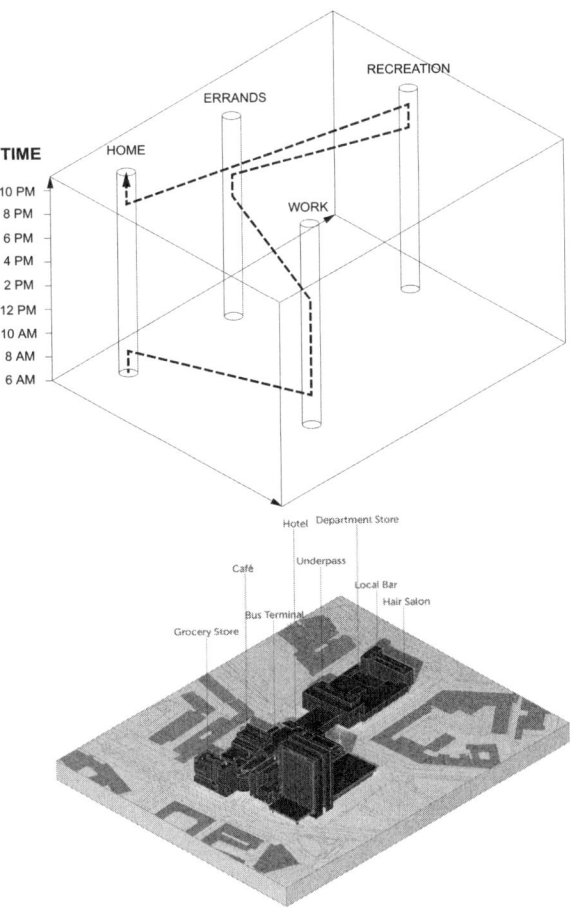

Figure 50. Hägerstrand's time-space constraints.

that can reach Darwin's on foot within a 10-minute walk. Census data in Cambridge tells us that there are 2,239 residents within this area who might be potential customers. Due to the distance decay effect, which makes visits less likely for residents that come from farther away, the gravity index is lower—it estimates that only 1,150 out of 2,239 people are likely to walk to the shop from their homes.[17]

But coffee shops and most other retail, food, and service establishments do not only value access from homes. Though indeed a portion of patrons might walk to shops from their houses, many more may that come from employment locations during lunch breaks.[18] Demand that originates from job locations thus also constitutes an important segment of overall visits to retail, food, and personal services. In 2012, American office workers spent, on average, $26.71 a week on

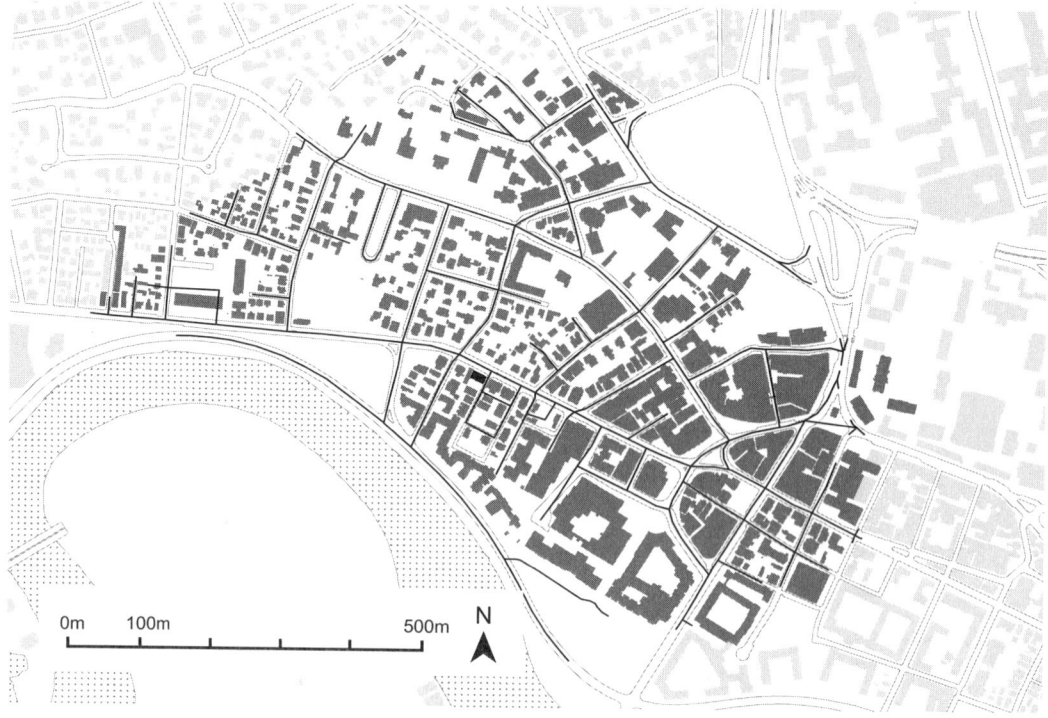

Figure 51. Time-space prism for residential access around Darwin's coffee shop in Cambridge, MA. The map shows buildings that lie within a 10-minute (600 m) walkshed from Darwin's (shaded).

eating and drinking around workplaces, accounting for roughly half of the national average expenditure on food away from home.[19]

In fact, street commerce tends to maximize access from a number of places simultaneously. In addition to homes and workplaces, shops also value proximity to transit stations, public institutions, recreational areas, parking garages, and, as we saw in the previous two chapters, other shops as well. All of these places can be added to the gravity index. Just like for residences, the weight for employment locations (e.g., office buildings) can show the number of employees found at each building and the weight for transit stations can show the number of daily passengers at each station.[20] The denominator of the index captures the distance or time cost required to get to each of them. There is no limit to what can be put into the gravity accessibility index as long as we have the data to represent places where potential customers' might be coming from.

Figure 52 shows the result of the gravity index in the same area of Cambridge, MA, as Figure 49 earlier, but now including access to jobs and transit stops in addition to homes.[21] Notice how the values have changed compared to the residential accessibility map above. The highest accessibility locations

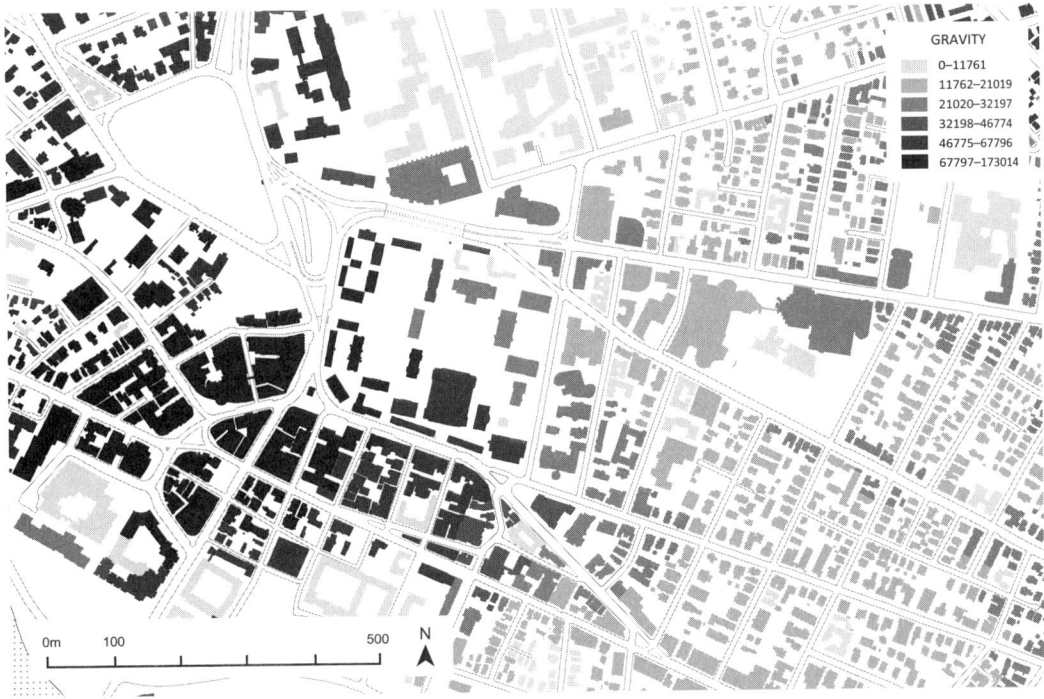

Figure 52. Combined gravity accessibility to residents, jobs, and transit stations from each building in Cambridge, MA.

are now located around the subway entrance and places with high employment densities that house tens of thousands of jobs within a square mile around the station. Subway stops are used by a lot of daily passengers—over 20,000 a day in this case. Proximity to the subway thus increases access to potential customers a great deal, given no single residential or commercial building comes close to having as many daily users. The previous peaks around student dormitories toward the bottom of the map have been outweighed by even more populous places. The residents of each building are still counted, but they simply do not dominate the outcome when workers and transit riders are included.

Impulse Shopping and How Businesses Locate to Capture Customers on the Move

Measuring accessibility from homes, workplaces, and transit stops is a powerful way to detect locations with great business potential. But even among a comprehensive list of destinations, many customers who visit a business may not come from a fixed location, but instead may just pass by the store during other trips to the area. It is much easier to step into a business if one is already walking by than if one has to make a separate trip. This is especially true for pedestrians, who, according to a study by Transport for London, spend 65% more on shopping than do drivers who pass a store.[22] This type of patronage is called *impulse* shopping or *en route* shopping. Impulse shopping is particularly important in dense urban environments, where people tend to move on foot. Retailers in inner-city commercial clusters often draw 30–60% of their customers from unplanned impulse visitors.[23] En route shoppers in cars also form an important demand segment for stores, which locate close to arterial roads and highways used by daily commuters.

The potential for impulse visits can be approximated using another spatial analysis index that predicts the amount of foot traffic on streets. The betweenness metric, proposed by the American sociologist and behavioral scientist Linton Freeman in 1977, is particularly useful toward this end. Unlike the gravity index, which describes accessibility as the ease with which a location can be accessed for *planned* trips by customers around a location, the betweenness metric can help us predict movement that passes through different streets and goes past particular locations, thereby capturing the potential for *unplanned* impulse customers.[24] The index is defined as the fraction of walks between pairs of locations that pass by a particular place.[25] By using origin and destination points that themselves are not retail venues, the index can estimate which routes trips between these other land uses are likely to take and which street segments or storefronts might be passed most often.

Think of a street segment in a city, which in and of itself does not have any pedestrian destinations, but which is nevertheless traveled by a lot of people who use it to commute somewhere else—a place with a high betweenness value. Historically, several famous bridges—London Bridge, the Vecchio Bridge in Florence, and the Rialto Bridge in Venice—have evolved from highly trafficked pedestrian links to full-fledged marketplaces (Figure 53). In an analogous manner, shopping mall customers most often walk by central locations within a mall. Most trafficked locations that are between other popular stores can be easily visited en route, without extra travel, resulting in impulse customers who would otherwise not undertake a separate trip to such stores. This benefit is reflected in the highest per-square-foot rents around central locations in shopping centers as well as top-dollar rents on urban streets with the most foot traffic.[26] When New York City decided to turn the world famous Times Square from a traffic intersection into a pedestrian plaza, retail rents along its edges almost tripled.[27]

Researchers who have studied retail patterns have found that betweenness estimates can significantly explain retail location patterns in a city.[28] Betweenness

Figure 53. Shops on the Rialto Bridge in Venice, Italy. Photo by Jorge Royan, 2009.

is also one of the best predictors of retail locations in Cambridge and Somerville, MA, as I show later in this chapter.

Just like with the gravity index, betweenness values of a specific street segment or address are inherently determined by the spatial configuration of origins and destinations around it. Streets that have more trip origins and destinations around them, or whose surroundings naturally channel more pedestrian trips through them, have higher betweenness values and thus more foot traffic. This is consequential for planners and urban designers since they shape the spatial configuration of the built environment, which in turn shapes pedestrian flows.

To see how the betweenness index works on a map, consider the example in Figure 54, where five people start from two different homes and take the shortest available path to the same destination, a transit station. During the first portion of both trips, each building is passed by five pedestrians, obtaining a betweenness value of 5. But at a certain point along the way, the paths converge onto the same street. From that point onward, each building is passed by all pedestrians, resulting in a betweenness value of 10. If we extended this example to thousands of homes around this transit station, we would get an aggregate estimate of foot traffic on all street segments during a peak travel period.

One of the shortcomings of the traditional betweenness metric is that it assumes that people follow shortest paths.[29] Even in the presence of several plausible walking routes, if one route is even slightly shorter than the others, a trip is only assigned to the shortest path, potentially inflating the importance of such paths—a

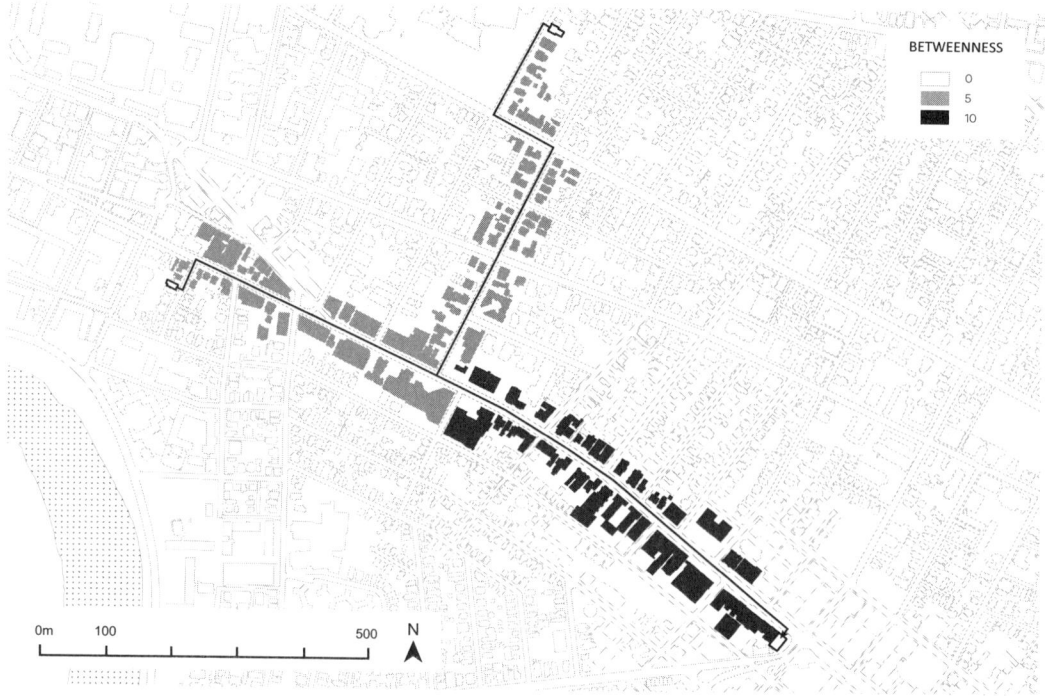

Figure 54. Betweenness results for five people walking from two home locations to the same destination using the shortest path.

methodological issue that makes the calculation simpler but doesn't necessarily match actual route choice behavior. This was my assumption in Figure 54.

Researches who have analyzed pedestrian movement have found that people do not necessarily know or prefer shortest routes and often take routes that are slightly longer even when plausible shorter alternatives are available. On average, detours up to 10–20% longer than the shortest path are common.[30] This makes intuitive sense—most of us do not try to time our meetings and errands with absolute precision and keep at least a few-minute buffer for our walks. When heading to meetings, this buffer enables us to choose alternative routes and visit places along the way. Naturally, the proportion of detours tends to be larger on shorter paths and smaller on longer paths, because the absolute value of a percentage of trip distance becomes much greater as lengths increase—walking 20% longer on a 5-minute stroll adds just 1 minute to the walk, but walking 20% longer on a 50-minute walk adds a whole 10 minutes.

In my research group—the City Form Lab—we have developed spatial analysis and pedestrian flow modeling tools that take such detours into account.[31] Figure 55 shows routes from the same two origins to the subway stop as in Figure 54, but

Figure 55. Betweenness results for five people walking from two home locations to the same destination using all paths that are up to 15% longer than the shortest path.

now distributes the 5 people from both origins equally across all routes that are up to 15% longer than the shortest paths. Each of the paths is given almost equal probability—the number of people from each origin are divided among all plausible paths such that shorter routes obtain slightly higher probabilities than longer routes.[32] The overall number of pedestrians does not change—five people still start from each origin and all end at the common destination. You can think of it as asking five uncoordinated people at both origins to walk to the destination along any path they prefer. Some will use the shortest route, some will prefer a quieter route, and some will choose a more scenic route. But across all plausible routes, certain street segments will get used more than others. Many of the routes overlap around the beginnings and ends of trips, for instance, where different trajectories inevitably converge (Figure 55). More importantly, adding these detours to the analysis ensures that we do not ignore slightly longer paths, but make them almost as likely as the shortest ones. Some pedestrians choose quieter routes, others like busier routes, some prefer greener routes, yet others more interesting routes. Restaurants and shops that cannot or choose not to locate along the main pedestrian spines capitalize on these idiosyncrasies and locate along different streets.

Adding a detour to the betweenness index is equivalent to adding a buffer such as Hägerstrand's time-space prism around walking routes. If the shortest available route only takes 10 minutes, but the person actually has 20 minutes available, then she can afford a 10-minute detour to take care of an errand along the way. Adding these detours to the betweenness index is a handy way of accounting for somewhat random behavior by pedestrians, who do not walk like robots on predetermined shortest paths.

If we enable detours around the betweenness metric, and include not just two, but thousands of origins and destinations, we obtain a more realistic estimate of pedestrian flow. We no longer assume that each walk strictly follows the shortest route, but instead calculate a probability distribution on a number of plausible routes.[33]

It is impossible to predict all the trips people make within even a small area of a city, but fortunately, it is not necessary to model every trip to detect locations with high impulse shopping potential. The set of important origin-destination pairs that generate the greatest amount of pedestrian traffic is typically small enough to model and tends to provide a sufficiently accurate picture of pedestrian foot traffic and demand for shopping.[34] In dense urban environments, critical origin-destination pairs include employment locations, transit stops, and residential locations. Additional attractions may include other retailers, institutions, parks, public spaces, and major parking garages.

The set of pedestrian trip generators can also vary by context. Travel surveys and trip diaries conducted by local governments' transportation departments can be used to detect the most common pedestrian trip types. For instance, in larger cities transit stations form some of the most important origins and destinations for pedestrian movement. But the proportion of trips people make to transit stations also depends on their access to such stations. Just like the gravity index has a distance decay function that lowers the probability of longer walking trips, the betweenness index too can be configured to lower the number of trips as walks get longer.[35] Members of households within a 5-minute walk from a subway stop, for instance, could spend 50% of all of their walking outings traveling to and from the subway, with the remaining half scattered among numerous other destinations around the home—trips to the supermarket, to the park, to the neighbor's house, to the playground, and so on, if such destinations are available nearby. Households that are a ten 10-minute walk from the same subway might only spend 15% of their walking outings traveling to and from the station. Instead of trying to model each of these remaining trips separately, we typically only model the dominant flows (e.g., home or workplace to subway) and assume the rest to be based at the home location itself. This simplification is reasonable, since all these other trips begin or end at home.

Figure 56. Estimated peak hour pedestrian foot traffic on streets around Davis Square metro station in Somerville, MA, including walks from homes to the subway and from the subway to employment locations within an 800-meter walkshed.

The map in Figure 56 shows estimated morning peak-hour foot traffic around the Davis Square metro station in Somerville, MA. Trips are modeled from both homes and job locations within a 10-minute walk around the station, using all routes that are up to 15% longer than the shortest paths. The betweenness values show the estimated foot traffic on different streets. A similar analysis can be prepared for trips at different times of day. Lunchtime outings, for instance, produce fewer trips to transit stations and more trips between workplaces, eateries, cafes, and parks. Betweenness analysis can thus pick up flows that produce unplanned impulse visits to stores, something the gravity accessibility index ignores.

Retail Patterns in Cambridge and Somerville, MA

A few years ago, I analyzed retail and food service establishments in Cambridge and Somerville, MA. I built a spatial statistical model to test which location factors actually explained the pattern of stores we see in the area.[36] Using gravity and betweenness estimates, I examined every building in the two towns to see how access to various types of destinations as well as pedestrian foot traffic predicted

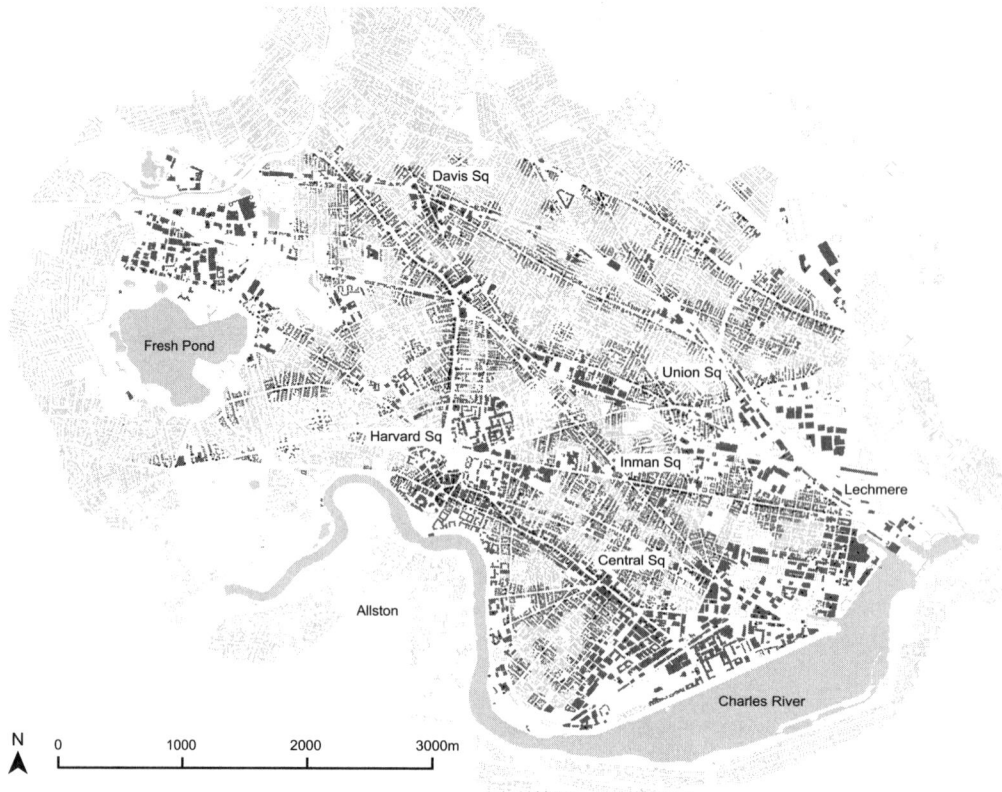

Figure 57. Retail and food-business locations in Cambridge and Somerville (marked as black dots) and the choice set of buildings used in location analysis (marked in dark gray).

with the betweenness metric affected their probability of containing stores. Many of the stores can be seen clustered around the squares of Cambridge—Harvard Square, Central Square, Inman Square, and Union Square—or strung along the city's primary streets (Figure 57).[37]

I measured detailed location qualities around each potential retail building—to homes, to workplaces, to transit stations, etc. Furthermore, retail location choices are not only affected by the built environment and demographics around them—they are also affected by location patterns of other retailers. As I discussed in the previous two chapters, stores often cluster with other stores, regardless of location. To include clustering between stores, I used a spatial statistical model known as a *spatial lag* regression, which can measure how a change in the outcome variable—a binary (0 or 1) indicator in my case, which detects the presence or lack of retailers in a given building—is affected by the presence or lack of neighboring retailers around it.[38] It allows the probability of observing retailers at a particular building to be impacted by the presence of other retailers around it. The model returns a spatial clustering coefficient rho,[39] which describes how colocation with other retailers affects location choices.[40]

The study thus integrated three important factors that are known to affect retail location choices simultaneously. First, a clustering coefficient estimated whether and how retail location choices were affected by groupings with other retailers. Second, the gravity index captured accessibility to transit, urban form, and land uses around a location, while the betweenness estimates captured the potential for foot traffic in front of each location.[41] And a third set of coefficients described the effects of site characteristics around each location—demographic indicators, as well as immediate parcel characteristics such as visibility, sidewalk width, and building size. In order to control for potentially important area characteristics, I also accounted for the median household income, vacancy levels, the proportion of renters, the proportion of African Americans, and the proportion of elderly in the immediate census tract surrounding each building. The results are shown in Table 7.

The clustering coefficient rho suggested that spatial clustering between stores was an important factor for explaining retail patterns in the two towns, regardless

Table 7. Estimated coefficients for location-choice variables of retail and food establishments in Cambridge/Somerville, MA (n=14,218). Binary dependent variable: presence (1) or lack (0) of retail/food establishments in each building.

Variable	Spatial Lag Model W matrix (d=100m)		
Rho (clustering)	0.28	***	(17.45)
Constant	−1.458E-01	***	(−12.85)
Bus stops (Gravity, r=600m)			
Subway stops (Gravity, r=600m)	6.210E-02	***	(5.66)
Built volume (Gravity, r=600m)	3.004E-09	***	(3.41)
Residents (Gravity, r=600m)	−6.686E-06	**	(−2.37)
Employees (nonretail or food, Gravity, r=600m)	9.813E-07		(0.67)
Betweenness (Weights=building volume, r=n)	3.254E-14	***	(10.38)
Parcel Type (# of streets directly accessed 1–5)	8.477E-02	***	(32.45)
Building footprint area (1000s of sq ft)	1.579E-07	***	(3.73)
Road width	5.276E-04	*	(1.92)
Sidewalk width	2.418E-03	**	(2.36)
Family median income (census tract)			
% Vacant	−1.324E-01	~	(−1.31)
% Black			
% Renters			
% over age 60	9.367E-02	*	(1.93)
R^2	0.147		
Likelihood ratio test for spatial dependence	313.720	***	
Significance level ~p<0.25, *p<0.1, **p<0.05, ***p<0.01			
Cell entries are coefficients, z-statistics in parentheses.			

of other location characteristics. If all neighboring buildings in a 100-meter walking radius contained retail establishments, then the probability that a given building would also accommodate a retailer was 28% higher than in the case where no retailers are found in the same walking radius. The presence of a single neighboring store in a 100-meter walkshed increased a building's probability of housing a store by 1% on average.[42] Retail location choices in Cambridge and Somerville were thus in part explained by clustering between stores, just as the theory in Chapter 3 predicted.

But treating all retail, food, and personal service establishments as a group meant that I couldn't be sure whether the nature of clustering observed here was complimentary or competitive. When I tested a similar model for each type of store separately, it became clear which types of stores were most likely to situate near their competitors—hobby, music, and book stores were most inclined to locate next to similar stores, followed by restaurants and drinking places, electronics and appliance stores, and then clothing and accessory stores (see Table 6 in Chapter 3).

The next set of coefficients in Table 7 describe how gravity access to surrounding locations correlated with store location patterns. Access to subway stations was a positive and significant predictor of store locations, while access to bus stops had no effect and was therefore eliminated from the final model. Buildings that were located within a 10-minute walk from a subway stop were 2% more likely to accommodate retail or food businesses than buildings that were further away. This effect increased to 5% when there was a subway station within 100 meters, keeping all other variables constant. The T, as the subway is known to Bostonians, works as an anchor attraction for stores.[43]

Gravity access to surrounding built floor area and jobs were also positively and significantly related to store locations. Holding other variables constant, a building in a high-density area (95th percentile) was 3.8% more likely to contain retailers than a building in a low-density area. This confirmed the importance of customer density: sites that could reach more built floor area had more stores. And retailers also located in buildings that had better access to jobs. Employment density was highly correlated with building density, which explains why the statistical significance of this effect was dampened when both factors were included in the model. When examined alone, proximity to jobs was strongly correlated with retail locations.

Surprisingly, sites with higher densities of residents around them did not have more stores. But access to residents in a 10-minute walkshed also varies much less than access to jobs and built floor area, which we already saw being significantly correlated with store patterns. Around 80% of all buildings are residential, so locating in one neighborhood rather than another can affect residential access to some extent, but the difference is much less than for jobs and nonresidential buildings. Access to jobs falls off rapidly as one moves away from main employment centers such as Kendall, Central, or Harvard Squares. Retailers in Cambridge and Somerville consequently chase job density more than residential density.

The betweenness coefficient, which describe the estimated number of passersby in front of buildings, was positively correlated with store locations and highly significant. It was, in fact, one of the strongest predictors of store locations. Buildings that lie on highly trafficked locations (95th percentile) were close to 6% more likely to house a retailer than buildings on less trafficked streets (5th percentile). This affirms that stores were not only drawn to places where they could be accessed on planned trips from surrounding buildings, but also to places that were passed by more people—where more unplanned impulse purchases were likely to take place.

The last six coefficients in Table 7 estimated the effects of site characteristics and demographic conditions on retail location choices. These suggested that retail and food establishments also tended to locate at places with better visual exposure, such as corners of two intersecting streets, or better yet, "end parcels" in a block, which face directly onto three surrounding streets. Direct access from one additional street increased a building's retail probabilities by 8.48% on average. To describe this common commercial typology, a number of languages have adopted a term translated as "corner shop."[44]

Building footprint area, sidewalk width, and road width were also positively related to store locations, suggesting that retailers tended to locate in bigger structures and on lots that front wider roads and sidewalks. When a sidewalk is expanded by three feet, the probability of having a store increased by an average of 0.73%. Wider sidewalks not only offer more space for pedestrians, they also tend to come with more tree cover, street furniture, and more active public space use—all qualities that benefit shops.

Household vacancy rates had a negative but barely significant effect on retail distribution, while other socioeconomic variables, except for the percentage of elderly residents nearby, had no significant effect. The percentage of elderly residents in a census tract was positively correlated with the presence of stores, which likely reflected senior citizens' preference to live in places with convenient access to services.

Overall, the detailed coefficients for location and access qualities explained why the store pattern was distributed the way it was, and why the clusters are situated on certain streets. The most significant factors explaining retail location

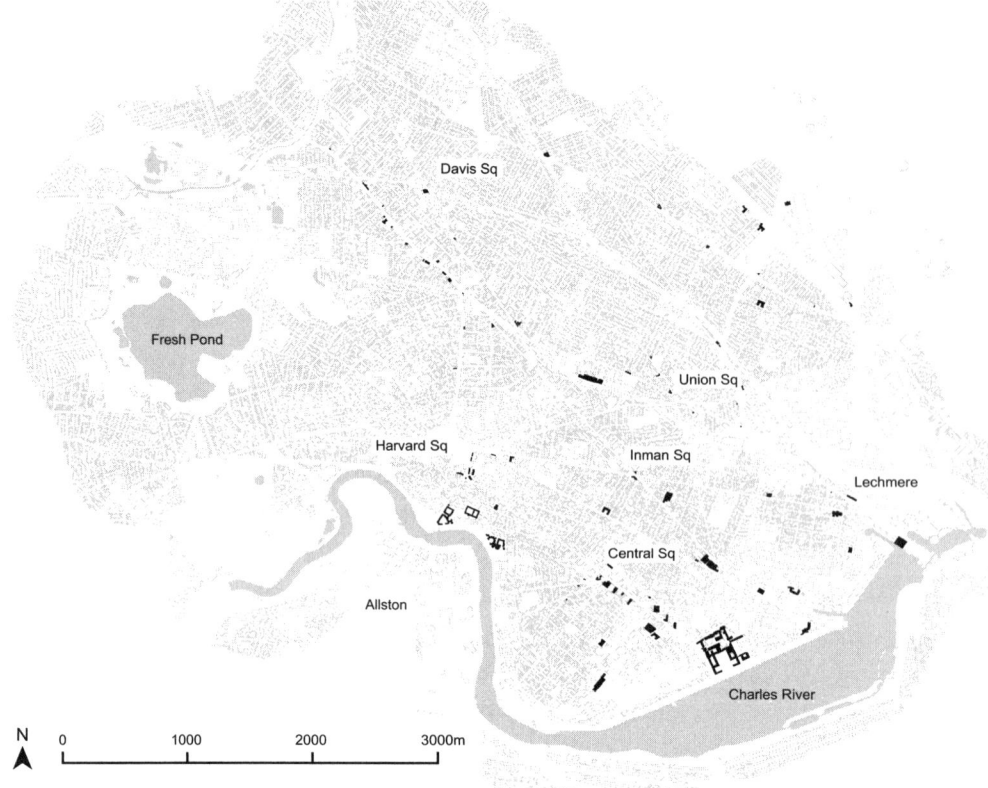

Figure 58. Buildings with negative standardized residual (<−1.5), indicating opportunistic locations for retail stores.

patterns in Cambridge and Somerville were visibility ("parcel type"), clustering, foot traffic in front of the store, proximity to the subway, and access to surrounding built floor area. They illustrate a field of location forces that attract retail and food establishments, which, like rubber bands, pull stores into some sites with greater tension than others, while agglomeration forces also ensure that most stores colocate in clusters.

An interesting by-product of such a spatial statistical model of retail probabilities are the model's residuals, which indicate how much each individual site was under- or over-predicted. Negative residuals are particularly interesting for planners and policy makers because they describe sites that have all-around excellent location characteristics but lack retailers at present. The model expects them to have stores, but they don't. These residuals can help us detect which locations might be ripe for retail uses and where zoning could potentially be altered to support commerce. Figure 58 shows a map of a part of my study area, outlining buildings that the model found highly likely for commerce, but where no retail or food businesses were found.

There can be numerous reasons why such locations did not have stores at the time. Some of these buildings house offices, fire departments, schools, public institutions, and other land uses on their ground floors, which may have preceded or outcompeted retailers. Some of their landowners or inhabitants may prefer not to have stores, and in some cases, historic value or zoning restrictions have outright banned shops in locations with otherwise high potential. However, good retail locations may also remain dormant because they have not yet been discovered or proven to work.

Andrew Caplin and John Leahey, economists from New York University and the University of Michigan, have illustrated how high-potential locations can remain underutilized for a considerable time due to first-mover's risk.[45] The first store that makes the decision to locate at a location with few or no previous retail establishments must do so by accepting considerable uncertainty. Should the location prove to be poor, then the losses are carried by the risk-taker alone. Should the location prove to be successful, however, then the payoffs not only accrue to the risk-taker but will also reveal the value of the location to potential competitors—through what they call information spillovers.

The authors examined first-mover risks among retailers in New York and used information spillovers to explain why lower Sixth Avenue remained inactive among retailers for years but witnessed a rapid turnaround after a Bed Bath & Beyond store opened there in 1992. Bed Bath & Beyond took on the first-mover risk by making a considerable investment in an uncertain location. The apparent success of the store quickly assured other retailers of the location's value and resulted in a rapid retail revitalization around it. Several other stores followed. Besides Bed Bath & Beyond, which is still there, the corner of Sixth Avenue and 18th Street now also has Marshalls, Lowe's, CVS, Staples, Men's Wearhouse, Old Navy, TJ Maxx, and many other stores, restaurants, and personal service providers. Analogous reasoning can explain why some locations in the Cambridge and Somerville map that appear promising due to their location characteristics might remain unexploited by commerce.

The statistical model described above is useful in two ways. First, it tells us which types of locations different stores and services gravitate toward. Where do clothing stores typically locate? What about shoe stores? Or restaurants? A similar statistical model, as shown above for all retail and food service establishments as a group, can be specified for each type of store.[46] Second, the model is also useful for detecting new locations for stores, as shown in the residual map. But the model does not tell us how many patrons we would expect to visit each of the locations or how much revenue a store at a new location might produce. This is where the Huff model comes in.

Predicting Visits to New Store Locations with the Huff Model

Having determined store locations, we can use the Huff model to estimate a probability for each consumer to spend at a specific shop among all available alternatives. The mathematical formulation of this probability can be found in an endnote,[47] but in a nutshell, the probability of going to shop at a particular store depends on how accessible the store is to the customer compared to all the other stores around. This accessibility is determined with the gravity index and depends simultaneously on the attractiveness of the store and the distance to it.

The approach hypothesizes that there is a degree of randomness in people's choices and picking a destination to shop does not follow deterministic patterns. Rather than assigning each customer to a single store that provides him or her with highest accessibility, the model assigns each person a probability to visit each of the stores around them. Just like in the gravity index, this probability increases when the destination is either more attractive or closer by. Waldo Tobler's first law of geography holds "everything is related to everything else, but near things are more related than distant things."[48] For instance, the model might assign a resident at a particular location a 70% probability to visit the most attractive or nearest shop, but the remaining 30% of his or her visits are distributed among other competing stores in the area. No store is left with a zero allocation, reflecting that even the worst-positioned and least-attractive stores could still get a few customers by virtue of random choices. The model keeps track of the probabilities assigned to each store or cluster of stores, which yields an estimate of how many customers in total we expect to patronize each site. It estimates patronage—or, alternatively, revenues—at each destination by taking into account both the accessibility of a site from surrounding customers and competition from other stores.

In order to see how the model works in practice, let us go back to the example of Dunkin Donut shops in Cambridge, MA. Dunkin has 19 stores in Cambridge. It is a franchise business, which means that individual shop owners apply to use the Dunkin brand in their stores and Dunkin, in return, takes a share of their revenues as compensation. Dunkin therefore does not own the coffee shops we analyze, but it does have significant say in where they allow shops to be operated. Their strategy and marketing teams do careful analysis as to where new shops might be needed and which franchise agreements are worth continuing when they expire.

Using Dunkin Donuts stores in this example is not coincidental. Keeping the retail destination type constant—the same donut shop—allows us to analyze how differences in patronage at various shops are primarily attributable to differences in location. If we keep the destinations in our analysis constant, we eliminate the difference in patronage that might be attributable to quality, branding, and pricing and focus only on the impact of location.

Like most retail businesses, Dunkin does not publicly disclose how many customers each of its stores attracts. The lack of such data can be a significant barrier to performing retail location analysis. In the example below, I use a workaround to tackle this issue. Together with the students from the Graduate School of Design at Harvard, we visited all Dunkin Donuts shops in Cambridge and examined their customer receipts. Dunkin receipts, and many other retail receipts, carry a number stamp that describes the consecutive order of customers at the franchise. A number "169,432" on a coffee receipt, for instance, may tell you that you were the 169,432nd customer at this store since it opened. There are a few cashier systems and not all of them include a consecutive customer number on the receipt. Some restart the count every year. Some restart the count once they go over 100,000. But if a transaction number exists on the receipt, it can provide convenient public information about how many people have visited the store.

My students visited all the Dunkin Donuts stores in Cambridge twice, the second visit occurring roughly two weeks after the first. The difference between the second and the first count tells us how many people visited the store in the two-week period. If the first number was 169,432 and the second number was 180,982, then we know that 11,550 customers had visited the store in the two-week period. Dividing that by 14 days tells us the average number of customers per day.

Figure 59 shows a map of all 19 stores in Cambridge, MA, with the average number of daily customers at each store. The stores are distributed at different types of locations—some are in metro stations at Harvard and Alewife, others on large thoroughfare roads, and yet others inside shopping malls. There is one drive-through in Cambridge as well, which appears to attract a lot of customers, but most Dunkin stores in the area are at highly pedestrian locations near other street commerce.[49]

Among the 19 Dunkin stores in Cambridge, the average daily patronage varied between 400 and 1,500 customers, with a mean of 850. Stores at Harvard and Alewife stations and the drive-through store at Fresh Pond attract approximately three times more customers a day than less popular stores in more residential areas. How do location qualities explain these differences? Do the high-performing locations have more customers living, working, and walking around them, or do they instead have less competition and therefore more spatial monopoly power?

Figure 59. Dunkin Donut shops in Cambridge, MA, indicating average number of daily customers.

In order to compare the estimated patronage at each of the 19 stores with the actual patronage, we measured access to each of the stores from a range of potential customer locations around Cambridge. These included homes, workplaces, and transit stations. We also distributed some of the demand from the static home and work locations to walking routes leading to metro and bus stops around them, using the betweenness metric to capture potential impulse shoppers. The full set of factors we used in a Huff model thus included residents, jobs, public institutions, and estimated foot traffic around each store (Figure 60).

A comparison of the visits predicted using the Huff model and the actual visits from the receipts we collected showed that the results were 80% correlated. Location is indeed a critical determinant of revenues for Dunkin outlets. Access to customers at home, work, and transit origins, combined with the estimated pedestrian flux on streets and competition from other shops, explained most of the variation in Dunkin visits in Cambridge.

More importantly, the Huff model demonstrates how we can predict patronage and revenues at new locations where businesses don't yet exist. Whereas the

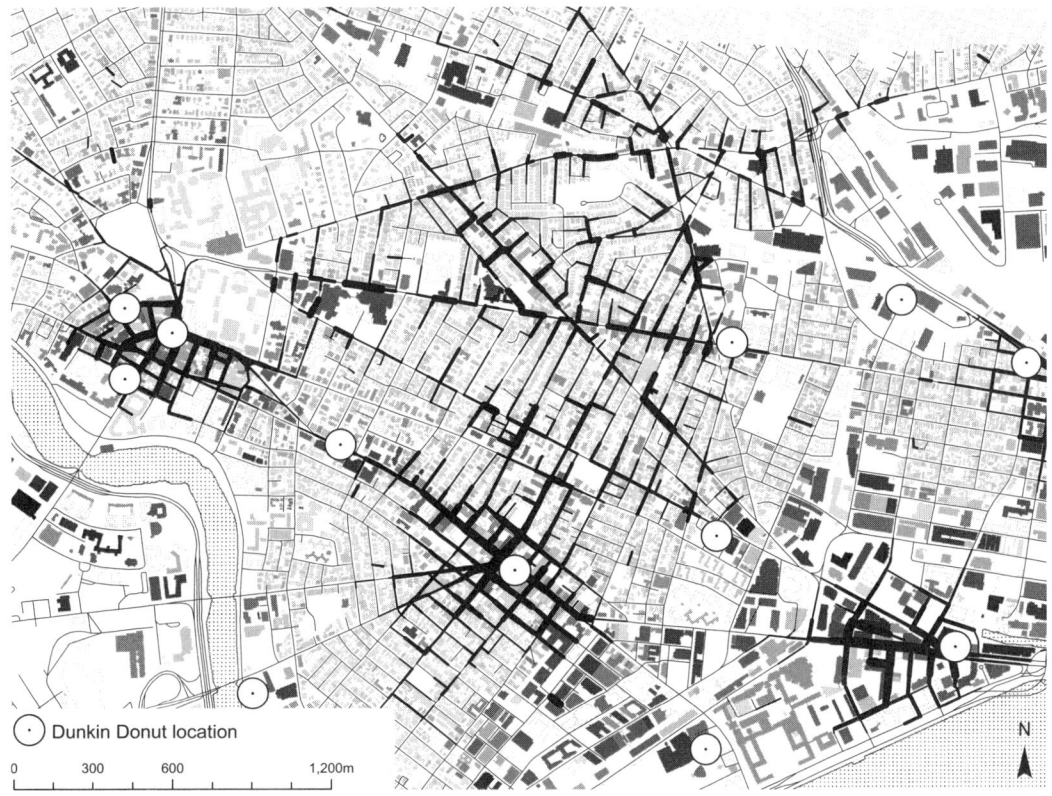

Figure 60. Estimated distribution of fixed and mobile demand origins for Dunkin Donuts stores in Cambridge, MA.

residuals of the spatial statistical model I described above could provide insight as to where a new business might work, the Huff model can estimate how many patrons a location is likely to attract in the presence of competing stores. And the patronage result can be compared with projected fixed costs of a location to determine whether the location would be economically viable.

However, even if a location appears ripe and revenue prediction favorable, new stores and restaurants may not be feasible at new sites. As we saw above, first-mover risk can incentivize businesses to hold out. In Chapter 2, I also discussed how zoning regulations and competition from other land uses can hold back stores from ground floors whose location attributes are promising. But another influential factor welcoming or deterring businesses is also at play—architectural typologies of buildings and streets. Excellent locations with favorable business regulations sometimes keep businesses out because the floor plates, facades, building types, and street configurations they offer simply do not work for shops. This is what the next chapter will explore.

CHAPTER 6

How Urban Design and Building Typologies Affect Retail Location Patterns

Whether or not particular buildings or streets at seemingly good locations can accommodate retailers that want to move there depends in part on their architectural typologies. Not all building types are equally suitable to accommodate commercial spaces and not all neighborhoods are equally fit to support commercial streets. I learned this firsthand through a natural experiment that took place in Annelinn, Estonia—the public housing district where I grew up—when, during the collapse of the Soviet Union in the early 1990s, it transitioned from a centrally planned retail environment to a market-based one.

Annelinn is a typical Soviet-era housing complex, made of 5- and 10-story prefabricated blocks. During the five decades of occupation, Soviet authorities built a series of dormitory districts in several Estonian cities. Annelinn, built in the 1980s, was home to around 35,000 people by the 1990s. Inspired by the modernist town-planning ideals of Le Corbusier and Walter Gropius,[1] freestanding standardized housing blocks were arranged in an orthogonal zigzagged pattern to maximize sun exposure (Figure 61). Buildings were set back from roads and they were all built using highly economical prefabrication techniques, in many ways similar to the HDB towns that I mentioned in Singapore in Chapter 2.[2]

Besides residential units, Annelinn housed a limited number of centrally planned stores, about 5,000 square feet each. Annelinn was ultimately served by four grocery stores, which were gradually added as the district expanded, and a single household-goods store that sold pots, pans, and the like. No street-corner bodegas, vegetable stores, or cigarette kiosks. Given the scarcity of retail space, most families had to walk considerable distances to get to a store, and once you got there, not much was on the shelves. Just like in countless other dormitory districts throughout the vast territory of the USSR, Annelinn had a clear deficit of retail facilities.

Figure 61. Aerial view of Annelinn. The U-shaped low-rise buildings to the left are Soviet-era schools and daycare centers. Photo from Toomas Paaver's collection.

The situation began rapid transformation after the Berlin wall fell in 1989 and Estonia regained independence from Soviet occupation in 1991. Almost overnight, the country had to leap from a centrally planned socialist economy to a capitalist system with free markets, private property, and commercial entrepreneurship. For retail space in Annelinn, this meant that a market correction was in order to make up for the underprovision maintained during the Soviet era. Residents were eager for new stores and more diverse products, and a nascent entrepreneurial market responded.

The first signs of new retail space appeared in the form of flea markets and kiosks. Setting up a table at an open-air flea market or a roadside kiosk required little startup capital and allowed merchants to try their luck. Kiosks were produced economically in underutilized metal factories left behind from the oversized Soviet industrial economy. As cheap alternatives to more durable construction, they imposed little risk on business owners and multiplied by the hundreds all over town. Their mobile and temporary character also enabled kiosk operators to avoid paying property taxes to the city.

About six different kiosks appeared within a five-minute walk around my house, more than tripling my family's retail offerings. Welded together from sheet metal and boasting a large acrylic window in the front, kiosks sold a surprisingly

Figure 62. Kiosk in Tallinn in the 1990s. Photo by Peeter Langovits.

large variety of groceries and other supplies—milk, bread, cheese, meats, juices, sweets, cigarettes, and alcoholic beverages (Figure 62). Some also prepared sandwiches and hamburgers with french fries. Despite their small size, their selection of merchandise was as good as in any Soviet-era grocery store. The illustrious social life that developed around such kiosks has been colorfully captured in the novels of the post-Soviet fiction author Victor Pelevin.[3]

Clothing and apparel items were rare in kiosks. These were instead offered at flea markets, where 50–100 vendors would compete side by side on tabletops covered with piles of clothes (Figure 63). A flea market, using makeshift wooden tables, was set up in a parking lot not far from my house. Plastic sheets were pulled over the tables to protect the merchandise from rain and snow. The variety of shirts, pants, winter coats, and other garments exploded due to an influx from even bigger markets in Poland and Turkey. People had never seen such variety and choice before and swept up the offerings with a newfound thirst for consumer products. Merchants dealt in cash and avoided paying taxes. The profits they earned attracted more vendors to the market.

Both the kiosks and flea markets were temporary retail typologies—cheap to establish and flexible in terms of location. But the shopping experience they offered was not on par with the street commerce or shopping malls we see in Estonia today. Goods and money were exchanged outdoors in a relatively cold climate, through a little window or over a market counter. Prices were often negotiable. There were no returns or exchanges—what you bought was what you got.

Figure 63. Flea market in Tallinn in the 1990s. Alamy stock photo.

Next came the slightly more durable basement stores. The residential building blocks in Annelinn were highly rationalized prefabricated concrete-panel structures. First floors were raised off the ground by half a floor to enable basements to have strip windows at the ground level. In typical five-story blocks, 15 apartments shared a staircase, with 3 units on every level and a series of small basement stalls below. For fire safety, the basements also had a back exit.

Both the architectural typology and site plans of these residential blocks made it difficult to install commercial spaces into the buildings. First-floor units were off-limits since they shared a staircase with 14 other households. With privatization, tenants in most buildings quickly formed tenant associations and preferred to lock their front doors to prevent thieves, loiterers, and vandals from entering. The idea of keeping the staircase door open for retail customers went against all this. Raising the level of first-floor units also cut off sightlines so that passersby could not see in the windows, making it difficult for stores to display their merchandise even if the residents allowed shops.

Basement spaces offered a somewhat better opportunity for stores (Figure 64). But their sightlines were almost as bad as first-floor units—a small strip window was placed only a couple of feet above the ground, far from ideal for displaying

Figure 64. Basement bar in the Lasnamäe housing district of Tallinn, Estonia. Photo by Vladimir Ljadov. Project "Commercial Lasnamäe."

merchandise. The size of basement spaces was also problematic—stalls were subdivided by load-bearing panels into 100–200 square foot spaces that were small for even mom-and-pop shops. But the fact that basements had a secondary entrance in the back of the block, which residents upstairs didn't use, made it possible to separate shop visitors from building residents and resolved an important safety issue. The diminished fire preparedness that came along with taking away a second exit wasn't much of a concern during these turbulent years. Some food kiosks moved to more permanent spaces in basements under residential slabs. A few clothing, shoe, and apparel stores, as well as bars, also took up basement spaces.

As it turned out, basement stores did not perform as well as the kiosks. One problem was that housing blocks were scattered throughout large open spaces not clearly aligned with any streets or popular sidewalks. Built ground coverage of such modernist housing districts is usually around 15–20%. The rest of the land area is open space, covered with patches of grass, dirt, and a web of pedestrian pathways (Figure 65). Few vehicular roads enter the area since Soviet planners never thought many residents would own cars. But in the 1990s, much of this open space was gradually turned over to parking, as cars were no longer centrally rationed and car ownership exploded. This meant that there was hardly any pedestrian flow next to the basement stores. Pedestrians used spread-out footpaths and would walk in front of a particular building only if they lived there or in one of the adjacent blocks.

With no jobs or commercial activities nearby, and with only housing units upstairs, pedestrian activity was minimal outside the morning and evening peak

Figure 65. Open space between residential blocks in Annelinn, Tartu, Estonia. Photo by Ivo Kruusamägi, April 2016.

hours and weekends, when residents were home. Occasional children and older adults used the nearby playgrounds or benches during business hours, but their numbers were far from sufficient to sustain the basement stores, which had to cover monthly rent payments to the apartment associations upstairs. Unlike kiosks, which were generally in good locations, basement stores suffered from poor patronage.

Soviet-era microdistricts (equivalent of neighborhood units) also included designated sites for schools and childcare centers (Figure 61). A number of these schools were converted to retail spaces in the 1990s. Typically 2–3 stories high and meticulously standardized, the school buildings offered large interior spaces that were attractive to newly formed stores, video game parlors, hair salons, and occasional bars. The size and number of spaces in these buildings allowed small retail clusters to form and attract a larger clientele than a basement store or kiosk could have alone. But the school buildings were not ideal for retail activities either. They did not have floor-to-ceiling windows to facilitate window shopping, and to circulate between stores, customers had to navigate double-loaded corridors or staircases between floors. In terms of location, schools had been built in areas easy to get to from homes, but not necessarily near popular bus stops or walking paths.

During this period of nascent market capitalism, developers in Annelinn also found it difficult to build between existing buildings. As part of privatization, ownership of open space between residential blocks was allocated to apartment associations so that land between buildings belonged simultaneously to several households around. Obtaining this land for development required agreements from all households who had a stake—not an easy task. Second, the modernist "free plan" layout of the town included very few sites where stores could find sufficient pedestrian flow and space for vehicular access and parking. The available building spaces were typically too small or required cumbersome access for deliveries.

Kiosks, flea markets, and occasional basement shops aside, no real street commerce emerged in Annelinn during the post-Soviet transformations, even though the demand for it was clearly there. Instead of adaptively reusing existing residential buildings or infilling developments between existing housing blocks, new commercial space popped up along more historic downtown streets that offered more malleable building types. The ground floors of these older perimeter blocks that faced busy sidewalks were quickly and successfully converted to nascent retail uses. And big-box shopping appeared on the edges of housing districts, close to traffic arteries and bus stops. But the inflexible structures that were optimized for residential uses in Annellinn have resisted commercial programming to this day. "We shape our buildings, and then they shape us," Winston Churchill once said.[4] Even though the necessary economic preconditions were in place—purchase frequency, density, low fixed costs, and a high pedestrian and public transit mode share—cumbersome building typologies and site plans discouraged stores from entering.

The story from Annelinn hints at a number of ways in which building forms and street typologies can affect retail viability—sizes of indoor spaces, ground-floor heights, relationships between buildings and sidewalks, and characteristics of internal circulation systems, as well as the design of building facades. We find similar examples of the ways in which street commerce is affected by design features of the built environment in cities and streets around the world. The remainder of this chapter will take a closer look at these features.

Floor Areas of Different Types of Shops

Different types of stores require different floor areas. Not all store sizes can be accommodated as part of street commerce—Walmart hyper-centers or Home Depot home improvement stores are too big to take part in street retailing. Yet a large variety of stores, ranging from small ice-cream counters to full-fledged department stores, can be found on pedestrian-friendly city streets around the world.

In an admittedly simplified taxonomy, the space requirements of street commerce can be divided into four size categories: small, medium, large, and extra large. Small stores range from about 250 to 1,000 square feet. This range can accommodate a coffee shop, a dry cleaner, an independent bookstore, a hair salon, or a range of other small operators. These stores do not necessarily need a back entrance, and the merchandise and services they sell tend to be relatively small and do not necessitate daily deliveries by 18-wheelers. Small spaces are ideal for many locally owned food and personal service businesses, since few chain operators compete for them. They can operate on streets with limited or no vehicular access.

The middle category involves stores of 1,000 to 5,000 square feet. This is a very typical size range for all sorts of chain operators and can fit full-service restaurants and medium-sized clothing and apparel stores, as well as established personal service providers such as beauty salons. The most common store size in shopping malls—around 30 feet of frontage and 80 feet deep—falls within this range, attesting to the high demand for space of this size. Many national and international brands can comfortably operate in a medium-sized retail space. A separate back entrance is usually needed for deliveries and services.

Large stores are between 5,000 to 20,000 square feet. These can accommodate chain stores with large space requirements, such as REI or supermarkets like Trader Joe's or Waitrose. Though common in malls, large retail floors are less common on city streets than medium-sized stores. This is partially because malls typically offer large stores lower per-square-foot rents than individual landlords on urban retail streets, as discussed in Chapters 3 and 4.[5]

Extra-large stores range from 20,000 to 150,000 square feet. Space in the top half of that range can accommodate a department store such as Macy's, Saks Fifth Avenue, or Marks and Spencer. Though extra-large stores form important anchors, they are rare among street retailers. Those that exist need to be cherished and supported because a large department store can provide a lifeline for many smaller stores around it. Closure of a department store in a downtown setting can result in the closure of series of small businesses that depend on customer spillovers from the department store.

Car-oriented big box stores, which the US retail market has relied heavily on in the post–Second World War era, also fall within the extra-large category. In many American cities, big-box stores represent most of a town's retail floor area. These stores are not accessed on foot like street commerce, but rather by car, from giant parking lots fronting stores. But this is beginning to change due to two simultaneous trends that I will discuss in Chapter 7—e-commerce and urban population growth.

Buildings that cannot provide space for any of these four size categories and streets along which their construction is impossible are unfit for retail activities.

Permeable Facades

Street retailers like to make their merchandise and services visible through large windows. The residential blocks in Annelinn had prefabricated, load-bearing facades. You couldn't just eliminate or create an opening in a facade panel to install a shop window—doing so would threaten the structural stability of the whole building. Permeable facades, on the other hand, allow openings and increase the visibility of goods and people in commercial spaces. People not only enjoy seeing merchandise but also other people in shops or restaurants before they step in. Many restaurant operators know this and seat their first lunch and dinner customers close to the street, where they can be seen by passersby and lure them in.

Even if new buildings' ground floors will not have stores in them immediately, building typologies can facilitate their addition as needs arise. Many city centers in Europe still have historic timber column-beam structures, clad in stucco. If you walk around the Marais district in Paris or Soho in London, you will see this typology everywhere. Timber beams can span about 12–16 feet, making sizable street openings possible. With a column-beam transfer solution, facades do not have any load-bearing wall elements on the ground floor, except at the very edges of the frontage. Historic buildings with commercial ground floors in European city centers are testaments to the flexibility of this solution. Having accommodated dozens of different ground-floor businesses over time, these buildings continue to host commercial uses elegantly today (Figure 66).

American taxpayer strips—cheap single-story commercial structures along busy roads—have also shown great versatility, partly due to their flexible front facades that do not carry structural loads and can be changed as needs arise. Predecessors of small-scale strip malls, taxpayer strips obtained their name from their temporary nature—such structures were historically built in newly expanding urban areas, where speculators bought up land early on and wanted to wait a few years for property values to increase before installing permanent multistory structures. During the interim period, taxpayer strips offered a convenient way to generate enough rental income to cover property taxes while waiting for property values to rise. But some of these strips, initially intended as temporary income-generating structures, grew and became permanent, as people got used to the shops and services they offered. A number of street corners in East Coast cities still have taxpayer strips with stores and restaurants in structures built a century ago.

Figure 66. A hat store in London housed behind a historic timber, column-beam, ground-floor facade. Photo by author.

Contemporary building technologies enable longer spans and openings. Construction with reinforced concrete and steel beams allows 30-, even 60-foot uninterrupted ground-floor openings on the street. The Office for Metropolitan Architecture has created a street front for a Prada store on Los Angeles's posh Rodeo Drive without any ground-floor facade whatsoever (Figure 67). An open-air passage underneath the seemingly floating second floor lures in shoppers all day long. Even when the store is closed, a solid panel is raised from a slit in the ground, which closes the opening just enough to deter nighttime access.

Ground-Floor Heights

Visual relationships between sidewalks and shop interiors also depend on ground-floor heights. If ground-floor spaces are not level with sidewalks, but instead are raised or lowered by half a floor—or in some cases, voided out altogether for parking or circulation uses—then even large openings cannot establish a relationship with the street. If a shop has windows toward the street but these windows start at five feet above the sidewalk, the visual bond between shop interiors and passersby is broken. It becomes hard to see the contents of the store from the street

Figure 67. Prada store on Rodeo Drive in Beverly Hills, CA. Photo by Phil Meech, courtesy of the Office for Metropolitan Architecture (OMA), Rotterdam, Netherlands.

and the onlookers' gazes will meet the ceiling ducts instead of the merchandise or visitors inside (Figure 68). Having to walk up or down a flight of stairs to get to the store also poses a physical inconvenience, especially for those carrying bags, baby strollers, or moving in wheelchairs.

Setbacks from the Street

Setbacks describe how far back building facades are from sidewalks or streets. Taxpayer strips were historically built right along the sidewalk. This makes peeking through the windows easy and attractive for passersby. But while a narrow setback is beneficial, some space between the sidewalk and shop windows is not necessarily bad for stores. Along the most popular shopping street in Boston—Newbury Street—which is located in the historic Back Bay district, many of the brick walkups are set about 10–15 feet back from bustling sidewalks. This allows restaurants to place outdoor seats in front of their doors. Some shop owners also maintain small front gardens, embellished with flowers, while others have used the setback to create direct access to basement stores downstairs (Figure 69). But when setbacks start exceeding 30 feet, sightlines break up. Passersby no longer see inside the store or recognize peoples' faces from a distance. Annelinn's

Figure 68. Elevated ground floors along Massachusetts Avenue in Boston. Photo by author.

residential blocks were often set back 30–50 feet, far enough to make any visual connections unlikely.

Independent Access and Circulation

In order to be able to accommodate commercial establishments in ground-floor units, shops also need autonomous access, separate from other activities in the building. Ideally, shops can be entered directly from the street. This ensures that customers do not share corridors or doors with upstairs residents or employees. In some cases, sharing a lobby space that splits access between shop visitors and residents can work, but this typically requires that some form of access control be established—a doorman or an access card reader that demarcates the private residential territory from public retail space.

Aside from separating residential and retail visitors' circulation routes, autonomous street entrances to stores also help animate streets, contributing to activities that take place on sidewalks. People enjoy peeking in shop windows and walking along sidewalks lined with commercial businesses. Pedestrian studies have found that people perceive walking distances to be shorter when the walk

Figure 69. Ten-foot setbacks on Newbury Street in Boston. Photo by author.

is stimulating and includes numerous shop entrances than when the walk is monotonous and lacks pedestrian-oriented uses.[6] Urban ethnographer William Whyte, who studied the use of outdoor plazas in New York City, found that the most important attractor for people to spend time in outdoor spaces was other people.[7] People like to see other people, look at what they wear or buy, and appreciate a serendipitous encounter with a stranger on the sidewalk. Turning shops toward the street can reinforce these behaviors.

A study by an MIT researcher found that this effect is even visible in peoples' subway transfer choices.[8] When streets contained more pedestrian-oriented businesses, people were more likely to get off a subway earlier and walk the last leg of their journey on foot, rather than transfer to another subway line underground that would take them closer. Where the street environment did not contain pedestrian-friendly frontages, people tended to prefer a subway transfer to a walk.

Historically, the invention of the corridor (hallway) as a circulation element inside buildings made it possible to avoid separate street entrances for different building users. Before the corridor typology was popularized in 17th-century building plans, most building interiors were organized around an enfilade system, where each room is simultaneously a destination and a through passage to additional rooms. If you have ever walked through old castles in Europe, you might have experienced walking through bedrooms or antechambers that led to other bedrooms, drawing rooms, and kitchens. Almost every room could be traversed to reach other rooms.

The corridor, now so common in modern buildings that we hardly even notice it, introduced a fundamental change to the enfilade system. With a corridor acting as a central trunk in a building's circulation structure, rooms could become end points that did not lead to any other rooms. This enabled different parts of buildings to be used by different tenants, giving rise to mixed-use buildings with unrelated neighbors. A law office in one room could operate autonomously from a clerk in another or a brasserie in a third. No tenant had to let other businesses' visitors walk through their space and establishments could independently operate at different times of the day.

For bustling sidewalks, interior corridors were bad news. Sidewalks themselves have historically been used as primary circulation trunks, providing direct access to tenants in different parts of a building. Corridors allowed people to walk from one part of a building to another indoors, without using the sidewalk outside. In the morning peak hour, different occupants of the building could arrive via the main door using the sidewalk to enter, but throughout the day, trips within the building no longer relied on open-air streets. For the overcrowded sidewalks in 18th- and 19th-century Paris, Milan, London, or Shanghai, this might have felt like a blessing, allowing people to avoid bumping into each other on shoulder-to-shoulder sidewalks. But on 21st-century shopping streets, overcrowded sidewalks are rarely a problem. Quite the opposite: cities more often struggle with getting pedestrians out on the sidewalk at all. Encouraging commercial ground floors with a series of direct street entrances offers one approach to stimulating more sidewalk activity.

Beyond the architectural typology of buildings themselves, the suitability of a place for retail activities also depends on the spatial relationships between adjacent buildings. For a street to be conducive to commerce, it is not enough for individual buildings to be suitable for retail stores, a group of buildings need to be connected together to enable the clustering dynamics and inter-store spillovers that stores value.

Sidewalk Quality

Good connectedness between different commercial, institutional, and transit destinations in a retail cluster requires high-quality sidewalks and public spaces, which can be achieved with multiple types of interventions. At the most basic level, pedestrian walkways need to be safe. That means that pedestrians need to be sheltered from dangerous and loud traffic with sidewalks that not only fit pedestrian flow but also enable eating and drinking establishments to spill out onto sidewalks, which

Figure 70. Brattle Street in Cambridge, MA. Photo by author.

slow down the flow and add eyes on the street. Parallel parking along the road can help establish a buffer between sidewalks and vehicular traffic. Landscaping elements, such as constructed or movable planter boxes, have a similar effect. Jan Gehl's studies from around the world have suggested that the maximum volume for comfortable pedestrian movement is around 12 people per minute per yard of sidewalk width. Throughput beyond this level can be uncomfortable.[9]

Good sidewalks also help shelter pedestrians from rain, sun, and snow, depending on climate and location. In northern cities, where sunlight is scarce during long winters, many people love to feel the sun, and streets fill up with pedestrians when the first good weather arrives in the spring. Blocking the sun in these settings can be counterproductive. Even as far south as Paris, retail rents on the south-facing side of the Champs-Élysées are notably higher than on the shaded side. But in Mediterranean cities and tropical environments, the sun can be too hot, and shelter in the form of tree canopies or architectural arcades can enhance pedestrian comfort. Traditional shophouses in Singapore and Malaysia, for instance, come with covered "five-foot-ways" in front of buildings, resulting in long covered walkways throughout the historic city center. A similar building type is common throughout the historic centers of Bologna, Italy. Trees, cantilevered buildings, and arcades can also improve pedestrian comfort in rainy and snowy climates. Zurich, for instance, has several arcades that keep pedestrians and shop fronts sheltered form snow rather than the sun.

The benefits of high-quality sidewalks go beyond pedestrian comfort. When New York City's Mayor Bloomberg transformed Times Square in 2009 into a pedestrian plaza by installing new landscaping features and street furniture and giving more space to pedestrians, retail rents in adjacent buildings rose by close to 300%. Public space improvements that are good for pedestrians are also good for stores. The shutting of Strøget—the main shopping street in Copenhagen, Denmark—to automobiles in 1962 and gradual improvements in public space design have significantly increased foot traffic in the city center. Today, Strøget is the longest car-free street in Europe, accommodating over 55,000 pedestrians, who are often shoulder-to-shoulder on pleasant summer days. Over time, retail revenues on the street have increased manifold. Investments made into sidewalks fronting retail clusters often reverberate back to city coffers in the form of property taxes.

Double-Sided Streets with Easy Crossings

Commercial streets work best when they are double-sided, lined with business on both sides—which doubles the number of destinations a visitor can reach within a short walk. This is a far more effective strategy for increasing destination access than extending out one-sided storefronts along a lengthy street.

For the shops both sides of retail streets to work together, it must be easy for pedestrians to cross the street (Figure 72). In some of the best cases, traffic-calming measures allow pedestrians to cross at ease along any point of the street. Traffic solutions called "shared spaces," which have gained popularity in Europe in the last decade, enable pedestrians and cars to share the street at the same grade, with no height or paving differentiation between roads and sidewalks (Figure 73). Signs alert drivers before they enter shared traffic zones that pedestrians can cross at any point. Driving speeds are reduced to 10–15 km/h, while stop signs, traffic lights, and ground markers are deliberately eliminated. This approach shifts the responsibility of traffic safety from signs to drivers and pedestrians themselves. Interestingly, several cities that have implemented shared spaces on their streets have seen accident rates decrease and, in some cases, traffic throughput increase. But in cases where traffic levels are high, pedestrians have also felt more stressed while competing for space with cars.

In more typical contexts, roads between double-sided shop fronts have marked zebra crossings on the ground. It is preferable to have pedestrian priority at crossings, requiring cars to yield to pedestrians any time someone wants to cross. Having such priority crossings at around 100-meter intervals on retail streets can

Figure 71. Strøget in Copenhagen is the longest pedestrian shopping street in Europe. Photo by Henrik Sendelbach, July 2005.

Figure 72. Impossible crossing on Tunjungan Street in Surabaya, Indonesia. Photo by author.

Figure 73. Exhibition Road following opening of shared-space scheme during 2012, South Kensington, London, UK. Photo by Romazur, May 2012.

generate good pedestrian access to both sides of the road. It is also beneficial to have no more than two traffic lanes in each direction and reduced speeds. More numerous lanes start inhibiting people's sense of safety and comfort while crossing streets. Pedestrian safety measures can help—pedestrian islands in the middle of the street make long crossings easier and safer, and sidewalk curb extensions improve the visibility of cars before pedestrians step onto the road. Using the same pavement at pedestrian crossings as on sidewalks can help signal drivers that pedestrians have priority at the crossing. The National Association of City Transportation Officials (NACTO) has made a notable effort in recent years to publish new street design guidelines for North American cities that encourage implementation of a wide range of pedestrian priority measures.[10]

The crossing problem disappears on pedestrian-only streets, where visitors can stroll freely between stores on both sides. The Third Street Promenade in Los Angeles, Church Street in Burlington, VT, the Strøget in Copenhagen, Via Dante in Milan, Bahnhofstrasse in Zurich, and Bourke Street Mall in Melbourne are all examples of successful city center shopping streets where cars are prohibited. Though pedestrian-only streets can work well for retailers, their success depends on where they are located and consequently how many people can conveniently access them. In the North American context, where the vast majority of trips are undertaken in cars, pedestrian-only shopping streets can pose an accessibility challenge. Pedestrian streets in the United States rarely entail people arriving to the area on foot or by public transit. More often, people drive to the area and then park their cars for a pedestrian shopping experience.[11] Near both Third Street Promenade in Los Angeles and Church Street in Burlington, significant parking is provided in multistory garages near the shops. Without undermining density and walkability of an area, parking is most efficiently resolved if individual stores are not required to build their own lots and instead share multistory structured lots built as part of public-private partnerships. Though the lots do need to be close to the stores, they work best if hidden from view. Yet, parking entrances on adjacent side streets can increase traffic in surrounding areas.

In the case of European and Australian examples, pedestrian-only shopping streets rely heavily on excellent public transit and pedestrian access in the city center. Zurich's Bahnhofstrasse starts at the city's main train station and is surrounded by world-class tram connections all along the street (Figure 74). Melbourne's Bourke Place restricts cars, but also has free light rail trams riding up and down the middle of the street. Milan's Via Dante lies at the heart of the historic city center and is anchored by major tourist attractions such as the Cathedral, the Galleria, and the Garibaldi monument on each side. Most successful pedestrian-only shopping streets benefit from good location and accessibility.

Shopping spines within malls are also effectively pedestrian-only streets with shops on both sides. Though shopping centers are typically enclosed and air-conditioned, developers have learned how traditional city centers work and replicated a stimulating street environment indoors. Through experimentation over time, shopping center developers have come to believe that the optimal distance between facing stores across the circulation corridor is 9–12 meters.[12] This is analogous to the width of city streets in many historic, pre-automobile town centers around the world.

Linear Density of Entrances

As important as crossings that link both sides of the street is the linear density of business entrances. A higher density of doors allows visitor to access more shops, services, and restaurants in a limited walkshed. A city block that has 20 rather than 10 shop entrances on one side of the street has double the choices and opportunities for visitors. If the same density increase is applied on both sides of the street, access to stores is quadrupled. Historically, a dense entrance pattern has been achieved with narrower parcel frontages facing the street (Figure 75). Narrow parcel fronts have led to narrow building fronts and a dense encounter

Figure 74. Bahnhofstrasse, the main shopping street in Zurich, Switzerland. Photo by author.

with diverse properties as one walks through a street. Five- to seven-meter frontages in historic city centers are common.

In Harvard Square in Cambridge, MA, the average distance between shop fronts on one side of the street is 26 meters. At a typical walking speed, it takes about 25 seconds to move from one store to another and on a 5-minute walk, one can reach around 12 storefronts along one side of the street. Being able to cross the road at any point doubles these encounters to around 24 stores in 5 minutes. Within a 10-minute walk along all available streets that run in multiple directions and wrap around small city blocks, pedestrians at Harvard Square can reach around 325 stores.

In Singapore's commercial Bugis district, which has a much higher density of businesses than Harvard Square, pedestrians can reach over 3,000 stores in the same amount of time. The average distance between businesses on one side of the street is still around 28 meters, almost the same as Harvard Square, but the much higher store accessibility is achieved with a multistory retail environment, where shops reach up to the sixth floor with another floor or two underground. Bugis has an extremely dense and interconnected network of walkways, connecting narrow stores together.

Newer commercial building typologies come with much larger footprints and wider frontages than historic buildings. A distance of 50 meters or more between entrances is common. From a pedestrian point of view, this leads to only 24

Figure 75. Haji Lane in the Bugis district of Singapore. Photo by author.

shop-front encounters on a 10-minute walk. Wide building blocks with few entrances tend to create underutilized facades, which lengthen the walk between businesses.

Boston's Waterfront District, right across the Fort Point Channel, is one of the newest developments in downtown Boston. The Waterfront District street grid is made of relatively small blocks, which normally would offer high potential for walkability. But unfortunately, the redevelopment of the area handed out very large land parcels to individual developers, usually in units of one city block—and most are being developed with only one building each, to the detriment of street commerce and activity. For instance, one might find a grand lobby entrance to a large single building on one, maybe two sides of the block and the garage and deliveries entrance on another side. As a result, much of the street frontage remains void of entrances and businesses.

To mitigate the problem of a low entrance density and underutilized street frontages, city governments could introduce urban design guidelines that require that ground-floor spaces around the block include small-footprint commercial spaces with direct access to the street. Such regulations can generate a high density of commercial activity along streets, even those that include large building footprints in newly developed commercial areas.

The city of Vancouver in Canada, which has a strong tradition of imposing urban design guidelines on new developments, has achieved relatively dense commercial facades, even in the newly developed Harbor area (Figure 76). High-rise

Urban Design and Building Typologies 165

Figure 76. Podium block in Vancouver, accommodating retailers with direct street entrances on the ground level. Photo by author.

residential towers are wrapped with 3- to 5-story commercial podiums lined with commercial entrances along the street. The internal circulation structure of the building pictured is kept separate from the commercial spaces, which are entered directly from the street. Grand lobbies for entering high-rise buildings still exist—these are important for maximizing residential values—but they become but one of many entrances around the block.

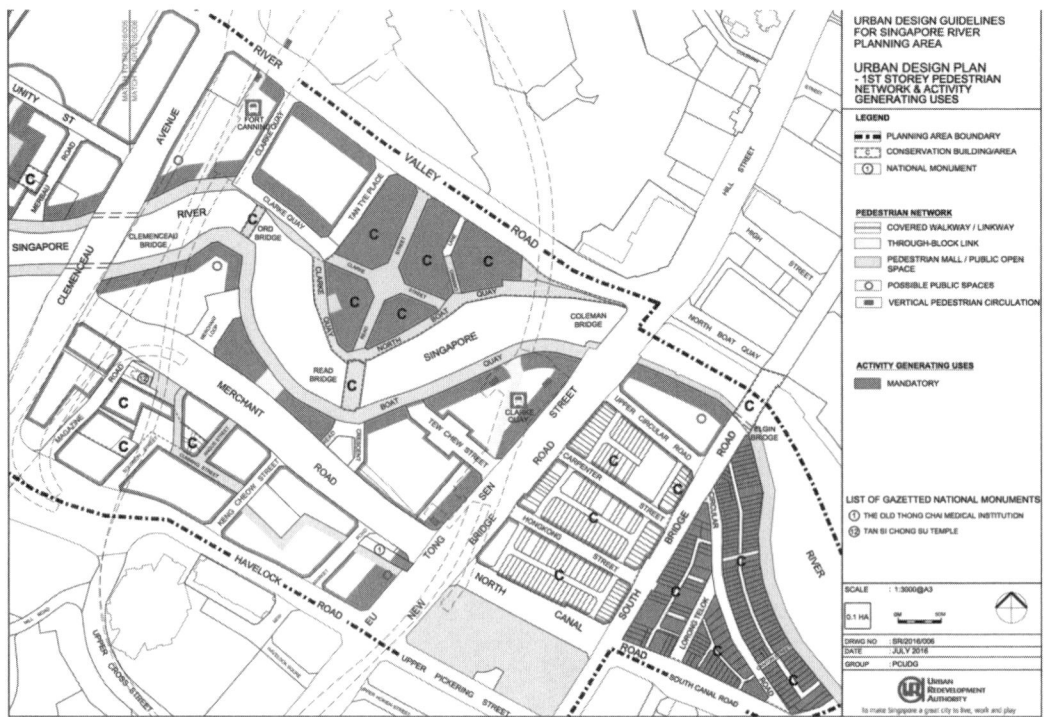

Figure 77. Urban Development Authority's urban design guidelines around the Singapore River. Source: Singapore Urban Redevelopment Authority.

Singapore's Urban Redevelopment Authority uses urban design guidelines in addition to zoning and land use regulations to shape developments in most of the downtown area. These guidelines include an "activity generating uses" category,[13] which requires developers to provide spaces for shops, services, restaurants, or equivalent publicly accessible amenities along street frontages. Wherever specified, developers need to deliver active ground-floor space with direct access from the sidewalk. This regulatory instrument allows the Urban Redevelopment Authority to ensure that any new downtown development will generate a robust density of business entrances along key streets (Figure 77). Several US cities have also introduced maximum frontage allowances for chain stores as part of an attempt to create more diverse and dense retail streets.[14]

The Shape of a Retail Cluster

Finally, the "fit" between retail form and function, as Kevin Lynch has called it, also depends on the spatial configuration of the cluster as a whole.[15] Some retail

Figure 78. The result of the Reach accessibility metric illustrated for a building that reaches 24 neighboring entrances within a five-minute (250 m) walkshed. Image by City Form Lab.

clusters are more compact and allow visitors to get to more stores in less time. Others stretch out over long distances.

A *reach* metric from spatial network analysis offers a simple yardstick to compare pedestrian accessibility to stores (and other building entrances) in any retail cluster.[16] This metric counts how many destinations you can reach within a specified walkshed within a street network. For instance, Figure 78 illustrates how a particular building has 24 neighboring entrances within a 5-minute (250 meter) walkshed.

Orchard Road, Singapore's most famous high-end retail corridor, is a two-and-a-half-kilometer street lined with shopping malls on both sides. But due to its elongated shape, few people make the walk from one end of Orchard Road to the other. Doing so would entail a long walk even in moderate climates, let alone Singapore's tropical heat and humidity. Carnaby Street in London, on the other hand, forms a gridiron retail cluster. Bounded by Regent Street to the west and Oxford Street to the north, Carnaby has a compact form, giving customers access to a high density of stores within a short walk. Third Street Promenade in Santa Monica, CA, is also wrapped around a gridiron street network with two anchor stores—Bloomingdale's and Nordstrom—at the eastern end of the street and a series of small and diverse stores spanning out along a double-sided, pedestrian-only promenade. Shops continue on the next block along both sides of Second and Fourth Streets (Figure 79).

Compact retail clusters provide access to more stores within shorter walking distances. Grid layouts, like the one around Santa Monica's Third Street Prom-

Figure 79. Plan of downtown Santa Monica, CA, and Third Street Promenade. Image by author.

enade, do this particularly well.[17] But squares form another compact spatial arrangement that makes street commerce easy to access. This pattern originated in historic European cities, where a *place, plaza* or *piazza*—an open space, typically with commercial edges—formed as an opening within an otherwise densely built city fabric. Modern squares are often found around highly connected street intersections. Squares are distinguished by name mostly in Anglo-Saxon settlements, but the typology can be found in greater or lesser concentration in most cities around the world. A highly connected street corner, usually at the intersection of more than four crossroads, serves as a central node of a square, with sidewalks lined and commerce spanning out along radiating streets in each direction. The densest concentrations of businesses, as well as the highest rents, are found around the intersections of the fanning streets—the places of heightened accessibility and visibility, as discussed in Chapter 5.

At typical walking speeds on a single-sided street, one reaches about 300 meters of street frontage in a 5-minute walkshed. If the street can be easily crossed to access shops on both sides, this goes up to 600 meters. But when you stand at the intersection of six fanning streets, with double-sided storefronts

Figure 80. Shibuya intersection in Tokyo.

and easy crossings, then you can reach close to six times that, or a 3,600-meter retail frontage within the same 5-minute walk. And if the street pattern contains not only outward fanning streets but also cross streets around relatively small city blocks, shop accessibility is even higher. Add to that the heightened visibility and memorability of such special intersections in a city's street network and it becomes easy to see why we often encounter street commerce clustered around highly connected intersections. Some of the most iconic shopping clusters in the world are found along intersections with six or more streets—the row of French department stores around the intersection of Boulevard Haussmann and Rue de la Chaussée-d'Antin, Potzdamer Platz in Berlin, the Shibuya crossing in Tokyo, Raffles Place in Singapore, Plaza Serrano in Buenos Aires, and the seven-dials circle in London's SoHo, among others (Figure 80).

The urban qualities of building types, streets, and street patterns I have explored throughout this chapter are present in most retail clusters. It is therefore difficult to evaluate how the lack thereof could adversely impact retail developments—stores don't tend to gravitate to buildings and streets that cannot accommodate them. But there is one example of a location that had all the economic prerequisites for retail density that I discussed in previous chapters—customer density, accessibility, public transportation, information about the location's performance—yet retail was inhibited by building types and urban design: Kendall Square in Cambridge, MA, at the heart of the Massachusetts Institute of Technology's campus.

When I arrived in Cambridge as a graduate student in 2004, I clearly remember my first impression of Kendall Square. I took the subway from the airport to MIT and got off at Kendall. Emerging from the underground staircase, I could see several tall office buildings and research labs surrounding the station. The time was five or six in the evening and lots of people were heading the opposite way toward the subway from which I emerged. I could hear the unusually loud humming of the industrial-quality HVAC systems in buildings all around, making me feel that MIT, and Kendall Square in the middle of it, were more like a laboratory complex than a traditional university campus or the city square that I had expected. Despite a high building density and hundreds of people on the street, there were only a couple of stores around the subway stop—a university bookstore, an MIT Press bookstore, a Legal Seafoods restaurant, a local bank, and a couple of coffee shops. Several buildings had uninviting load-bearing walls facing the street and some had elevated ground floors, with their lobbies up on a mezzanine. Instead of a lively retail environment where the subway let out, several parking lots fronted Main Street. Other buildings were little more than dull offices or long curtain-wall facades with no entrances facing the street. Commercial activities on the square were far below what the area's density and its adjacency to a major subway station would suggest.

Over the next few years I learned that the city of Cambridge had seen Kendall Square as a problem for a while. The city's planners were eager to see more retail, more restaurants, and more street life in the area, but it wasn't happening. MIT was the largest landlord around Kendall, and a couple of large developers, including Boston Properties and a federal transportation agency, were making good on their real estate investments by focusing on office space upstairs rather than street life downstairs. There were at most a half dozen stores within a five-minute walkshed around the subway entrance—a small fraction of what was available in other places with similar density and access to public transport.

The task of retrofitting Kendall Square was complicated by the fact that several building owners were not interested in having retail or food tenants on their ground floors. Large tech companies that had moved into the area, including Google, Microsoft, and Amazon, were providing free all-you-can-eat canteens inside their own offices, while MIT had its own food courts. Lucrative office space on the upper floors was commanding some of the Boston area's highest rents, bringing a windfall to the developers that had put up the buildings ahead of the area's tech revival in the 1990s and early 2000s. Dealing with a few extra ground-floor tenants, whose retail leases would pale in comparison to their main revenue sources upstairs, seemed like a hassle not worth having.

But the city persisted and started requiring that both MIT and other building owners in the area start placing retail and food tenants into both retrofitted street-facing ground floors of existing buildings as well as new buildings that were still in planning. As a result of a joint taskforce between the city, MIT, developers, the area's stakeholders, and urban design consultants, a Kendall Square Urban Renewal Plan was adopted. The plan suggested that Kendall continue as an innovation hub but significantly increase retail and food services, implement street and green-space improvements, introduce mixed-income housing to the area, and make Kendall work as an around-the-clock city square, on par with other nearby subcenters such as Central Square, Harvard Square, and Charles Street across the river.

In a Boston Properties–owned 255 Main Street building, ground floors were reconfigured and a formerly dead sidewalk facade rebuilt with new glazed openings; two new restaurants established shop there. A new, open, glass entrance for Microsoft's offices was built into what was previously a dead brick corner in the same building. Almost all the new buildings that have been added to the area since 2005 have come with commercial space requirements on the ground level, and the city has invested considerable resources into street improvements and pedestrian and bicycle amenities, as well as green-space enhancements.

While still in the early phases of a long redevelopment initiative, by 2017 the five-minute walkshed around the Kendall subway station boasted 12 eating and drinking places, 6 retailers, and 4 personal service providers. Within half a mile there were 91 establishments. This constitutes a 34% increase compared to 2006.[18] Though this increase has also been affected by rising job density in the area, highly paid tech workers, improved traffic solutions, and a few new multistory housing developments, the city's efforts in convincing developers as well as MIT of the value of a vibrant street environment lined with commerce and services has been instrumental. The conversion of formerly inactive ground-floor spaces and addition of newly built street frontages for retail and service uses through architectural and urban design planning has changed the area's image. Kendall is not yet a regional leisure destination like Harvard Square or Boston's Back Bay, and it still suffers from a lack of retailers and more affordable retail and housing that would bring students and other lower-income residents together with the high-income tech crowd around MIT, but if you go there at five or six o'clock on a weekday evening, you will find restaurants and cafés packed with workers who have discovered a newfound love for street life. More change is in the works, and if the city also adopted a resolution taxing large companies and institutions for housing internal canteens with free food and alcohol, like San Francisco has recently done,[19] more of the area's high earnings would flow to local neighborhoods, restaurants, and stores surrounding them.

CHAPTER 7

How Demographic Shifts and E-Commerce Are Reshaping the Retail Landscape

Target Corporation, the parent company of all Target stores in the United States, is headquartered in Minneapolis, MN. It ran 1,822 stores across all fifty states in 2018[1]—mostly big-box stores, though in recent years it has also introduced smaller urban stores and even little showrooms where customers can pick up online orders. Target is currently the second-largest retailer in the United States, after Walmart. The story of its expansion across America is not just one of another big-box chain following a well-established path. Target's trailblazing ascent is entangled with the very invention of the modern shopping mall. Interestingly, its history also traces back to an elegant six-story department store in downtown Minneapolis, which still stands across the street from Target's current corporate headquarters.

Donald C. Dayton became president of the Dayton Company in 1950. Founded by his grandfather George Henry Dayton in 1902, the original Dayton's was located in a six-story masonry structure on the corner of Nicollet Avenue and Seventh Street in downtown Minneapolis. Its stone and glass facades were ornate with entablatures, cornices, and half columns. The lavish interior, clad in terrazzo floor tiles, wood paneling, and stucco moldings, formed an elegant backdrop to the copper-trimmed glass counters, marble tabletops, and shelves that displayed a vast array of garments, shoes, accessories, jewelry, cosmetics, and toys. Dayton's was both the largest and the most prestigious place to shop in downtown Minneapolis in the 1950s.

Barely two years in as the company's president, Donald C. Dayton met Victor Gruen, an Austrian-born architect who was already widely known as America's preeminent retail designer. Gruen had recently completed a much-publicized Northland shopping center in the suburbs of Detroit for the Hudson Company, whose owner, Oscar Webber, was friendly with Dayton. Minneapolis, just like

Detroit, was restructuring, and Webber advised Dayton to refocus his business from the downtown streets of Minneapolis to the rapidly growing edges of the city.[2] Despite still having lively streets, the downtown core was beginning to lose out to the growing middle-class suburbs around the city. Racial inequalities and tensions in the historic city center led to occasional violence and unrest.[3] Webber and Gruen convinced Dayton to build a large suburban shopping center in Edina, a suburb south of downtown.

Working with Dayton, Gruen not only designed the store but reenvisioned the department store's future. Instead of targeting customers on bustling sidewalks and clustering with other competing department stores, Gruen saw the future of retailing in suburban middle-class customers. These customers would drive to malls in cars, which carried much larger and many more shopping bags than pedestrians could. They would come not just to shop and run errands, but to experience professionally choreographed civic life under private security and in segregated middle-class harmony. The mall was a place that could entertain primarily white, suburban families for a whole day.

To counter the cold winters and humid summers of Minneapolis, Gruen designed the large communal spaces between the shops as a continuous enclosed indoor atrium. This had never been done before. Every mall until then, even the one Gruen himself had just finished for Hudson's in Detroit, had outdoor circulation between the different stores, each of which was individually heated and cooled throughout the year. But for what became known as the Southdale Center, Gruen envisioned a giant communal atrium that was partially heated through skylights and partially through a heat-exchange pump that had never been tested in a large project before. Gruen said he was inspired by the Galleria Vittorio Emmanuele in Milan, Italy.[4]

Few engineers believed that heating, cooling, and maintaining this giant indoor area was financially feasible. But Gruen and his team discovered that if the atrium was climate controlled, then individual shops would no longer need their own heating and cooling systems. Considerable savings could also be achieved in the design of the front facades of individual stores, which would no longer be facing outward, toward parking lots, but rather inward, toward the common atrium and circulation spine. Stores would not require full-fledged facades and could simply have a glass or a sliding metal mesh door to close for the night. Their exterior facades were stripped down to the bare bones, and the mall had only three exterior entrances along a lengthy perimeter.

Southdale opened in 1956 with 72 shops and two anchors—Dayton's and Donaldson's.[5] Its indoor atrium—the largest in the United States at the time—was called Garden Court and was designed with utmost care. The Daytons, who were art collectors, commissioned Harry Bertoia to produce two three-story abstract sculptures for the atrium. Street furniture allowed customers to relax and watch passersby, and there were stages for music and fashion shows. A "Sidewalk Café," with umbrellas over indoor tables surrounded by trees in pots and on balconies, reminded visitors that the atrium was supposed to work like a bustling downtown street. Dayton's even organized evening symphony concerts and balls there. Gruen insisted that he had created a new form of civic space that would counter the otherwise sprawling, repetitive, and anonymous suburbia around it.

Southdale was the first air-conditioned, introverted, indoor mall. It became the model not only for future shopping centers in the United States but for the whole world. Contrary to Gruen's civic intensions, it also became a symbol for car-centric, consumerist, postwar suburbia. Though themselves an effect of suburban growth, Southdale and the many other malls it inspired enabled suburban, car-centric, and racially segregated lifestyles to prosper at a safe distance from historic inner-city streets.

As both purchasing power and stores started fleeing downtowns, traffic worsened. Problems for inner cities across the country were further compounded by the Federal Aid Highway Act of 1956—the largest public works project in American history at the time—which authorized $25 billion for the construction of a 41,000 mile-long interstate highway system. Cities that added highways connected to the interstate network recovered 90% of their costs from the federal government. A deal that at the time seemed too good to turn down for many economically stagnant and traffic-clogged municipalities led to massive demolitions of historic centers to make room for the sprawling new highways. Among others, the program funded I-94 from St. Paul to Minneapolis and the I-62 Crosstown Commons, which went right past Gruen's Southdale Center.[6]

But rather than producing higher land values in declining downtowns, highways opened up cheaper land outside of the city and sped up the exodus of white middle-class residents and jobs to the suburbs. At the same time, urban renewal projects cleared entire inner-city communities and commercial districts, displacing deeply rooted social networks and leaving many American downtowns socially and economically hollow. Many historically vibrant retail clusters and commercial corridors fell victim to racially driven neighborhood redlining, demolition, community destruction, and the flight of purchasing power that these policies enabled.[7]

Figure 81 shows population density in Minneapolis according to the 1950 and 1970 census counts. The residential population located within a one-and-a-half-mile radius around the original Dayton's department store in downtown Minneapolis dropped from 171,755 in 1950 to 105,862 in 1970—a 39% decline in 20 years. During the same period, the population in a three-mile radius around

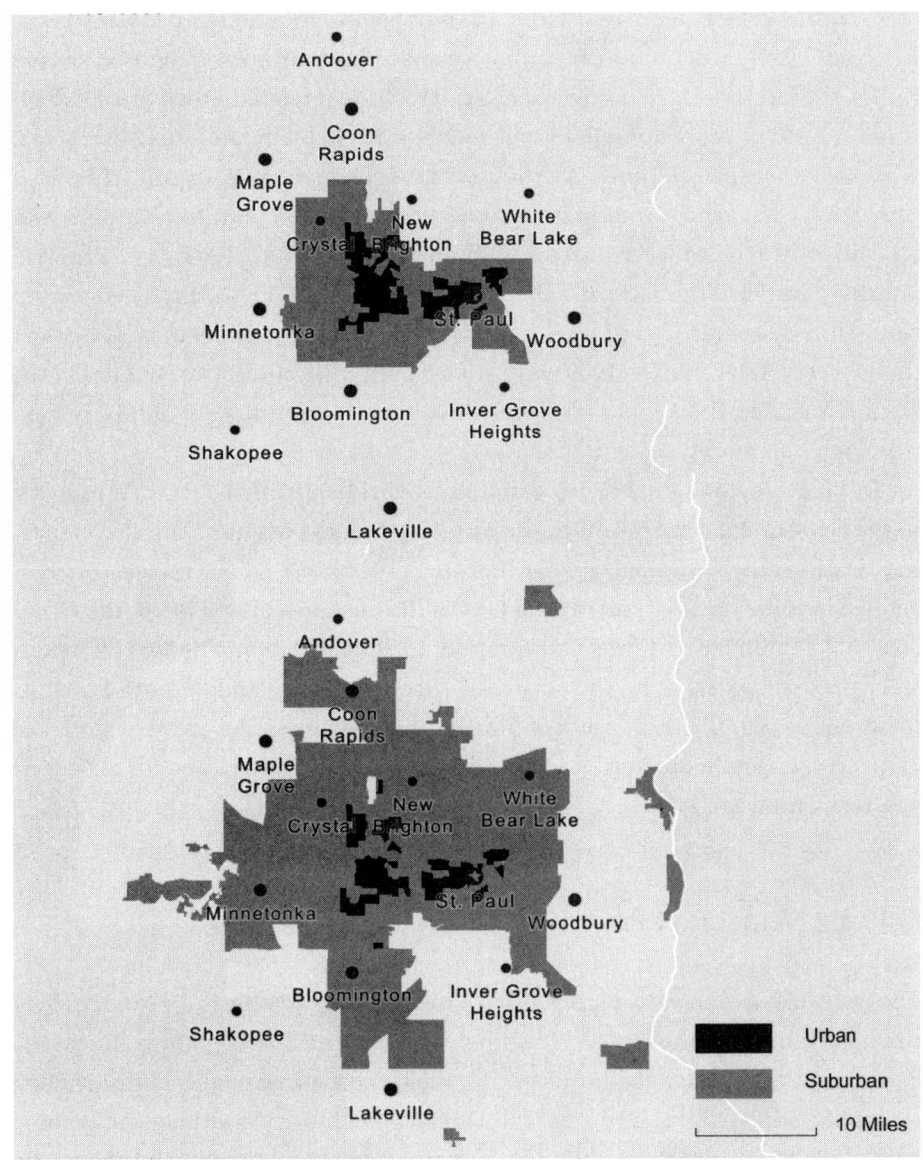

Figure 81. Minneapolis and St. Paul, MN, urban and suburban population densities in 1950 (top) and 1970 (bottom). Suburban population defined as 102–2,212 households per square mile and urban population as more than 2,213 households per square mile. Data source: U.S. Census Bureau. Population Density, 1950 and 1970. Prepared by Social Explorer (accessed January 2019).

the Southdale mall increased from 107,699 people to 206,045 people—a 91% increase. Using a definition of urban versus suburban areas proposed by Jed Kolko, the former research director at Trulia, I have rendered urban areas, which contain 2,213 or more households per square mile, in black, and suburban areas, which have between 102 and 2,212 households per square mile, in gray. This helps us see that what were formerly continuous urban cores in both Minneapolis and St. Paul in 1950 became fractured and discontinuous inner cities by 1970. Lower-density suburban tracts around them multiplied manifold during the same period. The city sprawled, and retail developers followed the white middle-class to the suburbs. "From 1965 to 1980 was a golden period," according to Arthur O'Day, from Associated and Federated Stores. "Everyone was running around like hell, throwing a shopping center up."[8]

In 1962, Dayton's established a discount subsidiary called Target. While still in the department store business, the company merged with its Detroit competitor, Hudson's, to form the Dayton-Hudson Corporation. By the mid-1970s, Target had become the highest-earning part of the business, and in 2000, the whole company rebranded as Target Corporation. In 2004, the company sold off its six-story department store on the corner of Nicollet Avenue and Seventh Street to focus on the national expansion of Target. The downtown department store became a Macy's in 2006, until it was sold to new owners and closed for an extensive renovation in 2017.

Shifting Demographics

The enclosed and inward-facing suburban shopping mall was a product of its time, during which the largest consumer base was the nuclear family. It was reflective of the postwar economic boom, rapid motorization and highway construction, white flight, and Federal Housing Authority mortgage insurance provisions favoring the suburbs.[9] But the forces that pulled department stores and street commerce out of downtowns across America in the 1960s, '70s, and '80s have weakened. Instead, signs of reversal are apparent in some American cities, shifting millennials and middle-class earners back to mixed-use centers and Main Streets.

Whereas in the 1970 census, 40% of American households were comprised of married couples with children, by 2010 this share had halved to only 20%. At the same time, the share of single-person households increased from 17% in 1970 to 27% in 2010. There are proportionately half as many nuclear families with children in 2018 and 50% more single-person households than during the heyday of malls. The privately securitized suburban mall has lost much of its target audience.

In addition, during the 2008 recession homeownership among households with children under the age of 18 fell by 15%, shifting more families to rental homes, which tend to be denser and more urban than single-family houses. These demographic shifts have reduced Americans' dependence on suburbs, centered around the nuclear family and a car-based lifestyle, and malls. They have instead catalyzed a demographic inversion that is bringing some of the middle class back to inner-city neighborhoods.

A recent report by the George Washington University School of Business found that walkable urban office space in the 30 largest metro areas in the United States commands a 74% rent-per-square-foot premium over rents in drivable suburban areas.[10] In Washington, DC, and Atlanta, for instance, walkable districts accounted for less than 1% of the total metro land mass but accommodated 50% of the metro area's office, retail, hotel, and apartment square footage developed after the 2008 recession, from 2009 to 2013. While baby boomers of the '60s and '70s preferred single-family suburban homes and corporate office parks centered around the automobile, the new generation is gravitating toward denser, mixed-use, walkable, and transit-oriented environments. Downtown housing prices in the largest US cities, including New York, Los Angeles, Chicago, San Francisco, Boston, and Washington, reflect what members of the new generation are voting for with their wallets.

According to a survey of millennials conducted by the National Trust for Historic Preservation and American Express, millennials primarily interact with historic buildings and neighborhoods by shopping and dining.[11] More than half of the respondents preferred to shop or dine in unique or historic downtowns as opposed to chain restaurants or shopping malls. Eighty percent also said they would rather patronize businesses that support historic preservation over those that do not.

And millennials are not alone in preferring amenity-rich built environments. A national Senior Living Preferences Survey, conducted by the nonprofit A Place for Mom, found that older Americans also value walkable urban centers. The survey asked 1,000 respondents around the country about their living preferences, and a majority said it was very important or somewhat important to live in a walkable neighborhood. Charlie Severn, head of marketing at A Place for Mom, concluded that "It's time to abandon the idea that only millennials and Generation X care about walkability and the services available in dense urban neighborhoods. These results show a growing set of senior housing consumers also find these neighborhoods desirable. It's a trend that should be top of mind among developers."[12]

As political scientist Alan Ehrenhalt points out in his recent book, *The Great Inversion and the Future of the American City,* the middle class is moving back to inner-city neighborhoods across the country en masse.[13] Many urban districts across the United States that lost middle-class residents and their purchasing power as part of white flight, violent street crime, and degradation of public schools in the postwar decades are now witnessing a return of more affluent residents. Central business districts and the blue-collar industrial areas around them, as well as former working-class housing districts nearby, are increasingly occupied by middle- and upper-middle-class households who used to stay in the suburbs. More poor people now live in American suburbs, outside of traditional city boundaries, than within.[14] As a case in point, the area around the original Dayton's in downtown Minneapolis has witnessed a 4.5% population growth between 2010 and 2016, while the total share of African Americans decreased during the same period.[15] Echoing the new downtown demographics, the ornate department store on the corner of Nicollet Avenue and Seventh Street that Dayton's sold to Macy's, which subsequently passed it on to a New York developer, is now going through a major renovation by Gensler architects, who are turning it into a hip center with co-working spaces, a food hall, a gym, and mixed-use retail and office space. The same elegant six-story building that Dayton's left behind in the 1950s in order to focus its business on suburban malls has sprung back to life, turning the tables on suburban shopping centers, including Southdale.

Several municipal governments are implementing initiatives that demonstrate the new urban-based economic development outlook. Boston is developing its first citywide master plan in 50 years, which envisions a significant densification of several inner-city neighborhoods around public transit. Los Angeles, the second-largest city in the United States, has embarked on its boldest investments into public transit and transit-oriented development since the 1930s. As part of PlanNYC, New York City has converted more than 40 acres of roadway into 70 new pedestrian plazas in locations that include the world-famous Times Square.[16] Walkability, active public spaces, and mixed-use developments have moved from the shadow of urban redevelopment policies, which have prioritized business and industrial interests since the 1980s, to occupy a central position in many cities' planning agendas.

The new era of urban economic development that New York City helped pioneer is captured in former mayor Bloomberg's commentary in 2015:

> Traditionally, urban economic development has focused on retaining industries and luring new businesses with incentive packages. But in the new century, a different and far more effective model has emerged: focusing first and foremost on creating the conditions that attract people. As cities are increasingly demonstrating, talent attracts capital more effectively than capital attracts talent. People want to live in communities that offer

healthy and family-friendly lifestyles: not only good schools and safe streets but also clean air, beautiful parks, and extensive mass transit systems. And where people want to live, businesses want to invest.[17]

Inner-city revival is in part fueled by knowledge workers—the largely white and wealthy "creative class," as Richard Florida has called them[18]—looking for density, vibrancy, and propinquity, and cities are competing to respond. After near bankruptcy in the mid-1970s, the urban environment of New York City has returned stronger than ever as the favored destination for a young, fun-loving, and highly educated workforce from all over the world. Silicon Valley, a long-standing magnet for technology-sector employment in the San Francisco Bay area, is now losing workers to San Francisco, which offers greater urban amenities, services, and density than the suburban settings of San Jose. In Seattle, Amazon has recently shifted its headquarters from a former hospital complex on a large highway intersection into newly constructed high-rise towers in a dense, mixed-use street grid amid 3,000 residential units and a large selection of shops and services, including 100,000 square feet of new ground-floor retail within Amazon's own buildings.[19]

Inner-city development is not only associated with wealthy tech firms and highly paid knowledge workers. Dudley Square in Boston, for instance, is the center of a diverse African American and Caribbean district of Roxbury, which has historically witnessed a number of damaging and neglectful planning initiatives by the city. Median incomes are well below the city average and many of the area's residents are recent immigrants. Yet Dudley Square is returning as a vibrant neighborhood center with active street commerce and well-utilized public space. Commercial spaces are located close to a popular bus depot behind the square—a former site of an aboveground subway stop that the city removed from the neighborhood in 1987—which helps keep businesses in use throughout the day. Several neighborhood organizations have set up shop in the square and work with both residents and the city to attract new business and employers to the area. Just like in wealthier downtown clusters, residents have voiced their preference for small, diverse, and locally owned business instead of big-box chain stores.

The Haley House Bakery Café offers one example of a community-centered business that does more than serve coffee to its visitors. In addition to healthy food and a popular gathering space, the café provides workforce and business opportunities for people with limited employment prospects, especially those transitioning out of incarceration, through the Transitional Employment Program, culinary education for underserved youth, and a forum for cultural and arts events.[20]

The City of Boston and especially former mayor Thomas Menino have played an important role in bringing public institutions and employers to Dudley Square.

The recently completed Bolling Municipal Building at the heart of Dudley Square houses the Boston Public Schools department, a community center, and retail spaces that offer rooms and theaters for public lectures, job-training events, and performances. City-led initiatives have helped attract new private sector retail and service establishments to the square. And as the city's advocacy and support for Dudley continues, it has now been earmarked as the next community-centric innovation cluster for the greater Boston area.

In Los Angeles, the Byzantine Latino Quarter south of Koreatown has emerged as a vibrant center of street commerce in lower downtown. The area is home to a largely Mexican, Central American, and Greek community with relatively low household incomes. But like Dudley Square, it has taken off as a popular street commerce cluster comprised of garment businesses, food vendors, and apparel stores. Sidewalks, pocket parks, and public art installations invite visitors to use the streets as public spaces to meet friends and people watch.

In the 1990s, the area had been almost abandoned by mainstream businesses, covered in graffiti, and neglected by city officials. The turnaround was made possible by a conscious organized effort by the area's residents, merchants, and representatives of local institutions such as religious, school, and community groups who formed a coalition called Genesis Plus. With the help of volunteers from UCLA's planning program, Genesis Plus obtained a modest Los Angeles Neighborhood Initiative seed grant and used the funds to establish a highly participatory and inclusive planning process to reenvision the neighborhood. The area was renamed to emphasize its multiethnic identity (it had previously been called Pico-Heights and subsequently Pico-Union). A series of volunteer-based initiatives reclaimed small public spaces, eliminated negative landmarks such as Jersey barriers and graffiti, decorated building facades and outdoor street furniture, installed new trees and planter boxes, and forged an entire new public identity through signage, landmark maps, and media outreach. The gradually strengthened public realm helped, in turn, to lure new businesses and employers to the area, turning a public space strategy into an economic development and neighborhood revitalization strategy.

American inner cities have been witnessing not only residential growth but also employment growth. A recent study by Daniel A. Hartley of the Federal Reserve Bank of Chicago and Nikhil Kaza and T. William Lester of the University of North Carolina examined the changing geographies of employment across 281 Metropolitan Statistical Areas in the United States.[21] For the first time in decades, they found that "the rate of job growth between 2002 and 2011 in inner cities—defined broadly as non-Central Business District (CBD) tracts in the largest principal city within a metropolitan area—was on par with that of suburban areas (6.1% vs. 6.9%) and even surpassed suburbs in the post–Great Recession recovery (2009–2011)."[22]

More jobs and a higher proportion of single-person, childless, and elderly households who demand more walkability and fewer houses with yards, who prefer to eat outside of their home, and who have more flexible leisure hours are catalyzing street commerce in many inner-city districts. Instead of malls, current real estate trends suggest that Americans increasingly prefer amenities that are closer to their homes and workplaces and accessible by foot and public transit. Rather than undertaking daily or weekly trips in a car to a remote shopping center, they increasingly prefer stopping by stores near transit stations on their way home and going to neighborhood centers on weekends to shop, dine, and meet people.

Unequal Inner-City Revival

But the story of urban revival is also uneven. Large coastal cities such as New York, Los Angeles, San Francisco, Boston, Washington, Philadelphia, Portland, and Seattle are witnessing more growth in inner cities than suburbs. According to research done by Jed Kolko, Seattle was the fastest urbanizing metro area between 2010 and 2016, with a 3% increase in average population density at the neighborhood level, followed by Chicago (+1.2%) and Minneapolis (+0.8%).[23] But of the 50 largest metro areas in the country, 41 still saw an overall decrease in population density, not an increase. The fastest sprawling cities are not on the water-bound coasts but in the middle of the country, where land is abundant and populations keep growing. San Antonio witnessed the largest decrease in population density (-5.3%), followed by Austin (-5.0%), and Oklahoma City (-4.1%). Houston, the fourth largest city in the nation, witnessed a 3.8% decline in average population density between 2010 and 2016. Suburbs are still growing in middle America and inner-city revival is not affecting all cities equally.

Access to urban amenities is also uneven within economically booming coastal cities. A typical middle- or lower-middle-income family cannot afford to move back to the city. According to a study by Anthony Alofsin, a family of four with a moderate middle-class income could commit up to $8,120 for a down payment in 2018, plus closing costs, to buy a home for $232,000.[24] This will get them a suburban home with three to four bedrooms, two bathrooms, a garage, and a piece of ground for a front and back yard. Meanwhile, according to the real estate portal Zillow.com, a median home in Boston costs $588,200, in San Francisco $1,358,500, in Seattle $764,200, in Los Angeles $677,400, and in Washington, DC, $568,600. A family would need to make $135,000 to meet the mortgage payments without even factoring in a down payment. Less than a quarter of all households in these metropolitan areas fall in an income bracket that can afford this. And even if the prices are somewhat lower in the formerly lower-income parts of inner cities, buying an urban home close to public transit and amenities remains out of reach for most households.

Employment growth in American inner cities is similarly unequally spread. The same study by Daniel A. Hartley, Nikhil Kaza, and T. William Lester that examined employment growth in the inner cities of 281 Metropolitan Statistical Areas across the country found that inner-city employment growth was geographically skewed. During the 2009–2016 recovery, the share of all new jobs grew faster in inner cities than suburbs in all but two US regions—East South Central and West South Central. In these two regions, which includes Arkansas, Louisiana, Oklahoma, Texas, Alabama, Mississippi, Tennessee, and Kentucky, employment typically grew faster in suburbs than inner cities.[25] However, in all of the other regions of the United States, including New England, Mid Atlantic, East North Central, West North Central, Mountain, and Pacific, jobs in inner cities surrounding the historic CBD grew faster than suburbs.[26]

In the regions where inner cities have witnessed a comeback, their growth has largely been driven by white, relatively high earners, whose arrival has also contributed to pushing former city-center residents—often minority and immigrant populations—out to further suburbs and towns. In another longitudinal analysis on the 120 largest metropolitan areas in the United States, Nathaniel Baum-Snow and Daniel Hartley found that "neighborhoods near central business districts of US metropolitan areas have experienced remarkable rebounds in population and their residents' socioeconomic status since 2000. Our decompositions reveal that this turnaround in population has primarily been driven by the return of college-graduate and high-income whites to these neighborhoods, coupled with a halt in the outflows of other white demographic groups. At the same time, the departures of minorities without college degrees continued unabated."[27]

Communities of color, which up until recently occupied central neighborhoods that few moneyed middle-class groups competed for, are witnessing steep rent increases and pressure to relocate to cheaper areas away from downtown. For established residents, especially those who do not own their homes, the influx of higher-income residents tends to produce rent hikes and displacement. This influx has produced a lot of friction. "It's a war zone here," said Paula Tajeda, who owns an empanada shop in the Mission—a historically Latino district of San Francisco—to a *New York Times* interviewer in 2015. "This is not like the Lower East Side" of Manhattan, "this is happening a lot faster."[28]

Both residential and job density data since the 2010 census suggests that the what Alan Ehrenhalt calls the *great inversion* is really at work in the coastal and northern parts of the United States and is largely driven by affluent and educated suburbanites who are returning to city buzz. Many southern metropolitan areas remain unaffected, with their dominant growth still driven by suburbs. Further-

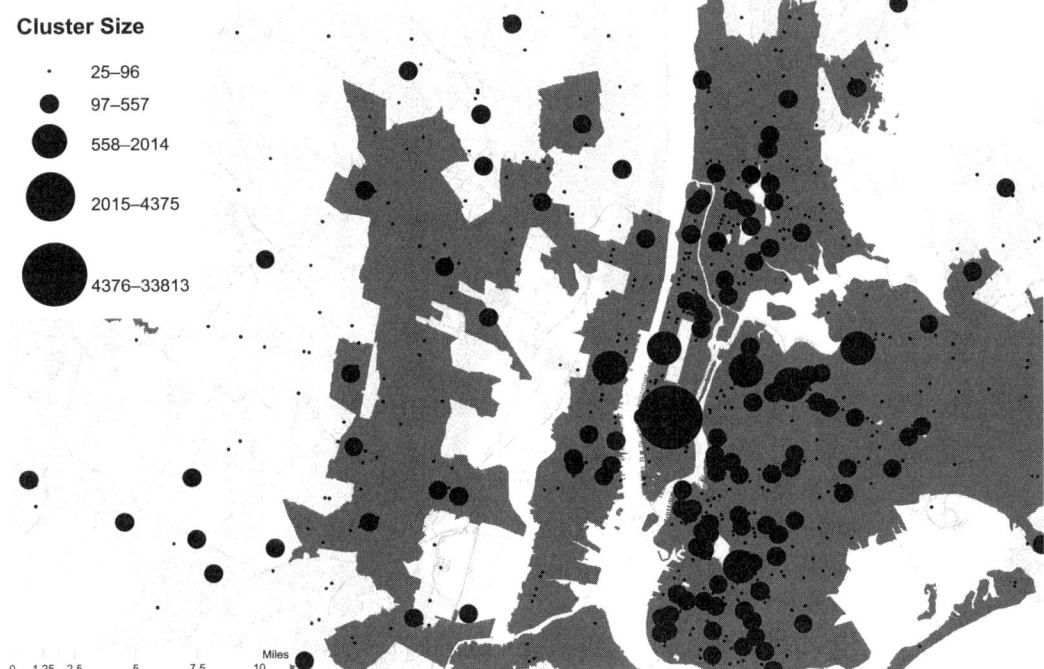

Figure 82. Retail clusters around greater New York City. Dots indicate retail agglomerations of 25 or more retail, food, or personal service establishments. Dot size corresponds to number of establishments. Gray areas are considered "urban" with zip code densities above 2,213 households per square mile. Data Source: Infogroup 2010 Business Listings, provided as part of ESRI Business Analyst software; U.S. Census Bureau. Population Density, 2010.

more, even in coastal cities such as Boston, San Francisco, Los Angeles, and Seattle, inner-city boom is not benefiting everyone. Just as the population with greater means and historic advantages drove housing to the suburbs in the postwar period, a similar demographic is now driving inner-city return. But while suburbs were developed on underpopulated exurban fields, inner-city revival is occurring on historic, contentious, and often minority-populated terrain.

At the same time, inner cities are not the only, or even the dominant, areas of street commerce growth. New commercial clusters are popping up in both urban and suburban parts of metropolitan areas. The maps of retail clusters I presented in Chapter 1 from different American cities (Figure 3–Figure 9) indicated street commerce clusters everywhere, not just inner cities.

Figure 82 illustrates the distribution of retail clusters around New York City. Relying on the same definition of urban versus suburban areas used above, I have rendered the urban areas, which contain 2,213 or more households per square mile, in black. The superimposed circles are centroids of retail clusters, their radius corresponding to the size of each cluster. While the largest clusters remain in historically dense urban areas, there are several retail agglomerations in suburban areas around the Big Apple. The story of street commerce is not just a story of inner-city neighborhoods, but of suburban ones as well.

In fact, 73% of all retail clusters in the country are in environments that can be described as suburban. And of all new retail cluster formations that emerged in the United States between 2000 and 2016, 78% are found in suburban zip codes.[29] Even though inner-city retail developments tend to be newer, more fashionable, and geared toward higher-earning millennials and knowledge workers, street commerce is also growing in suburbs, where most Americans still reside.

As ethnic minorities and lower-income residents are being displaced from inner cities, new ethnic retail clusters are growing around their new suburban communities. Wei Li, a professor at Arizona State University, describes ethnic suburban enclaves as follows: "Ethnoburbs are suburban ethnic clusters of residential and business districts within large metropolitan areas. They are multiracial/multiethnic, multicultural, multilingual, and often multinational communities, in which one ethnic minority group has a significant concentration, but does not necessarily comprise the majority."[30]

In the Boston metro area, the city of Quincy, located south of Boston, has become a vibrant Chines and Vietnamese "ethnoburb." About a third of the city's population is ethnically Asian, including a third of the city council. The influx of Asians and Asian Americans to the city has brought along a diverse business mix, with Chinese and Vietnamese restaurants, bakeries, and grocery stores. In the Los Angeles metro area, Artesia is known as Little India. At the center of Artesia, around Pioneer Boulevard and 183rd Street, lies a vibrant cluster of sari shops, Indian and Korean grocers, restaurants, tailors, doctors, travel agencies, and dry cleaners. Street commerce in Artesia also includes numerous Latino, Filipino, and Chinese businesses. When relocating to the suburbs, ethnic communities often catalyze new patterns of street commerce.

E-commerce

While changing demographic and employment patterns are partly responsible for the rising demand for street commerce, technological change has started to challenge this trend. E-commerce, which has been developing since the late 1990s, has now achieved a scale that forces every brick-and-mortar store to pay attention. Online purchases in the United States reached nearly $395 billion in 2016, accounting for 11.7% of total retail sales in the country. This statistic is sometimes used to argue that e-commerce is not as big as the popular media makes it out to be—almost 9 out of 10 purchases are still made in physical stores. However, the disruptive effects of e-commerce are not captured in its current market share but rather in its impressive growth rate. Between 2006 and 2016, online sales grew by $300 billion in the United States. A 2018 *New York Times* study suggested that 40% of all retail growth in that period was attributable to retailers with no physical presence.[31]

For brick-and-mortar stores, the two major forces affecting street commerce in American cities today—demographic restructuring and e-commerce—exert pressure in somewhat opposing directions. Demographic restructuring, discussed above, is bringing higher-earning middle-class residents back to city neighborhoods and creating a demand for shops and services that can be visited on foot, as part of a new social and recreational culture. One of the most commonly cited reasons behind the rediscovered popularity of center-city neighborhoods is the convenience that these areas offer. Shops and services are nearby and you don't have to have a car to access them. But at the same time, e-commerce is making it easier for these middle-class families to shop without leaving their homes or offices. Analogous to the way in which the automobile led to a rapid decline in transportation costs during the 20th century, e-commerce has led to a sudden decrease in transportation costs for consumers who order goods and services from their laptop or phone. As more and more people have goods shipped to their houses, fewer will need to step foot on the very streets whose convenience they pay high rents for. Will e-commerce therefore end up working against the return-to-the-city movement?

My guess is no. Current indications suggest that competition from e-commerce is forcing a wedge between shopping as a chore and experience shopping, where browsing goods, trying on garments, talking to people, and meeting friends over a meal constitutes an end in itself, rather than a means. Routine shopping is increasingly threatened by more convenient e-commerce, which enables chores to be completed without leaving one's house. Experience shopping is becoming an increasingly important part of street commerce. Goods that people like to compare in person and services that involve an essential element of human interaction are on the rise on Main Streets.

Amazon, the largest e-commerce store in the world, started in 1994 with three people selling books in a Seattle garage. The company now employs over 340,000 people globally and ships 1.6 million packages a day. In 2015, Amazon surpassed Walmart as the most valuable retailer in the United States, and by 2016 it became the fourth-highest-valued publicly traded company in the world. Alibaba is the largest e-commerce store in China. Established in 1999, the company now delivers over 57 million packages a day. In 2014, on China's peak shopping day, known as Singles' Day, the company received and shipped 278 million orders—significantly more than the number of orders shipped by Amazon on the Friday after Thanksgiving, the busiest shopping day in the United States.[32]

Several online merchants, including the behemoth Amazon, offer free or inexpensive delivery for their orders. Amazon Prime, a popular loyalty program, offers members free deliveries with unlimited purchase frequency for $99 a year. It requires no minimum spending or item size—you can get a pair of socks delivered free of charge to your house as often as you wish. And people increasingly do. According to investment bank Piper Jaffray, in 2009, before Prime was launched, the average customer who paid for deliveries spent $400 a year on various Amazon purchases. After joining Prime, average spending went up to $900.[33] The reduction in transportation costs increased shopping frequency 2.25 times, exceeding even the expectations of Amazon's own executives. "In all my years here, I don't remember anything that has been as successful [as Prime] at getting customers to shop in new product lines," said Robbie Schwietzer, vice president of Amazon Prime, to *Businessweek*.[34]

The rise of e-commerce is currently causing a lot of concern among traditional retailers, who are trying to figure out how the brick-and-mortar retail market will change due to online shopping. Until recently, the effects of e-commerce on brick-and-mortar stores were unclear. Some retail sectors had felt shocks earlier than others—many music and DVD stores, for instance, closed around 2005 as people started downloading music rather than collecting physical discs. Book and electronics stores were also shaken early on. In 2010, one of the largest bookstore chains in the United States—Borders—declared bankruptcy after 40 years of operation. Emerging competition from e-commerce was a key factor in pushing the company out business. Borders lagged behind Barnes & Noble in starting a viable online bookstore, and in 2001 it made the mistake of linking its online store to Amazon, losing control over the most important arm of its future business. In 2008 it restarted its own e-commerce site, but by then its debt and losses had grown to unsustainable levels, forcing the company to shut all of its 511 superstores across the United States.

But other types of stores, such as mid-market clothing and apparel stores, shoe stores, and household goods stores, appeared to be less affected by e-commerce, at least up until 2017, which started with a wave of bankruptcies among some of the largest clothing and apparel brands in the country. In the first three months of 2017, at least 14 major chains filed for court protection, almost surpassing a full year's worth of chain bankruptcies in the previous years. The new wave of liquidations affected discount shoe sellers, outdoor gear stores, consumer electronic stores, and clothing stores as well as general stores. Well-known brands such as American Apparel and RadioShack have been forced to close their doors. In February 2019, Payless Shoe Source announced that it would close all of its

400 stores around the country. Of all US computer, electronics, apparel, and accessories sales that took place in 2016, 45% were online sales.

Big-box stores, which primarily compete on price and whose merchandise is relatively affordable to ship, are most directly affected by e-commerce. Many of these stores have set up brick-and-mortar stores at locations where land is inexpensive, forcing customers to trade low prices for higher transportation costs. This model of discount retailing is finding it increasingly difficult to compete with online stores that deliver the same goods at similar prices with close to zero transportation costs. On top of that, many discount chains have been growing their business by continuously expanding brick-and-mortar facilities—a process that has put them into over-leveraged debt. Connecting a network of sellers electronically, from whom millions of packages are shipped directly to the buyers' addresses, turns out to be more economical than running hundreds of big-box stores and distribution centers around the country. The latter face considerable rent, upkeep, and labor costs, while e-commerce offers lower prices and doesn't require travel to access a store.

Experiences Are Part of the Sell

Stores that offer an in-person "experience" as part of their service, on the other hand, are best positioned to withstand competition from e-commerce. A key reason why grocery shopping hasn't quite gone online yet is that it involves tactile and sensory experiences. Choosing bananas, tomatoes, cheese, and bread in person, or sampling new treats as part of the visit to the store, can be as important to customers as prices. A drop in transportation costs isn't necessarily worth giving up the pleasure of tasting cheese or smelling flowers in person. Even if routine grocery shopping—the replenishing of standard orders of weekly milk, bread, vegetables, and meats, which do not involve an essential element of pleasure—is likely to move online, experiential food buying could increase rather than decrease in a society whose incomes are higher, schedules more flexible, and outlooks more informed by trends that spread via digital communication networks.

In June 2017, Amazon surprised the world by announcing that it was buying up the organic food chain Whole Foods for a staggering $13.4 billion. The acquisition gave Amazon a major stake in the vast grocery business, worth $700–800 billion a year in the United States alone. Having a physical presence via Whole Foods' 460 stores in the United States, Canada, and Europe extended the online juggernaut's physical reach to within a couple of miles from millions of well-to-do households.

It is no accident that the online giant chose grocery stores—where an in-person experience at the store is part of the lure—as its vehicle for venturing into brick-and-mortar retailing. This move will further blur the line between online and physical retailing, enabling grocery stores to work as physical showrooms that combine online orders and physical delivery systems with the social pleasures of shopping. The merger also opens up the possibility of expanding Whole Foods' physical outlets into smaller and more numerous urban showrooms that display the retail giant's vast organic offerings, but only carry physical supplies of some unpackaged groceries that customers might want to palpably inspect and personally choose before buying. The rest of the order could be combined with packaged goods from larger stores that carry full stock, all shipped to the customer's home in a single box.

Similarly, clothing, shoe, apparel, or outdoor equipment stores that offer customers an experience—personalized attention, on-site tailors, well-trained staff, and enticing environments—generate sales not because of their affordable prices, but because of the experience that customers get. Of course prices remain critical—few people are willing to pay double for a shirt because a sales associate told them how good they look in it. But just as small premiums are paid for being able to handle mangos before making a purchase at a market or to flip through books on physical shelves at a bookstore, customers will also pay small premiums for other types of merchandise in brick-and-mortar stores if the experience itself is part of the lure. Many people are willing to forego lower transportation costs to partake in more interesting shopping experiences. While routine, weekly shopping will increasingly move online, optional and social shopping are likely going to grow in brick-and-mortar stores.

Nike has recently opened a series of flagship stores that not only sell its sports apparel, but also offer full-scale arenas and equipment to play the sports. Its store in the SoHo neighborhood of New York City, for example, boasts a basketball half-court with adjustable hoops and digital video screens, an indoor soccer trial area, a treadmill facing a jumbotron that simulates outdoor running, and dedicated, on-call coaches to help customers improve their skills. The store works as an activity center, where fitness and shopping are hard to tell apart.

Nordstrom's—a high-end American department store, which typically occupies a 175,000-square-foot floor plan—introduced a "Local" store model in 2017, which comes with a tiny footprint and carries no merchandise at all. One such "Local" is situated on Melrose Avenue near Beverly Hills. It has curbside pickup for purchases made online and a whole suite of personalized services offered inside a boutique interior: alterations and tailors, personal styling, a nail salon, coffee, and drinks. A Trunk Club offers made-to-measure designer clothes.

Target has come out with a similar concept for discount retailing. It now offers small urban stores where customers can pick up goods they ordered online.

Increase in Dining Establishments

Across all retailers, the fastest growing type of physical store is the eating establishment—restaurants, bars, and coffee shops. These types of stores offer services that e-commerce cannot: their services can only be enjoyed around a table or a counter in person. Restaurant sales grew 19% between 2012 and 2015, surpassing all other retail categories. They now make up around 15% of all retail sales. The rise of food services among brick-and-mortar street retailers is visible on many cities' streets. While retailers selling goods find it difficult to pay increasing rents, restaurants, bars, and coffee shops can weather rent hikes by raising food prices and offering more personal services. A number of historic retail clusters are witnessing a turnover in tenants, resulting in fewer retail stores and more food service providers. As a result, street commerce is increasingly becoming food-and-beverage commerce.

When I lived in Singapore, several restaurants in my neighborhood that were facing high rents started splitting their space with another tenant. In the morning, a space would operate as a traditional breakfast café, serving soft-boiled eggs, kaya toast, and coffee with condensed milk. In the afternoon, the same space would be taken over by a high-end Japanese sake bar and yakitori restaurant. At another corner, a traditional Chinese noodle shop, which made most of its income before 10 a.m., transformed into an Italian pizza shop in the afternoon. Splitting the space helped both businesses lower their costs, enabling shops that would otherwise be priced out to stay in business.

Bricks and Bits Becoming More Intertwined

The majority of shoppers (78%) now conduct product research at home before they head to the store, and 72% of shoppers buy some goods online after seeing physical samples in stores.[35] E-commerce has expanded window shopping to everyone's pocket phones, but the same phones have also brought their users back to the streets. Like Target and Nordstrom's, several other retail chains now offer "online pickup" services in their brick-and-mortar stores. Amazon has also recently opened several brick-and-mortar stores where checkout lines have disappeared. Instead, customers enter Amazon's stores through rows of electronic gantries, much like modern subway stations, and a network of motion sensors and computer vision cameras track the visitors in the store and automatically charge them for what they basket from the shelves. Other stores' efforts to streamline the experience of shopping include free deliveries from the physical checkout, allowing customers to focus on other activities while their purchases are being shipped to their doorstep.

Street commerce made up of smaller and more personalized stores is likely to do well in this climate. If pedestrian environments along streets are safe, comfortable, interesting, and equitable, then a walk along a street can be as much part of the experience of going out as visiting shops or eateries themselves. Visiting shopping streets in Boston, downtown Los Angeles, San Francisco, New Orleans, and many other cities is an experience of it its own that no online retailer can match. Urban retail clusters produce a diverse environment rich in sensory experiences, which is itself an asset that invites people to a place not only to shop but also to experience surprise, intrigue, diversity, and chance encounters.

An Unequal Restructuring of the Retail Market

The current wave of big-box liquidation in America is partly a market correction. The United States has the most retail space per capita in the world—five times more than the United Kingdom, for instance. I mentioned the alarming growth of big-box stores in Tallinn, Estonia, in Chapter 2, where I noted that the city now has 1.35 square meters of retail space per person—more than any other European capital. But this still pales in comparison to the Los Angeles metro area, which boasts 2.32 square meters of retail space per capita. Much of American retail space consists of suburban malls and big-box stores, built in the 1970s, '80s, and '90s. The US retail market is oversupplied and is based on an outdated notion of ballooning suburban demand, low energy prices, and cheap land. The correction triggered by e-commerce will trim some of the excess.

At the same time, the replacement of historic retail businesses with upscale food establishments is threatening the sustainability of street commerce as a typology that reduces urban energy consumption and makes strides toward increasing spatial equality and livability. Pricy eating establishments target a narrow set of middle- and upper-middle-class consumers. Replacing brick-and-mortar clothing, apparel, electronics, and home appliance stores with pricy restaurants or online alternatives leaves families who do not have credit cards and who live from week to week on meager paychecks without close access to basic goods and services. Some delivery companies refuse to deliver e-commerce packages to low-income and minority neighborhoods.[36] A lack of convenience retail around one's home—food markets, household goods stores, electronics stores, and clothing stores—forces residents to travel longer distances, spending a disproportionate share of their income and time on transportation and lowering their productivity.

Lower-income families who cannot afford Amazon Prime, who do not have access to credit cards and high-speed internet connections, who do not have a car, and whose neighborhoods remain poorly served by delivery companies are negatively affected by the current restructuring of the retail market. With affordable clothing, shoe, apparel, and household stores moving online, these families' quality of life suffers. While experience shopping remains unaffordable to many families, it is the decrease of routine grocery, clothing, apparel, and household goods in brick-and-mortar stores that could hurt lower-income households the most. In many American cities, the ability to drive to opportunities still constitutes an important step on the ladder of upward mobility.

Throughout the 20th century, shopping centers replaced myriad historic amenity-rich streets with highly curated and financially coordinated consumption environments, leaving no city in the United States untouched. Shopping centers rose to power not merely as a result of inevitable market forces, but due to the demographic reality in which the largest consumer base was the nuclear family, as well as to a highly pro-market political climate, rapid motorization, and housing policies that favored low-density suburban growth. The accumulation of capital in malls allowed developers to maximize profits by orchestrating an entire retail cluster to behave as one profit-generating apparatus.

Amazon arguably represents the latest iteration of centralized retail provisions, similar to, and yet bigger and more powerful than, earlier shopping centers. Despite Amazon's reliance on digital purchasing and home delivery, we should remember John T. Riordan's point, that "a shopping center is not a building but a management concept, a way common management causes separately owned businesses to behave as one."[37] Amazon clearly fits that description. In order to avoid undesirable consequences to street life once again, cities need to plan with e-commerce in mind.

Planning Streets with E-commerce in Mind

Competition from e-commerce has created an opportunity for city governments and planners to rethink how plans and policies can help physical stores along city streets thrive in the 21st century. The market for retail space in the United States is oversaturated with peripheral big-box stores. Given that big-box clothing, apparel, hobby, book, and discount stores are most directly affected by online competition, city governments should proactively plan for smaller retail spaces in more central and transit-oriented locations. Medium-scale retail spaces in the range of 1,000 to 20,000 square feet can accommodate a huge variety of shops and services in denser urban settings. This scale of retail space is not only attractive to smaller stores, but also to national and international chains who have started downsizing their suburban operations and who have started to bet increasingly on showrooms and pickup facilities. Target, Circuit City, and Nordstrom's are but a few examples of a more general trend of national chains downsizing into smaller spaces at more urban locations.

Meanwhile, underutilized big-box stores and suburban shopping centers can be rezoned and repurposed for uses other than retail—office space, mixed-use residential redevelopment, schools, sports facilities, warehouses, etc. Such conversions are already happening across the United States. Amazon is repurposing what was once the world's biggest shopping center in North Randall, OH, outside of Cleveland, into a new e-commerce warehouse. The entire mall will be demolished and much of the land on which it stood restructured for the very corporation that helped bankrupt the mall in the first place. In McAllen, TX, an underutilized 124,000-square-foot Walmart store was turned into the nation's largest single-story public library.[38] Julia Christensen, an artist and author from Oberlin College, has documented dozens of such transformations of malls into housing, gyms, schools, smaller retailers, and parks in her book *Big Box Reuse*.[39]

Municipal governments would also be wise to adopt more flexible zoning for brick and mortar retail spaces. Instead of strictly limiting commercial space to retail operations, more open-ended use requirements for street commerce spaces could provide a hedge for property owners against uncertain demand. Whereas traditional occupancy categories in municipal zoning codes may distinguish between retail space where customers walk out with purchased goods and service space where services are delivered onsite, the lines between retail and services are increasingly blurred. Zoning codes should be updated to reflect these ambiguities, enabling more flexible uses of traditional retail spaces. I mentioned Singapore's policy for "activity generating uses" in Chapter 6. This innovative zoning designation enables a variety of commercial uses to occupy ground-floor retail space, including retail, food and beverage, entertainment, sport and recreation (such as gyms and fitness centers), art galleries, and other similar uses.[40] Such broad use designations can help fill commercial spaces in uncertain markets, where retail demand fluctuates.

Zoning codes and business policies should allow commercial tenants to share risk and occupancy costs by splitting rent between multiple tenants in a single space. This would allow two different restaurants to occupy the same space at different hours of the day—a café or breakfast place in the first half of the day, a restaurant in the second half of the day. Allowing multiple businesses to occupy the same space enables smaller businesses to survive in rapidly gentrifying property markets and benefits customers with more diverse offerings.[41]

City governments can also facilitate or spearhead initiatives to host special outdoor events, such as Car Free Sundays or First Fridays, on key retail streets. By banning vehicular traffic for the duration of these events, populating roads with temporary street furniture and potted plants, and inviting mobile food vendors to participate, cities can create major attractions that bring a community together and benefit stores and visitors alike. The City of Boston recently established Car Free Days on its preeminent commercial spine—Newbury Street. The event, known as Open Newbury Street, draws thousands of visitors. Restaurants, food trucks, and tents line the streets and set up tables in parking spots. Local musicians perform in the street and the Public Works department sets up chairs, tables, and a range of games to lure in families. One of the Open Newbury weekends overlaps with the Massachusetts's Tax Free Weekend, during which customers are exempt from paying the 6.25% sales tax on goods and services they purchase. But the Newbury Street initiative currently takes place only three or four times over the summer. It could be regularized into a weekly or monthly event. Implementing car-free days on retail streets on a regular basis helps extend awareness of local street commerce, provides an attractive reason for people to see and be seen by others in their community, and helps bolster store visits with experiences that online retailers cannot match.

Furthermore, just like it is important to make housing affordable, it is equally important that residents be able to access commercial goods and services suitable to their incomes and tastes. To prevent the exclusion of more affordable, community-oriented retail, city governments should adopt innovative policies to support below-market-rate rents for businesses that support community needs but cannot sustain asking rents in an area. I speculated on such policies in Chapter 2, but more innovation is certainly needed.

Finally, in order to tackle the challenges posed by online commerce head on, city governments would also be wise to establish staff positions for retail planners in their economic development or planning departments. Such roles could help coordinate the various parallel efforts that support street commerce via zoning amendments, urban design guidelines, transportation investments, street upgrading projects, events and festivals, as well as through the development of new policy tools to enable inclusionary retail.

Neither demographic restructuring of inner cities nor technologies that support e-commerce invalidate the retail location theory or change the nature of fundamental forces shaping street commerce that I have described in the preceding chapters. Instead, they alter the magnitude of some of the key forces. Demographic change in American cities changes how customer density factors into the retail density model I discussed in Chapter 2. The shift of wealth and purchasing power to inner-city districts will alter both the purchasing frequency for different types of goods and the customer density that seeks these goods. Similarly, e-commerce does not transform the underlying factors that shape brick-and-mortar commerce; it instead alters their relative balance. E-commerce particularly changes how transportation costs for goods and services affect end consumers—instead of having to undertake trips to stores, people pay to get the merchandise delivered to their doorsteps. Because it is cheaper to pool lots of deliveries in a single UPS truck than for every customer to travel to the store on their own, e-commerce lowers transportation costs and increases shopping frequency. These shifts in the balance of forces can be strong enough to alter the pattern of stores we observe on city streets. Yet the fundamental forces shaping street commerce remain—purchase frequency, transportation costs, customer density, fixed costs, regulatory environments, and urban design still matter.

And neither of these trends—demographic and technological—plays out the same way in each city. Both of their trajectories depend on the spatial, socioeconomic, and institutional environments in each town. Inner-city restructuring depends on housing policies, development allowances, planning, urban design, and tenants' rights, as well as job opportunities and economic development. The influence of e-commerce on brick-and-mortar stores depends on what the retail landscape of a city looks like at present, the extent of big-box versus Main Street outlets, and the land use pattern and transportation system of a city, as well as the institutional and financial mechanisms that a city deploys to incentivize commercial and economic development.

Conclusion

How the fate of street commerce plays out in different cities, neighborhoods, and streets each year depends on a range of factors, which I have described in the preceding chapters. These include the cost of operating a business, customers' density and purchase frequency for various goods and services, prices, transportation costs, transportation mode share, competition among stores, location, clustering dynamics, inter-businesses organizing, building typologies, and urban design features around stores. Shifts in any of these factors can change a city's amenity pattern balance. And as we saw in the last chapter, demographic and technological trends play an important role too. Together, these factors constitute a complex set of spatial and economic forces that can be hard to disentangle. It is tempting to lump them all together and call their joint action on street commerce the "invisible hand."[1]

Yet, there is a whole suite of factors affecting retail and service establishments on city streets that are not uncontrollable market forces producing an inevitable outcome, but that instead reflect the social, environmental, and economic policies and plans put to action by local governments, individuals, and firms. Elected officials, planners, developers, and community groups can do a lot to improve the health of street commerce and the public space where it takes place.

In this final chapter I attempt to summarize five key lessons that emerge from the previous chapters and speculate on what it might entail to create greater access to street commerce citywide.

The first important takeaway is that there are no one-size-fits-all prescriptions for improving street commerce from one city, one neighborhood, or even street to another. I have tried to demonstrate with stories from around the world that the kinds of issues cities face regarding street commerce depend a great deal on local context and history. The challenges of revitalizing commerce in Soviet-era panel housing structures in eastern Europe's high-density residential districts have little in common with those of Los Angeles's inner-city neighborhoods,

New York's Business Improvement Districts or in Indonesia's neighborhoods of street vendors. But despite the vast differences between these disparate contexts, I have also tried to emphasize that there are consistent, overarching forces at play that shape street commerce in all urban settings.

Planners and urban designers that engage with cities, neighborhood associations, community groups, or developers to improve street commerce should start with an assessment of strengths and weaknesses in each context to determine which of the factors work well, which could be improved, and which might be lacking all together. The example of Kendall Square in Cambridge, MA, which I alluded to in Chapter 6, suggested that a whole list of critical factors that benefit street commerce were already in place: the area is surrounded by a high density of jobs; the square had excellent walking and public transit access; and area residents and visitors had ample disposable income, suggesting quite a bit of local spending. But architectural typologies of office and lab buildings were not well suited for ground-floor street commerce and the companies managing the high-rise office space upstairs were drawing so much income from booming technology firms that leasing out ground-floor retail space did not seem like a worthwhile undertaking. An assessment of street commerce at Kendall Square led the city government to negotiate with commercial property owners to open their ground floors for shops and services. As part of the process, the city rezoned allowable uses on a number of parcels, and several commercial property owners, in turn, reconstructed ground-floor facades and interior layouts in several buildings around Kendall Square. Furthermore, the area around the square didn't have enough residents who would frequent businesses on mornings, evenings, and weekends. Residents were predominantly high income and stayed in luxury serviced apartments on short-term leases, which do not create sustained patronage patterns or encourage the establishment deep social networks via repeat encounters and interactions. This assessment prompted the city to add provisions to its zoning code that will lead to the development of new student and affordable housing. While these interventions will take years, even decades to materialize, initial outcomes suggest that both public and private efforts to encourage more street commerce are starting to pay off.

The vibrant street-vendor culture in Solo, Indonesia, which I described in relation to low fixed-cost investments in Chapter 2, has substantially benefited from former mayor Jokowi's platform to support small-scale retail, service, and food entrepreneurs though legal restrictions on shopping center development. The city also invested heavily into the reconstruction of existing and the creation of new open-air markets that support of micro-vending practices that involve only one or two staff per kiosk. These policies benefited small-scale retailers and allowed the city to maintain a high density of traditional shops and services even during periods of rapid economic growth and real estate development.

Among international examples, London stands out not only due to its historically vibrant structure of street commerce, which I described with my personal experience in the opening paragraphs of this book, but also because of a number of current, progressive policies that aim to improve street commerce in hundreds of high street clusters throughout the metropolis. Under Boris Johnson's leadership, and extended under Mayor Sadiq Khan, the Greater London Authority (GLA) has implemented an "Action for High Streets" program that provides direct investments into tens of high streets throughout the city in the form of public space improvements, commissions for public art, transportation, and landscaping.[2]

The Mayor's Business Improvement Districts grant program provides financial support for existing and emerging business improvement districts in London to encourage establishment, coordination, and background research. The Outer London Fund, launched in 2011, is a £50 million investment program dedicated to helping London's high streets grow and become more vibrant. Supplementing this fund is the offer of project support and professional advice aimed at providing necessary skills and additional capacity among high street businesses. The fund specifically targets many parts of London that have benefited less directly from prior strategic investments in Crossrail—a new high-frequency rail line that will cross London from east to west—and urban improvements made prior to 2012 Olympic games.[3] Additionally, following the 2011 riots across London, the mayor announced another £70 million toward major long-term improvements to the affected town centers and high streets. The city's transport agency—Transport for London—also set up a Future Streets Incubator Fund that supports small-scale tactical projects that can be implemented short term with the aim of discovering new ideas on how to make London's roads and streets fit for future needs. All these programs are further coordinated with the mayor's Street Tree Initiative and Pocket Parks Program, which provides resources and services to add greenery to London's high streets. By 2015 the program had spent £5.7 million planting over 20,000 trees along a number of streets and parks citywide. These broad-ranging initiatives demonstrate that London not only takes pride in its high streets, but also keeps investing in their future.

Among the less successful examples, we saw from the experience of Estonia how siloed and myopic transportation policies can produce significant damage to the structure of street commerce citywide. Tallinn's exceptionally rapid motorization in the last three decades led to the replacement of many historic city center shops with big-box shopping centers on the urban edge. Transportation and urban growth policies are perhaps hardest to change, but fortunately, a number of inspiring precedents from Melbourne, London, Zurich, and other cities demonstrate how shifts toward more active and public transit–oriented mode share are indeed possible when there is political will and strong grassroots organizing by civil society actors.

The experiences of London, Cambridge, Solo, Tallinn, and other cities highlight a second important lesson: successful street commerce almost never emerges or survives as a result of pure market forces alone and usually represents the fruits of conscious planning and strategy. City streets do not get better via a laissez faire attitude, where planners, local governments, and regulators take a back seat and wait for the market to work. Quite the opposite: good streets with diverse retail and service choices, run by diverse owners, and serving diverse interests require conscious planning and management. Shared outdoor spaces—sidewalks, squares, and parklets—require public coordination and investment since the public benefits they provide go well beyond the interests of any individual store. Their planning is often led by forward-looking city governments, which coordinate policies and investments in support of community vitality. This was the case in London. In other cases, as we saw in the Byzantine Latino district in Los Angeles, initiative stems from citizen groups and civil society organizations, who introduce tactical interventions, organize businesses and community members, mobilize around branding, and advocate community interest to the municipal government. Business improvement districts and business associations, discussed in Chapter 4, illustrate how the business community too can mobilize behind a shared need for coordination and joint action, collecting additional funds and working with public officials to support street commerce through event organization, street cleanup and management, additional capital investments, as well as business recruitment. In each case, conscious planning, policy, and design play an essential role in transforming the quality and diversity of street life.

A third key takeaway is that public investment into community-oriented streets produces multipronged and cross-sectoral public benefits that are hard for other infrastructure investments to match. While access to many social opportunities in a city—to schools, to jobs, to healthy lifestyles, or to social networks—is often unequally distributed, favoring the wealthier and historically dominant groups, street commerce can offer one important strategy for equalizing opportunities for everyone.

On the one hand, Main Streets provide significant employment opportunities. The types of retail, food, and personal service business I have analyzed as part of street commerce generate over 20% of all jobs in the US economy. Alongside these, a whole range of nonretail businesses locate on Main Streets—various professional and service sector jobs in office buildings, cultural and entertainment establishments, public institutions, and even in clean urban manufacturing that is returning to city streets with the advent of new rapid-prototyping technology. Together, both retail and nonretail jobs along Main Streets represent an even larger share of a city's job pool, which may only be second to a Central Business District (CBD), and at times even surpass the CBD in total employment. In London, for instance, 47% of all firms outside of the CBD are located along high streets and 18% of the city's population lives within a three-minute walk of a high street.[4] Public investment into these streets reaches a large and diverse set of constituents.

Beyond the sheer volume of employment, many of the jobs around commercial streets are particularly important to marginalized groups and recent immigrants who seek entry-level service sectors employment and access to professional social networks. A large portion of visitors to retail clusters include job seekers, the elderly, immigrants, students, as well as temporarily unemployed parents and caretakers of young children. The GLA's surveys of high streets in London revealed that 51% of high street visitors were not currently in employment, compared to the citywide average of 27%.[5] Scholars who have studied activity patterns in American Main Streets and public spaces have noted a similar pattern of visitors.[6] Furthermore, fully 45% of visitors' primary reasons for visiting high streets was nonretail related—evidence that Londoners value the social and cultural exchange that high streets provide. Nonretail activities were especially important for vulnerable users, particularly the elderly, who greatly value face-to-face interaction, people watching, and strolling.[7] Investing into community-oriented streets benefits the more vulnerable user groups the most.

From a social perspective, commercial streets work as places of encounter. Some of these encounters are planned—get-togethers with friends, acquaintances, or first-time meetings with recently established contacts at local coffee shops or restaurants. These encounters represent what sociologist Mark Granovetter refers to as weak social ties, as mentioned in the Introduction—ties that bring people together once a week, once a month or even once in a few years. Street commerce plays a particularly important role for these interactions, since most planned meetings occur in indoor spaces—at coffee shops, restaurants, cinemas, lobbies, or atria. Stanford Anderson has called such venues along city streets the "occupiable realm"—privately owned spaces that are open for public use with different degrees of access.[8]

Commercial streets also produce unplanned encounters that take place both inside businesses—shops, hair salons, libraries, restaurants, or supermarkets—and outside—on sidewalks, benches, stoops, street corners, tables, and in parklets. These unplanned encounters represent latent ties, fostered by economically vibrant, walkable, and equitable streets. The latter are even more important for building mutual awareness and transmitting information across society than planned encounters. Serendipitous meetings that take place on a street establish the first synapses for the formation of Granovetter's weak ties. We often start the first conversation with someone we have already seen before. We talk to our family members and colleagues about what or who we encountered on a street. And our political views adapt when we experience folks whose backgrounds, views, incomes, ages, cultures, and genders differ from ours. Encountering what sociologist Richard Sennett has called "otherness" on city streets shapes our perception of a city in a visceral and tangible manner and deeply informs the understanding of "community" and "society" around us.[9] Commercial streets thus function as barometers of city life, helping us gauge how healthy, prosperous, livable, equitable, fun, or interesting the city and the community around us are. If a city's street commerce is inclusive, in terms of both store offerings as well as its geographic reach to more vulnerable users, if it benefits the city's economy with multiplier effects and hiring, if it helps create inclusive, high-quality public space for social encounters and interactions, and if it is accessible on foot and by public transportation, then a city tends to do well overall.

To capture these benefits in public plans, policies, and investments, cities need a more deliberate spatial definition of street commerce. Common administrative designations of commercial areas as central business districts, commercial districts, Main Streets, cultural districts, and arts districts typically include only a small subset of actual amenity clusters and street segments that connect them. Yet these administrative definitions are associated with resource allocation and annual budget cycles. Instead of strictly allocating public funding and improvements around such existing boundaries, cities would be wise to monitor their evolving clusters of street commerce annually and target improvements to sidewalks, pocket parks, roadways, and intersections according to their functional, rather than administrative importance. Throughout this book I have defined street commerce as clusters of retail, food, and personal service amenities that include at least 25 stores and where each store is no more than 100 meters away from its closest neighboring store. Cities can adopt their own definitions and adapt them to local needs. Yet in each case, it would beneficial to have a comparable definition that allows us to map all clusters of street commerce and spatially target deliberate public space improvements to deliver more immediate, effective, and felt benefits to both the visitors and businesses who use them.

Unfortunately, many cities, neighborhoods, and streets struggle with capturing the social and economic benefits of street commerce. As I discussed in both the Introduction and Chapter 7, the benefits of good street commerce are not equitably distributed to everyone. On the one hand, there is the question of how less profitable, older, or more community-oriented businesses can survive on growing or upscaling city streets. I suggested that new affordable retail policies are needed to generate inclusive retail space, analogous to inclusionary housing policies that were implemented to combat similar challenges on the housing market.

But inequalities also arise based on ability to afford housing close to street commerce. Revitalized city streets, rich in offerings and public space, tend to attract wealthier, whiter, and more privileged residents to their vicinities. Along with new policies that would enable community-oriented businesses to weather speculative rent hikes, Main Street improvements also need to offer existing tenants protection from displacement.

This forms the fourth takeaway point—equitable street commerce requires both stores that cater to all income groups and policies that ensure that improved amenities and high-quality public spaces enable the more vulnerable residents to stay and benefit from such investments. There is nothing about pedestrian-oriented street commerce that inherently exacerbates inequality or gentrification—rather, pedestrian-oriented street commerce often becomes commodified by speculative, capitalist housing markets. It is up to cities, their planners, community groups, and developers to integrate Main Street improvements not only with inclusionary zoning and affordable housing requirements in new development projects that benefit from such streets but also provisions to preserve existing affordable housing, including tenant protections, rent control, public housing preservation, and even public housing expansion, something not seen in American cities in decades. Gentrification, displacement, and the exacerbation of historic inequalities in the American housing markets disproportionately affect renters and lower-income communities of color. But this does not mean we should stop investing in and improving these streets. Cities should invest in streets in historically marginalized neighborhoods, but also ensure that low-income communities of color can stay and benefit from these improvements.

Besides social and employment benefits, investments into street commerce can also address important citywide environmental goals. As I showed in Chapter 1, around 15% of all Americans already live within a 15-minute walk of an amenity cluster that has at least 25 stores. Twice as many Americans are therefore able to conduct at least part of their retail and service errands on foot than ride heavy- or light-rail transit from their homes. Given that around two-thirds of all trips involve going to recreational, retail, and social destinations, conducting some of these trips without a car near homes or workplaces can yield considerable reductions in traffic, transportation energy use, and carbon emissions.

To imagine what types of built environments could provide the majority of the population an amenity cluster within a 15-minute walk from their home, we don't have to venture into utopias or look for distant examples—data presented in Chapter 1 demonstrated that a number of existing US cities already achieve this. Municipalities where more than 50% of the population has at least one retail cluster in a 15-minute walkshed included New York City, San Francisco, Boston, Miami, Honolulu, Los Angeles, Washington, DC, and Oakland. Yes, even Los Angeles, which is often referred to as the car capital of the world. And this list only includes cities with populations over 350,000. Many smaller cities also achieve a highly accessible amenity pattern. That these cities come with very different urban forms, land use patterns, and building typologies speaks to the fact that widespread access to street commerce can be achieved in myriad different typologies and configurations; no single template offers a silver bullet.

Yet, a few broad parameters of urban form and density nevertheless commonly describe highly retail-accessible cities. These parameters become apparent if we examine the highest and lowest pedestrian-accessible retail cities in Table 8. The top- and bottom-tier cities shown in the table are ranked according

Table 8. Comparison of urban form and population density metrics across US cities larger than 350,000 residents, which provide a high (top) and a low (bottom) share of their populations with walking access to retail clusters. Fields marked with "-" had no data available.

Rank	City	Population within 1000m of a retail cluster	Population 2010	Land area (km^2)	Residential density per km^2	FAR	Built coverage
1	New York, NY	88%	8,175,133	783.0	10,890	1.66	35.38%
2	San Francisco, CA	84%	805,235	121.5	7,174	0.43	27.42%
3	Boston, MA	69%	617,594	125.4	2,700	0.71	16.14%
4	Miami, FL	67%	399,457	93.2	4,866	-	-
5	Honolulu, HI	62%	337,256	156.7	2,236	1.50	14.16%
6	Los Angeles, CA	55%	3,792,621	1,214.0	3,275	1.40	18.67%
7	Washington, DC	54%	681,170	158.1	4,308	0.83	16.47%
8	Oakland, CA	51%	390,724	144.8	2,901	0.69	17.04%
9	Chicago, IL	41%	2,695,598	589.6	4,572	-	14.15%
10	Atlanta, GA	40%	417,735	344.9	1,211.17	-	-
	Mean	61%	1,831,252	373.1	4,413.4	1.03	19.93%
31	Omaha, NE	9%	383,964	329.2	1,166.35	-	-
32	Jacksonville, FL	9%	822,050	1,934.7	425	0.05	1.23%
33	Tucson, AZ	9%	520,116	611.7	868	0.21	6.52%
34	Cleveland, OH	8%	396,815	201.2	1,972	-	-
35	San Antonio, TX	7%	1,469,845	1,193.7	1,147	-	-
36	Oklahoma City, OK	7%	579,999	1,556.9	360	-	-
37	Columbus, OH	7%	787,033	562.5	1,399	-	-
38	Fort Worth, TX	6%	854,113	886.3	842	-	-
39	Memphis, TN	6%	646,889	816.0	770	0.26	6.42%
40	Detroit, MI	4%	713,777	359.4	1,900	0.25	14.78%
	Mean	7%	717,460	845.2	1,084.9	0.19	7.24%

to the share of the population that has at least one retail cluster in a 15-minute walkshed.

The table suggests that city size does not play an important role in affecting the distribution of retail clusters. Even though the average population in the most retail-accessible cities is larger (1.83 million residents on average), as opposed to the lower-ranking cities (0.7 million residents on average), the first mean is heavily skewed by the fact that three of the largest cities—New York, Los Angeles, and Chicago—are included. Even cities with population sizes between 350,000 and 400,000 can have more than 50% of their residents near a retail cluster, as is the case in Honolulu, Oakland, and Miami.

While overall population matters little, population density is clearly related to retail accessibility. Top-tier cities have, on average, four times higher population densities (4,413 people per square kilometer) than the bottom-tier cities (1,085 people per square kilometer). This difference is also partly skewed due to two outlier cities that have exceptionally high population densities in the US context—New York City (10,890 people per square kilometer) and San Francisco (7,174 people per square kilometer). But even when these two cities are left aside, most accessible retail cities still have three times higher residential densities, on average, than the bottom cities. Higher residential densities make higher retail densities. Chapter 2 of this book discussed how this relationship works via a two-part benefit that density creates. First, a higher residential density enables more retailers to remain economically viable by placing more customers near stores. And second, a higher residential density also tends to generate shorter, local, nonretail trips on foot, creating a secondary benefit for stores in the form of impulse purchases.

Data in Table 8 suggests that at a citywide level, a minimum residential density of about 2,700–3,000 people per square kilometer is associated with achieving majority walking access to retail clusters in cities with populations over 350,000. Honolulu, which has over 60% of its population within walking reach of retail clusters with a population density of only 2,236 residents per square kilometer, is an exception—much of the city's land area is covered by unbuildable mountain ranges. This geographic limitation distorts the population density estimate for the city as a whole. Residential densities in the built-up areas of Honolulu are much higher than the citywide average.

Floor Area Ratio (FAR) and built coverage indicators in the last two columns of Table 8 offer crude metrics to describe the built forms of the cities. FAR illustrates the ratio between gross floor area that is found within all buildings in the city and the land area of the city. A ratio of one, for instance, means that floor area within buildings is the same as the city's overall land area. Given that around 40% of urban land is typically devoted to streets and most cities also have sizable parks and natural areas where building is restricted, even a FAR of 1 means high built density at the citywide level. For instance, in Tucson, AZ, a relatively low-density place, citywide FAR is 0.21.

The built coverage metric, on the other hand, describes the percentage of a city's land area covered by building footprints. The two metrics are complimentary and should be explored together.[10] It is possible, for instance, to have a high FAR and low coverage—this would typically mean that the city has high-rise buildings with large unbuilt spaces between the buildings, as in Singapore. The reverse, where a city has high built coverage but low FAR, usually means that much of the buildable land is occupied by buildings, but the buildings are low, single-story or double-story structures. This scenario is common, for instance, with low-rise wall-to-wall terrace houses in London or other low-rise typologies in rapidly developing cities in the Global South. Finally, a high coverage and high FAR jointly mean that most of the buildable land is used up and buildings are also tall. New York City is a perfect example of the latter. Among all the cities in Table 8, it has both the highest coverage and the highest FAR.

Comparing the top- and bottom-tier cities in the table illustrates that cities with a majority of their residents within walking distance of a retail cluster have five times higher FAR, on average, than cities at the bottom ranks of the table. A denser built environment means more residents and jobs per unit area of land and more patrons who need retail, food, and personal service amenities.

Overall, a minimum citywide FAR of about 0.5 and ground coverage of 15% are typically needed to achieve an environment that gives most residents walking access to urban amenity clusters. At such densities, all the top-ranking cities in Table 8 also have rail-based public transit systems in operation or, in the case of Honolulu, under construction, pointing again to the mutually supportive relationship between street commerce and transit.

These metrics do not offer steadfast limits and are indicative mileposts at best. Citywide population density, building coverage, and FAR are notoriously sensitive to the way the city boundary is drawn—cities that encompass large unbuilt areas, water bodies, or reserve lands will be difficult to compare to those where the boundary only encases fully built-up areas.

But more importantly, it is possible to achieve a high population share with walking access to street commerce even in municipalities that boast very low citywide densities. A city with a very large land area and very low coverage and FAR can indeed have most of its development channeled into few, higher-density hubs, creating enough population and development density to support diverse commercial activities in each hub, while at the same time having the majority of its inhabitants within a short walk from street commerce or transit stations. This

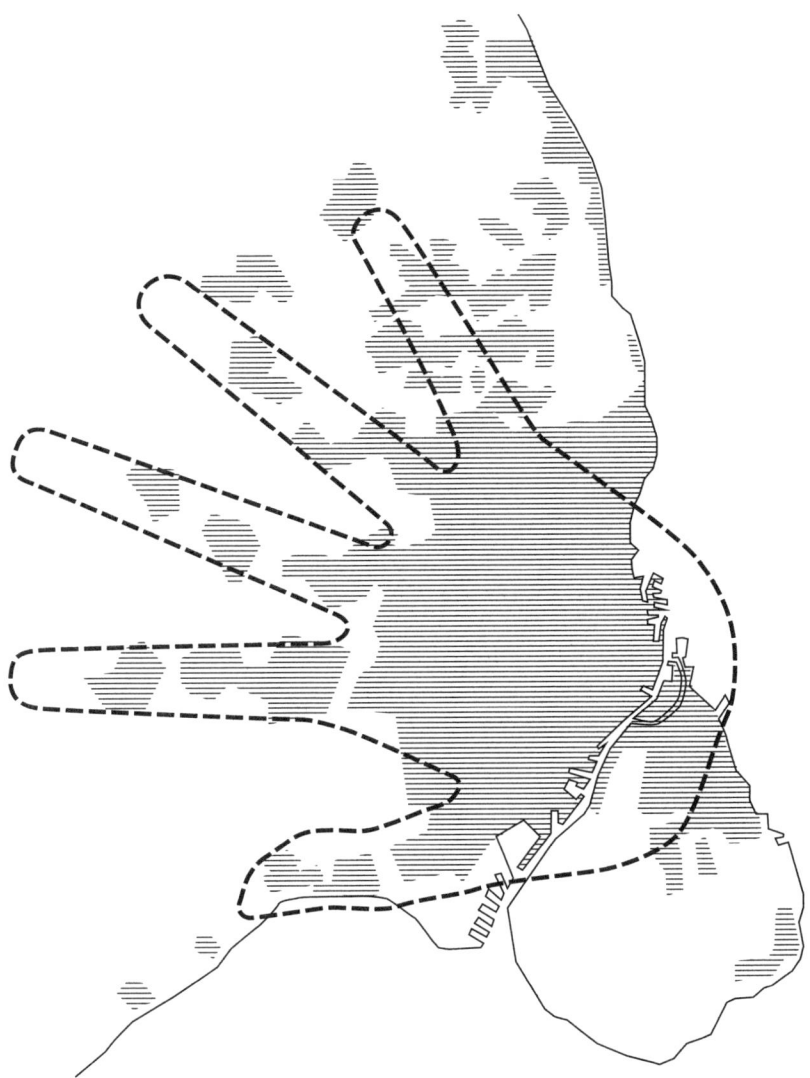

Figure 83. Copenhagen's regional transit-oriented "Finger Plan" of 1947. Image by author.

can be achieved with a polynuclear development pattern, where both residential and commercial development is concentrated around specific, transit-oriented corridors, leaving large swaths of land in between undeveloped or sparsely developed. Copenhagen's famous Finger Plan of 1947 (Figure 83) and Stockholm's transit-oriented plan are structured this way, incorporating large undeveloped areas within the municipal boundary while warranting relatively high development densities around transit-oriented subcenters. In the American context, an analogous spatial structure is seen in Washington, DC, Seattle,

WA, and Miami, FL, where wetlands and waterbodies have historically forced development to concentrate into scattered, but relatively high-density districts.[11]

This forms the fifth and final takeaway from this book—the benefits of economically vibrant, socially inclusive, and walkable street commerce are not reserved for towns of particular size, history, or income. They can be achieved in small or big cities, in historic or new developments, in private and public developments, and in low- as well as high-income districts. A vibrant cluster of street commerce in Atlanta's suburban neighborhoods can be as good a retail cluster as one in a much wealthier neighborhood around Boston's university campuses. Ethnic retail clusters in Queens or Flushing, NY, can function better than a historic cluster in downtown Philadelphia. Inclusivity, local benefit, public space quality, and pedestrian accessibility are urbanistic qualities that can be achieved in all towns and communities that value the quality of life of their members.

But this does not mean that very low-density suburban areas, with no appetite for more density, land use mixing, and public transport can develop street commerce without changing business as usual. You still cannot have your cake and eat it too.

Achieving walkable street commerce does require polynuclear planning and development around locally denser urban form and more mixed land use patterns. It also requires coordinated investing into public transportation and walkability improvements. Given the extent and pervasiveness of suburbs around American cities, the future of street commerce will, to a large extent, depend on the creation of denser, mixed-used, and economically diverse suburban subcenters. Despite their overall low population density, FAR, and built coverage, if suburban municipalities channel new real estate growth toward transit stops and amenity clusters, then walkable commerce can indeed become a reality for many more Americans.

Places with moderately dense urban form and mixed-use developments that put diverse retail and food service establishments along with accessible, high-quality public spaces near homes and workplaces, and which are connected by walkways, bikeways, and public transit, offer a template that promises positive outcomes for several 21st-century sustainable development goals that governments on all levels have established. From an environmental perspective, retail clusters that are accessible on foot and by public transit reduce a city's energy bill, contribute to cleaner air, and improve public health. Having a higher proportion of visitors arrive without a car helps lower traffic congestion, encourages exercise, and reduces per capita fossil-fuel consumption. If most errands and commercial trips can take place on foot or by public transit, to places not too far from one's home or workplace, then more valuable urban space can be converted from roads and parking lots to functional economic destinations, public spaces, and recreational areas.

From an economic standpoint, a significant share of revenues from street commerce have a multiplier effect as payments to local suppliers and employees and improvements made in the public infrastructure reverberate back into the local economy. This makes towns more resilient to economic downturns and fosters social cohesion.

Street commerce also incentivizes people to experience the city on foot, generating serendipitous face-to-face encounters and helping establish "latent" social ties—social connections that do not preexist, but which can sprout from casual encounters, unplanned conversations, or simple eye contact. These connections are critical for social awareness and urban resilience.

The 20th-century's biggest innovation in retailing was the shopping center. The shopping center replaced myriad historic amenity-rich streets with highly curated and financially coordinated consumption environments, leaving no city in the United States untouched. Shopping centers rose to power not merely as a result of inevitable market forces, but because of demographic changes that made the nuclear family the largest consumer base, as well as the development of a highly pro-market political climate, rapid motorization, and housing policies that favored low-density suburban growth. The accumulation of capital in malls allowed developers to maximize profits by orchestrating an entire retail cluster to behave as one profit-generating apparatus.

Indeed, there is reason to believe that the tendency toward larger accumulations of retail capital will continue in the future. We should not expect developers to desire smaller, more diverse forms of retail. Instead, it is the job of municipal governments, planners, and community groups to work with, push back against, and negotiate with developers to set allowances on what sorts of urban retail environments are better for communities. The rules of development must incentivize street commerce that offers greater collective benefits than the car-oriented suburban mall has so far. The experience of many cities that have vibrant street commerce has shown that once such constraints are established and both retailers and developers see what successful street commerce can be, they are willing to engage, as commercial town centers in many of the most livable cities in the world demonstrate.

Commercial streets define community centers and bustling streets from Italian hill towns to informal settlements in Brazil, from villages in Indonesia to metropoles in China. Even in the United States, only a few cities have lost the opportunity to visit commercial amenities on foot entirely. Most still have pedestrian-oriented retail clusters along their downtown sidewalks and, as we saw, these are now growing again in many parts of the United States.

Planners should seize this opportunity and respond to citizens, who have demonstrated their preference for more sustainable urban form along with street commerce by voting with their wallets via their housing and employment location choices. Developing cities around commercial streets is not just about convenience and consumption, just like investing into urban mass transportation is never just about moving people. It is also about the built forms, land use mixes, and urban experiences that are catalyzed by such developments. "Always design a thing by considering it in its next larger context," argued Eliel Saarinen, "a chair in a room, a room in a house, a house in an environment, an environment in a city plan."[12] Planning street commerce offers an opportunity to consider its next larger contexts—building better districts, and ultimately, better cities.

We need to collectively ensure that the cities we develop in the 21st century are more livable, healthy, equitable, prosperous, and stimulating than those of the 20th century. Instead of relying on personal automobiles, cities need to become less energy consuming and more reliant on public transit. Instead of spatially segregating land uses, cities need to provide more opportunities for people to mix. Instead of allowing market dynamics to sort people into rich and poor neighborhoods, cities must enable everyone to live in locations that maximize their potential to society and allow them to benefit from the public goods and infrastructure that urban societies generate. Street commerce can play a modest but nevertheless important role in fulfilling these aims.

Appendix

Table 9 shows the application of Zipf's Law to the two most populous cities, New York and Los Angeles, and the top five most populous cities in each of the next four population tiers. Whether in large cities, such as New York or Los Angeles, midsize cities such as Charlotte, NC, or smaller cities such as Oceanside, CA, the rank-size pattern of retail clusters shows a correlation with Zipf's Law of 85% or higher. There is a lot of variation in the proportional sizes of the largest clusters in different towns. This discrepancy explains in part why Zipf's Law applies differently to individual cities. Even if retail-cluster sizes follow a predictably exponential hierarchy, with few large and many smaller clusters, the starting point of that hierarchy—the largest cluster in town—varies proportionately in different cities. Second, the estimated slopes (x-coefficients) and y-intercepts for Zipf's trend-line equations also vary considerably across towns, suggesting that clusters scale differently in different cities. While the conformity of the linear (log-log) trend line to data in individual cities suggested that cluster sizes are inversely proportional to their ranks, as Zipf's Law predicts, these trend lines have different slopes in different cities. Zipf's Law suggests that cluster rank should be inversely proportional to its size, so the rank "2" cluster should be one-half the size of the rank "1" cluster, and the rank "3" cluster one-third the size of the rank "1" cluster. It thus suggests a trend-line slope of "−1" in log-log scale for all cities. But an actual application to 2,500 individual cities showed that slopes fluctuated considerably, between −4.4 and 0, confirming large discrepancies in the ways in which business clusters scale in individual cities. In New York City, for instance, the log-log rank-size trend of retail clusters is best described by a slope of −0.77, in Phoenix, AZ, by a slope of −0.97, and in Las Vegas, NV, by a slope of −0.58. Simply knowing the size of the largest cluster in town as "n," and predicting that the remaining clusters should correspond to "1/n" does not lead to a very useful forecast. It therefore also follows that if we try to apply either a national average trend of cluster size hierarchies to a specific city, or even a more customized Zipf's trend line that characterizes the average trend in cities of a particular population tier to a particular city in that tier, the outcome is less impressive than the average macro patterns we saw above.

In order to see how closely Zipf's Law can approximate the presence of particular rank-size retail clusters in specific cities, I have derived the average of all Zipf's trend equations in each population tier—tier 3 cities for instance, which describe municipalities that have between 439,000 and 790,000 inhabitants—and used it to predict how many retail clusters of each size there are in any individual city that belongs to this population tier. The average trend-line equation for tier 3 cities comes out as $y = -0.736x + 2.271$, where y is the log of the size of a cluster and x is the log of the rank of a cluster. I used a similar approach in the other four population tiers and derived the average trend equation for each tier.

To predict the presence of clusters of a particular size in a particular town we also need to define some thresholds for cluster sizes. Table 10 uses the Jenks' natural breaks for the sizes of all retail clusters in the United States to illustrate the thresholds for eight cluster-size categories. I use these thresholds to check whether the actual number of clusters observed in a town corresponds to what the Zipf's trend predicts. For instance, we can examine how many clusters there are with

Table 9. R-squared values, showing how closely rank-size distributions of retail clusters in US cities conform to linear log-log relationships predicted by Zipf's Law.

Population bracket	City	R-squared value from rank-size linear regression analysis
1	New York, NY	0.9701
1	Los Angeles, CA	0.957
2	Chicago, IL	0.8816
2	Houston, TX	0.9696
2	Philadelphia, PA	0.9635
2	Phoenix, AZ	0.951
2	San Antonio, TX	0.936
3	Columbus, OH	0.8858
3	Fort Worth, TX	0.8754
3	Charlotte, NC	0.8247
3	Detroit, MI	0.9848
3	El Paso, TX	0.9773
4	Virginia Beach, VA	0.9123
4	Atlanta, GA	0.9704
4	Colorado Springs, CO	0.9366
4	Omaha, NE	0.8889
4	Raleigh, NC	0.9903
5	Overland Park, KS	0.9709
5	Garden Grove, CA	0.8442
5	Santa Rosa, CA	0.9555
5	Chattanooga, TN	0.9343
5	Oceanside, CA	0.9866

Table 10. Jenks' natural breaks for the sizes of all retail clusters in the United States.

Group	Cluster size
1	25
2	53
3	105
4	200
5	429
6	1,054
7	2,015
8	4,376

Table 11. Predicted number of retail clusters of different sizes in five Tiers of city sizes.

Precited cluster size	Tier 1 cities	Tier 2 cities	Tier 3 cities	Tier 4 cities	Tier 5 cities
4,376–33,183	0	0	0	0	0
2,015–4,375	0	0	0	0	0
1,054–2,014	2	0	0	0	0
429–1,053	6	0	0	0	0
200–428	6	2	0	0	0
105–199	37	3	2	1	0
53–104	101	9	3	1	1
25–52	309	25	10	4	4

25–52 businesses, 53–104 businesses, and so on. The average trend-line equations for cities in each population tier can produce predictions for cluster size ranges shown in specific cities. For example, they predict that there will be 6 retail clusters with 429 to 1053 businesses in a population tier 1 city, and these will be the third- through eighth-largest clusters of that city, since 2 more clusters are predicted to be larger, in the 1,054–2,014 establishment range (see Table 11). These predictions can be compared to the actual cluster sizes in individual cities across the country. In Phoenix, AZ, which is a tier 2 city based on its population, the trend line predicts 25 retail clusters with 25–52 establishments, while the actual number of such clusters is 23. The trend also predicts 9 clusters with 53–104 establishments, while the actual numbers is 8. And the predicted number of clusters with 105–199 establishments is 3, which exactly matches the 3 actual clusters. But based on the population of Phoenix, AZ, the trend line does not predict any retail clusters with more than 428 establishments. Yet Phoenix has a retail cluster that falls into the 4,376–33,813 establishment range. The average prediction error across cluster sizes in Phoenix is 30%.

Phoenix is among the better-predicted cities. The formula predicts retail patterns in many other cities less accurately. In Atlanta, GA, for instance, the model predicts four clusters with 25–52 establishments, while there are eight of them. It also predicts only one cluster with 53–104 amenities and one more cluster with 105–199, while the actual number of such clusters are five and two respectively.

The average error across all cities and cluster sizes is 68%, which is not great, but not terrible either. It simply suggests that using population tiers and average Zipf's distributions to predict size ranges of retail clusters in specific cities is much less accurate than it is for predicting the higher-level statistical trend in the nation.

Notes

Introduction

1. Sennett, R. (2018). *Building and dwelling.* New York, NY: Farrar, Straus and Giroux; Bakhtin, M. M. (1982). *The dialogic imagination: Four essays.* V. Liapunor & K. Brostram (Trans.). Austin: University of Texas Press.

2. Granovetter, M. (1973). The strength of weak ties. *American Journal of Sociology, 78*(6), 1360–1380.

3. Civic Economics. (2002). *Economic impact analysis: A case study, local merchants vs. chain retailers.* Retrieved from https://d3n8a8pro7vhmx.cloudfront.net/liveablecityatx/pages/29/attachments/original/1404368422/Eco_Impact_Independents_vs_national_chain.pdf?1404368422.

4. Shuman, M. H. (2007). *The small-mart revolution: How local businesses are beating the global competition.* San Francisco, CA: Berret-Koehler Publishers.

5. US Department of Transportation. Federal Highway Administration. (2009). *Summary of travel trends: 2009 national household travel survey.* Retrieved from http://nhts.ornl.gov/2009/pub/stt.pdf.

6. Cohen, N. E. (2002). *America's marketplace: The history of shopping centers.* International Council for Shopping Centers. Lyme, CT: Greenwich Publishing Group. (p. 10)

7. Jacobs, J. (1961). *The death and life of great American cities.* New York, NY: Random House. p. 433.

8. Proudfoot, M. J. (1937). City retail structure. *Economic Geography, 13*(4), 425–428.

9. Some planning scholarship has indeed focused on commercial redevelopment as part of neighborhood economic development planning, but no one has directly focused on retail environments. One of the exceptions is the Clinton administration's creation of a federal program of economic empowerment zones in the 1990s, which aimed to bolster economic activity in distressed urban and rural areas. Modeled after the "enterprise zones" proposed by Peter Hall in the UK in 1977 and administered by the Department of Housing and Urban Development (HUD), renewal communities, empowerment zones, and enterprise communities offered highly distressed communities a combination of grants, tax credits for businesses, bonding authority, and other benefits that support local businesses. The Clinton administration created six urban empowerment zones, each receiving $100 million in block grants, and three rural empowerment zones, each receiving $40 million. Private enterprises that invested in these areas received tax credits and deductions for business expenses when hiring local residents. The program established additional "supplemental zones" in other cities. In total, 91 communities received enterprise community designations. The programs have targeted relatively small towns and communities with populations under 200,000 with moderate degrees of success (Matias, B., & Kline, P. [2008]. *Do local economic development programs work? Evidence from the Federal Empowerment Zone program.* Cowles Foundation Discussion Paper 1638. Cowles Foundation, Yale University, New Haven, CT.)

A second exception is a body of thought focused on urban commercial development that is often associated with economist Michal Porter's ideas on commercial agglomerations and business clustering. (Porter, M. E. [May–June 1995]. The competitive advantage of the inner city. *Harvard Business Review*, 55–71.) This approach too seeks to bolster private enterprise, but it focuses on investigating the endogenous externalities that businesses create toward each other when they locate close in space. It argues that governments should support the private sector in new economic initiatives "rather than allocating resources to public programs that tackle social problems." (Porter, M. E. [1998]. Location clusters, and the "New" microeconomics of competition. *Business Economics*, 33[1], 7–13; Moss, M. L. [2010]. Reinventing the central city as a place to live and work. *Housing Policy Debate*, 8[2], 471–490.) According to Porter, the greatest economic benefits are achieved by productive economic agglomeration effects between businesses themselves and the role of public policy should be to support the private sector in achieving these agglomeration benefits.

A third strand of literature has focused on community activism and grassroots planning initiatives that empower local stakeholders to set the planning agenda in contested public spaces and communities. The proponents of activist planning have advocated for strategic or "tactical" physical interventions that might be small, but which create visible and symbolic impacts that transcend individual cases and locations. (Loukaitou-Sideris, A. [2011]. *Sidewalks: Conflict and negotiation over public space*. Cambridge, MA: MIT Press; Brenner, N. [2015]. Is "Tactical Urbanism" an alternative to neoliberal urbanism? *POST: Notes on modern and contemporary art around the globe*. Retrieved from https://post.at.moma.org/content_items/587-is-tactical-urbanism-an-alternative-to-neoliberal-urbanism.) This literature rightly suggests that unless urban communities and their grassroots representatives get involved with local plans and policies, their interests are unlikely to materialize in buildings and public spaces.

10. Schuetz, J., Kolko, J., & Meltzer, R. (2012). Are poor neighborhoods "retail deserts"? *Regional Science and Urban Economics*, 42(1–2), 269–285.

Chapter 1

1. Bettencourt, L. M. A., Lobo, J., Helbing, D., Kuhnert, C., & West, G. B. (2007). Growth, innovation, scaling, and the pace of life in cities. *Proceedings of the National Academy of Sciences*, 104(17), 7301–7306; West, G. B. (2017). *Scale: The universal laws of growth, innovation, sustainability, and the pace of life in organisms, cities, economies, and companies*. New York, NY: Penguin Press; Ensenat, E. C. (2014). *Beyond city size: Characterizing and predicting the location of urban amenities*. BS thesis, Massachusetts Institute of Technology, Cambridge, MA. Retrieved from https://dspace.mit.edu/handle/1721.1/100296; Bettencourt, L. M. A. (2013). The origins of scaling in cities. *Science*, 340(June 2013), 1438–1441; Bettencourt, L. M. A., Lobo, J., Strumsky, D., & West, G. W. (2010). Urban scaling and its deviations: Revealing the structure of wealth, innovation and crime across cities. *PloS One*, 5(11), e13541.

2. Ensenat, E. C. (2014). *Beyond city size: Characterizing and predicting the location of urban amenities*. BS thesis, Massachusetts Institute of Technology, Cambridge, MA. Retrieved from https://dspace.mit.edu/handle/1721.1/100296.

3. Federal Highway Administration. (2017). 2017 National Household Travel Survey, U.S. Department of Transportation, Washington, DC. Available online: https://nhts.ornl.gov.

4. MacDonald, J. F. (1987). There are over 900 CBSAs in the US. *Journal of Urban Economics*, 21, 242–258.

5. Giuliano, G. & Small, K. A. (1991). Subcenters in Los Angeles region. *Regional Science and Urban Economics*, 21(2), 163–182.

6. García-López, M. A. (2007). Estructura espacial del empleo y economías de aglomeración: El caso de la industria de la región metropolitana de Barcelona. *Architecture, City &*

Environment, 4, 519–553; Muñiz, I., & García-López, M. A. (2009). Policentrismoy sectores intensivos en información y conocimiento. *Ciudad y Territorio Estudios Territoriales, 160*, 263–290.

7. City Form Lab surveys in Cambridge, New York City, and Los Angeles.

8. Openshaw, S. (1984). The modifiable areal unit problem. In *Concepts and Techniques in Modern Geography* (no. 38). Norwich, UK: Geo Books.

9. Author's analysis using the 2010 US census and 2010 InfoGroup Business locations (https://www.infousa.com/lists/business-lists/), which were grouped into clusters as explained in this chapter. Overall, 45,560,890 people lived within a 1,000-meter radius from a retail cluster, which constituted 14.76% of the total US population (308,745,538) in 2010.

10. Spatial analysis performed by author based on 2010 census records and 2010 InfoGroup establishment locations (https://www.infousa.com/lists/business-lists/).

11. This is excluding Washington, DC (54.33%), which as a district, is much smaller and more urban than a state.

12. George Frederick Jenks was a 20th-century American cartographer. He developed a method called Jenks' natural breaks, which groups values into a predefined number of classes, such that variance within classes is minimized and variance between classes is maximized.

13. With around seven million square feet of retail space on a bit less than a square kilometer of land, this Penn Station area is sometimes referred to as the largest retail concentration in America.

14. See Appendix, Table 9.

15. See Appendix, Tables 10 and 11.

Chapter 2

1. I should qualify that I assume store owners don't run their shops as a hobby, operating at a loss. There are indeed some mom-and-pop and boutique stores out there, which owners run for fun without breaking even financially. It seems that the last financial crisis drove some Wall Street bankers to try something "real," such as operating a cute café or running a bed and breakfast in the wine country. I will also assume that the shops are not recuperating losses in other forms of benefits, such as advertisement and branding. This too happens to some businesses—high-end boutique stores at premium locations, such as airports, prestigious streets, and city squares or luxury malls, where businesses may run at a loss in return for advertisement value. Having a shop front on Times Square, for example, can be prohibitively expensive for most retailers, but being seen on Times Square is great marketing.

2. Space and utility costs are also called *occupancy costs* because they relate to occupying a space.

3. Taxation can be considered a fourth category, but I am leaving it out for simplicity here. Taxation might involve not only government taxes, but also franchising fees for parent companies, location-based Business Improvement levies, etc. In the United States, corporate income tax is only charged on profits that go beyond the breakeven income. In Massachusetts, coffee shops are charged a minimum of $456/year, plus 8% corporate excise tax, plus 15–39% federal corporate tax, depending on income level.

4. InfoGroup 2010 US business location data.

5. InfoGroup 2010 US business location data.

6. The 2010 data reflects that some of the book and news business had moved online.

7. Lösch, A. (1954). *The economics of location*. New Haven, CT: Yale University Press; Christaller, W. (1933). *Die zentralen orte in Süddeutschland*. Jena, Germany: Gustav Fischer.

8. Ibid.

9. Kant, E. (1933). *Ümbrus, majandus ja rahvastik Eestis. Ökoloogilis-majandusgeograafiline uurimus.* Tartu, Estonia: Tartu University.

10. Berry, B. J. L. (1967). *Geography of market centers and retail distribution.* Englewood Cliffs, NJ: Prentice Hall.

11. DiPasquale, D., & Wheaton, W. C. (1996). *Urban economics and real estate markets.* Englewood Cliffs, NJ: Prentice Hall. (p. 132)

12. The optimal purchase frequency v^* for any type of good is given as a function of inventory storage costs of the good at home (i), the amount of the good consumed annually (Pu), and transportation costs (k):

$$v^* = \left(\frac{iPu}{2k}\right)^{1/2}$$

13. The total delivered price is the sum of the purchase price P and the travel cost kD (travel costs per mile k times distance D). In equilibrium, each store offers identical prices and has an equal-size double-sided market area ($2T$), where it offers the lowest delivered price for consumers located within its catchment area. The market boundary between two stores is defined as the point where the total delivered cost is equal between two stores (dashed vertical line in figure 19).

14. The distance (D) between stores is given as:

$$D = \left(\frac{\textit{fixed costs } C}{\textit{transportation costs } k \ * \ \textit{purchase frequency } v \ * \ \textit{buyer density } F}\right)^{1/2}$$

A complete explanation of how we arrive at this solution is given in DiPasquale, D., & Wheaton, W. C. (1996). *Urban economics and real estate markets.* Englewood Cliffs, NJ: Prentice Hall. (p. 136).

15. World Bank. (2016). *Indoneisa's urban story: Role of cities in sustainable urban development.* Jakarta, Indonesia: World Bank Group.

16. Majeed, R. (2011). Defusing a volatile city, igniting reforms: Joko Widodo and Surakarta, Indonesia, 2005–2011. *Innovations for Successful Societies.* Princeton University. Retrieved from https://successfulsocieties.princeton.edu/publications/defusing-volatile-city-igniting-reforms-joko-widodo-and-surakarta-indonesia-2005-2011.

17. Gyourko, J., Mayer, C., & Sinai, T. (2013). Superstar cities. *American Economic Journal: Economic Policy, American Economic Association,* 5(4), 167–199.

18. Kurutz, S. (2017, May 31). Bleecker Street's swerve from luxe shops to vacant stores. *The New York Times.* Retrieved from https://nyti.ms/2rpTlo0.

19. Milosheff, P. (2015, October 16). Bronx leads all boroughs in court evictions of businesses, Up 30%. *The Bronx Times.*

20. Center for an Urban Future. (2015). *State of the chains.* New York, NY: Center for an Urban Future.

21. For instance, the grocery giant COSTCO generated about 13% gross profit margins in 2017 according to Financial Data Research Platform Ycharts. Retrieved from https://ycharts.com/companies/COST/gross_profit_margin.

22. A high-end jewelry store—Tiffany's—generated a 63% gross margin in 2006 according to Financial Data Research Platform Ycharts. Retrieved from https://ycharts.com/companies/COST/gross_profit_margin.

23. About the Legacy Business Program. Office of Small Business, City and County if San Francisco. (n.d.). Retrieved from https://sfosb.org/legacy-Business.

24. This also includes people who work at home.

25. NYC Department of Planning. (2010). *Peripheral travel study. Modal split by borough for NYC residents.* Retrieved from https://www1.nyc.gov/assets/planning/download/pdf/plans/transportation/peripheral_travel_02.pdf.

26. Los Angeles Department of Transportation. (2009). *The city of Los Angeles transportation profile 2009*. Los Angeles, CA. Retrieved from https://handels.gu.se/digitalAssets/1344/1344071_city-of-la-transportation-profile.pdf.

27. Author's calculation using 2015 InfoGroup business location data.

28. Luberoff, D. (2019). Coalition politics and expansion of the transit system in Los Angeles. In D. E. Davis & A. Altshuler (Eds.), *Transforming urban transportation: The role of political leadership* (pp. 62–93, 326). Oxford, UK: Oxford University Press.

29. See chapter 5 in Cervero, R. (1998). *The transit metropolis: A global inquiry.* Washington DC: Island Press.

30. Estonian Ministry of Economic Affairs and Communications, EMOR survey 2015.

31. Ober Haus Real Estate Advisors. (2016). *Real estate market report '16: Baltic states capitals*. Retrieved at https://www.ober-haus.lt/wp-content/uploads/Ober-Haus-Market-Report-Baltic-States-2016.pdf.

32. Cervero, R. (1998). *The transit metropolis: A global inquiry.* Washington DC: Island Press.

33. Ibid.

34. Ibid.

35. Singapore had 17,000 stores per 5.3 million people on 277 km^2 of land—61.3 retailers/km^2 and 7,340 people/km^2. The central part of Solo had 217 retailers/km^2 and 6,250 people/km^2.

36. Niemira, M. P., & Connolly, J. (2013). *Office-worker retail spending in a digital age.* New York, NY: International Council of Shopping Centers.

37. Figure 15 shows that across the 50 largest cities in the United States, 1,800 people, on average, correspond to a single grocery store. This estimate includes grocery stores of all sizes, many of which are small corner stores.

38. Street commerce clusters are here defined as agglomerations that have at least 25 retail, food, or service businesses (NAICS codes 44, 45, 721, 811, 812) and where businesses within a cluster are no further than 75 meters from their nearest neighboring business.

39. But it is important to emphasize that district density alone cannot explain densities of retail clusters—a share of customers also arrive from more remote parts of the city, some of whom visit retailers while passing them on other trips.

40. Jacobs, J. (1961). *The death and life of great American cities.* New York, NY: Random House.

41. Alonso, W. (1964). *Location and land use.* Cambridge, MA: Harvard University Press.

42. CBRE. (2015). *Singapore office and retail market overview.* Retrieved from http://www.mapletreecommercialtrust.com/services/view_file.aspx?f=%7B56334E4B-19D3-447F-A923-F22BD616CF10%7D.

43. Colliers International. (2015). *Greater Los Angeles Basin market report.* Retrieved from http://www.colliers.com/-/media/D3F225AF06D345C3AF5720F21EBCD1F4.ashx.

44. Fixed costs for running a business and transportation costs are higher in Singapore than in Los Angeles, which Wheaton and DiPasquale's model does include, but Singapore's retail density is still lower that the model would predict.

45. Corbusier, L. (1973). *The Athens charter.* New York, NY: Grossman Publishers.

46. Subway overtook McDonald's as the biggest global fast-food restaurant by number of outlets in 2010. The rapid growth of the company is explained, in part, by its offering of more healthy alternatives to burgers and fries and in part by its efficient franchising model. The brand now boasts more than 40,000 restaurants worldwide, all franchised, and continues to expand by opening an average of 2,000 new shops each year.

47. Special Coffee Association of America Resources. Retrieved from: http://www.scaa.org/?page=resources&d=facts-and-figures.

48. US Census Bureau.
49. 2009 National household travel survey. US Department of Transportation. Federal Highway Administration. Retrieved from https://nhts.ornl.gov/2009/pub/stt.pdf.

Chapter 3

1. Proudfoot, M. J. (1937). City retail structure. *Economic Geography*, *13*(4), 425–428.
2. Bacon, R. W. (1971). An approach to the theory of consumer shopping behavior. *Urban Studies*, *8*, 55–64; Mullingan, G. F. (1987). Consumer travel behavior: Extensions of a multipurpose shopping model. *Geographical Analysis*, *19*, 364–375.
3. Hanson, S. (1980). Spatial diversification and multipurpose travel: Implications for choice theory. *Geographical Analysis*, *12*, 245–257.
4. O'Kelly, M. E. (1981). Model of the demand for retail facilities. *Geographical Analysis*, *13*, 134–148.
5. Rushton, G., Golledge, R. S., & Clark, W. A. (1967). Formulation and test of a normative model for spatial allocation of grocery expenditures by a dispersed population. *Annals of the Association of American Geographers*, *57*, 389–400.
6. Clark, W. A. (1968). Consumer travel patterns and the concept of range. *Annals of the Association of American Geographers*, *58*, 386–396.
7. Brueckner, J. K. (1993). Inter-store externalities and space allocation in shopping centers. *Journal of Real Estate Economics and Finance*, *7*, 5–16. Note that space is used as a proxy variable for capturing the choice of merchandise at the store.
8. Anikeeff, M. A. (1996). Shopping center tenant selection and mix: A review. In J. Benjamin (Ed.), *Megatrends in retail real estate: Research issues in real estate* (vol 3.). Dordrecht: Springer; Nelson, R. (1958). *The selection of retail locations*. New York, NY: Dodge.
9. Eppli, M. J., & Schilling, J. (1993). Accounting for retail agglomeration in regional shopping centers. In *American Real Estate and Urban Economics Association Annual Meeting*. Anaheim, CA.
10. There is a debate over the question of whether these discriminatory rents favor mall owners or mall tenants. See Wheaton, W. C. (2000). Percentage rent in retail leasing: The alignment of landlord-tenant interests. *Real Estate Economics* *28*(2), 185–204.
11. Benjamin, J. D., Boyle, G. W., & Sirmans, C. F. (1990). Retail leasing: The determinants of shopping center rents. *Journal of the American Real Estate & Urban Economics Association*, *18*(3), 302–312; Benjamin, J. D., Boyle, G. W., Sirmans, C. F. (1992). Price discrimination in shopping center leases. *Journal of Urban Economics*, *32*, 299–317.
12. Eppli, M., & Benjamin, J. (1994). The evolution of shopping center research. *Journal of Real Estate Research*, *9*(1), 5–32.
13. Hotelling, H. (1929). Stability in competition. *Economic Journal*, *39*, 41–57.
14. With inelastic demand, the quantity bought by customers is not very sensitive to price changes. Proportionately, a 1% increase in price will reduce quantity sold less than 1%.
15. Eaton, B. C., & Lipsey, R. G. (1975). The principle of minimum differentiation reconsidered: Some new developments in the theory of spatial competition. *Review of Economic Studies*, *42*, 27–49.
16. Author's observations in October 2016.
17. This assumes that the students are coming from the dormitories along the river, which are in the opposite direction from the alternative store.
18. Dudey, M. (1990). Competition by choice: The effect of consumer search on firm location decisions. *The American Economic Review*, *80*(5), 1092–1104; Dudey, M. (1993). A note on

consumer search, firm location choice, and welfare. *The Journal of Industrial Economics*, *41*(3), 323–331.

19. Scitovsky, T. (1952). *Welfare and competition*. London, UK: Novello & Co. (p. 17)

20. Nevin, J. R., & Houston, M. J. (1980). Image as a component of attraction of intraurban shopping. *Journal of Retailing*, *56*, 77–93.

21. Hise, R. T., & Kelly, J. P. (1983). Factors affecting the performance of individual chain store units: An empirical analysis. *Journal of Retailing*, *59*, 22–39.

22. Ingene, C. A. (1984). Structural determinants of market potential. *Journal of Retailing*, *60*, 37–64.

23. Bloch, P. H., Ridgeway, N. M., & Nelson, J. E. (1991). Leisure and the shopping mall. *Advances in Consumer Research*, *18*, 445–452.

24. Sevtsuk, A. (2014). Location and agglomeration: The distribution of retail and food businesses in dense urban environments. *Journal of Planning Education and Research*, *34*(4), 374–393.

25. The previously combined group of retail and eating establishments (NAICS categories 44, 45, 722) splits into 13 individual three-digit NAICS categories. Of these 13 categories only 6 offer a sample, where the number of buildings containing the corresponding types of stores is large enough for statistical estimation (NAICS 443, 445, 448, 451, 453, 722). A separate spatial lag model was estimated for each of these 6 categories.

26. The percentage of all retail, food, and service establishments that fall in NAICS category "722" (drinking and eating places) is 34% in Inman Square (34 out of 70) and 36% in Davis Square (44 out of 121). Based on Infogroup 2014 business listings.

27. The formation of retail clusters is in reality an evolutionary process whereby the clusters and their surrounding urban environment grow and change at the same time.

Chapter 4

1. Downtown Los Angeles had also witnessed the effects of urban renewal. In the decades following World War II, several vibrant, mixed-use neighborhoods and commercial districts were bulldozed and displaced, including the famous Bunker Hill.

2. Though organizations, such as those behind the Los Angeles Fashion District, are best known as business improvement districts or BIDs, private place-making efforts come under different names and structures—business improvement zones, downtown improvement districts, municipal management districts, special assessment districts, community benefit districts, and others. There is some variation between their missions and services, but in this chapter, I generally refer to all these types of organizations using the term business improvement district or BID. See more in: Becker, C. J., Grossman, S. A., & Santos, B. Dos. (2011). *Business improvement districts: Census and national survey*. Washington, DC: International Downtown Association.

3. NYC Small Business Services. (2015). *New York City fiscal year 2015 business improvement district trends report*. Retrieved from https://www1.nyc.gov/assets/sbs/downloads/pdf/neighborhoods/fy15-trends-report-final.pdf.

4. Becker, C. J., Grossman, S. A., & Santos, B. Dos. (2011). *Business improvement districts: Census and national survey*. Washington, DC: International Downtown Association.

5. Caruso, G., & Weber, R. (2006). Getting the max for the tax: An examination of BID performance measures. *International Journal of Public Administration*, *29*, 187–219.

6. Ha, I., & Grunwell, S. (2014). Estimating the economic benefits a business improvement district would provide for a downtown central business district. *Journal of Economic and Economic Education Research*, *15*(3), 89–102.

7. MacDonald, J., Bluthenthal, R. N., Golinelli, D., Kofner, A., Stokes, R. J., Sehgal, A., & Beletsky, L. (2009). *Neighborhood effects on crime and youth violence. The role of business improvement districts in Los Angeles*. Retrieved from RAND Corporation website: http://www.rand.org/content/dam/rand/pubs/technical_reports/2009/RAND_TR622.pdf.

8. Ibid.

9. Sutton, S. A. (2014). Are BIDs good for business? The impact of BIDs on neighborhood retailers in New York City. *Journal of Planning Education and Research*, 34(3), 309–324.

10. Ibid.

11. Brooks, L., & Strange, W. C. (2011). The micro-empirics of collective action: The case of business improvement districts. *Journal of Public Economics*, 95, 1358–1372.

12. Ibid.

13. Rivlin-Nadler, M. (2016, February 19). Business Improvement Districts Ruin Neighborhoods. *New Republic*. February 19, 2016.

14. Becker, C. J., Grossman, S. A., & Santos, B. Dos. (2011). *Business improvement districts: Census and national survey*. Washington, DC: International Downtown Association.

15. Westbury Village Business Improvement District website: http://westburybid.org.

16. Two Rivers Company. (2015). *Rent/Lease Assistance Incentive Program for New Businesses*. Retrieved from http://tworiverscompany.com/tcg/wp-content/uploads/2016/05/TRC-Rent-Lease-Assistance-Incentive-Program.pdf.

17. Minnesota has a long history of cooperatives and more favorable laws toward their creation that other US states.

18. Northeast Investment Cooperative. (n.d.). Our Story. Retrieved from http://www.neic.coop/our-story/.

19. Kennedy, D. (2002). Limited equity coop as a vehicle for affordable housing in a race and class divided society. *Howard LJ*, 46(85), 85–125.

20. Greater London Authority. (2012). *Action for high streets*. London, UK: Greater London Authority.

21. Author's analysis based on InfoGroup 2014 business establishment location data.

22. Al, S. (2017, March). All under one roof: how malls and cities are becoming indistinguishable. *The Guardian*. Retrieved at https://www.theguardian.com/cities/2017/mar/16/malls-cities-become-one-and-same?utm_content=buffereel4d&utm_medium=social&utm_source=facebook.com&utm_campaign=buffer.

23. Cohen, N. E. (2002). *America's marketplace. The history of shopping centers*. Lyme, CT: Greenwich Publishing Group. (p. 124)

24. Lawless, S. (2014). *Black Friday: The collapse of the American shopping mall*. Artivist Publishing.

25. Sanburn, J. (2017, July 17). Why the death of malls is about more than shopping. *TIME*. Retrieved from https://time.com/4865957/death-and-life-shopping-mall/.

26. In some cases, however, BIDs and other merchant organizations can also impose more stringent oversight of public space. BIDs have been found to actively report unauthorized street vendors in New York City, for instance. See, Qadri, R. (2016). *Mapping contestation of sidewalk space in NYC*. Unpublished MCP thesis, Massachusetts Institute of Technology, Cambridge, MA.

27. Mattera, P. (2011). *Shifting the burden for vital public services: Walmart's tax avoidance schemes*. Retrieved from Good Jobs First website: https://www.goodjobsfirst.org/sites/default/files/docs/pdf/walmart_shiftingtheburden.pdf.

28. Americans for Tax Fairness. (2014). *Walmart on tax day: How taxpayers subsidize America's biggest employer and richest family*. Retrieved from http://americansfortaxfairness.org/files/Walmart-on-Tax-Day-Americans-for-Tax-Fairness-1.pdf.

29. Mitchell, S. (2006). *10 Reasons why Maine's homegrown economy matters: And 50 proven ways to revive it*. Retrieved from Institute for Local Self-Reliance: https://ilsr.org/10-reasons-why-maines-homegrown-economy-matters-and-50-proven-ways-revive-it/.

30. In 2016, more than 100 Walmarts around the country shut down for good, many in small towns and rural areas that lack alternative shopping options.

31. Civic Economics. (2002). *Economic impact analysis: A case study, local merchants vs. chain retailers*. Retrieved from https://d3n8a8pro7vhmx.cloudfront.net/liveablecityatx/pages/29/attachments/original/1404368422/Eco_Impact_Independents_vs_national_chain.pdf?1404368422?.

32. Song, L. K. (2012). *Race and place: Green collar jobs and the movement for economic democracy in Los Angeles and Cleveland*. PhD thesis, Massachusetts Institute of Technology. Retrieved from https://dspace.mit.edu/handle/1721.1/77842#files-area; Song, L. K. (2016). Enabling transformative agency: Community-based green economic and workforce development in LA and Cleveland. *Planning Theory and Practice*, 17(2), 227–243.

Chapter 5

1. Park, R. E., & Burgess, E. W. (1925). *The city: Suggestions for the investigation of human behavior in the urban environment*. Chicago, IL: University of Chicago Press. (p. 22)

2. Stahl, K. (1987). Theories of urban business location. In E. S. Mills (Ed.), *Handbook of Regional and Urban Economics* (vol. 2, pp. 759–820 of chapter 19). Amsterdam, Holland: North-Holland. (p. 1322)

3. Hurd, R. (1903). *Principles of city land values*. New York, NY: Record & Guide. (p. 13)

4. Hansen, W. G. (1959). How accessibility shapes land use. *Journal of the American Planning Association*, 25(2), 73–76, 73.

5. Thünen, J.-H. von. (1826). *The isolated state*. Wirtschaft & Finan; Alonso, W. (1964). *Location and land use*. Cambridge, MA: Harvard University Press; Christaller, W., & Baskin, C. W. (1966). *Central places in southern Germany*. Englewood Cliffs, NJ: Prentice-Hall.

6. Weber, A. (1909). *Über den standort der industrie*. Tübingen, Germany: J. C. B. Mohr (Paul Siebeck).

7. Hansen, W. G. (1959). How accessibility shapes land use. *Journal of the American Planning Association*, 25(2), 73–76.

8. Wachs, M., & Koenig, J. G. (1979). Accessibility, mobility and travel demand. In D. A. Hensher & P. A. Stopher (Eds.), *Behavioral Modelling* (p. 861). London, UK: Croom Helm; Handy, S., & Niemeier, A. D. (1997). Measuring accessibility: An exploration of issues and alternatives. *Environment and Planning A*, 29, 1175–1194; Bhat, C., Handy, S., Kockelman, K., Mahmassani, H., Chen, Q., & Weston, L. (2000). *Development of an urban accessibility index: Literature review*. (Report No. 7-4938-1). Retrieved from Center for Transportation Research at the University of Texas at Austin website: http://ctr.utexas.edu/wp-content/uploads/pubs/4938_1.pdf.

9. Bhat, C., Handy, S., Kockelman, K., Mahmassani, H., Chen, Q., & Weston, L. (2000). *Development of an urban accessibility index: Literature review*. (Report No. 7-4938-1). Retrieved from Center for Transportation Research at the University of Texas at Austin website: http://ctr.utexas.edu/wp-content/uploads/pubs/4938_1.pdf.

10. From a perspective of a storeowner, households that surround the stores represent potential destinations to which we quantify accessibility. For each household found, a weight is recorded on the numerator of the index. This weight represents the attractiveness of the destination, in this case the number of residents at a household. In order to also account for

transportation costs, this weight is divided by the travel distance required to get to each home location. Analogous to Newton's definition, the gravity index is a sum of ratios between all destination weights and travel costs that are reached within a given travel radius. See more details in Hansen, W. G. (1959). How accessibility shapes land use. *Journal of the American Planning Association, 25*(2), 73–76.

11. Using the GIS or Rhinoceros3D Urban Network Analysis toolbox for example.

12. The index is mathematically defined as follows:

$$\text{Gravity}[i]^r = \sum_{j \in G-\{i\}, d[i,j] \leq r} \frac{W[j]^\alpha}{e^{\beta \cdot d[i,j]}}$$

where is the gravity index at origin "i" within network "G" at search radius "r," "W" is the weight of destination, "d" is the shortest travel distance between locations "i" and "j," α is the exponent that can controls the destination weight or attractiveness, and β is the exponent for adjusting the effect of distance decay. The gravity index thus captures both the attraction of the destinations as well as the spatial impedance of travel required to reach those destinations in a combined measure of accessibility. If no weight attributes are given, then the weight of each destination is considered to be "1." The default value for alpha is also set at "1," so that the destination weight has a linear effect.

13. The index I used in New York is also known as the Reach accessibility index or the cumulative opportunities index.

14. Analysis performed with the help of the Urban Network Analysis toolbox. Retrieved from City Form Lab website: http://cityform.gsd.harvard.edu/projects/una-rhino-toolbox and http://cityform.gsd.harvard.edu/projects/urban-network-analysis.

15. Though small blocks do usually lead to higher residential accessibility this is not always the case. Sevtsuk, Kalvo, et al. show how pedestrian access can increase with larger blocks in a number of circumstances: Sevtsuk, A., Kalvo, R., & Ekmekci, O. (2016). Pedestrian accessibility in grid layouts: The role of block, parcel and street dimensions. *Urban Morphology, 20*(2), 89–106.

16. Hägerstrand, T. (1970). What about people in regional science? *Papers of the Regional Science Association, 14*, 7–21.

17. Using a decay coefficient beta of 0.002 for distance measured in meters, and a 600-meter search radius. How longer distances affect the gradual drop-off in visits is controlled by the parameter beta. A larger beta value assumes a stronger dislike for travel and produces a sharper decay rate. The appropriate beta value can be empirically estimated by studying trip distribution data or conducting a small survey in an area. If we ask 100 visitors at coffee shops in Cambridge how long they walked to get to the shop and then organized the responses by distance into bins at equal distance intervals, we would see the shape of the distance decay curve traced out by the peaks of the bins. My students estimated that a beta value of 0.002 works well for pedestrians in Cambridge if distance is captured in meters as units of distance. Note that the beta value differs for different travel cost units (meters, miles, minutes, etc.) and for different travel modes (walking, biking, driving, etc.). This is what I have used in the index above.

18. In areas, where ample retail and food service options were available, the expenditures on eating and drinking were roughly two and a half times higher than in areas with limited retail choices.

19. Bureau of Labor Statistics. (2015). *Consumer expenditures 2014*. [News release]. Retrieved from http://www.bls.gov/news.release/pdf/cesan.pdf; Niemira, M. P., & Connolly, J. (2012). *Office-worker retail spending in a digital age*. New York, NY: International Council of Shopping Centers.

20. Note that since many of the passengers who come to a location by subway may be going to the residences or employment locations around the station, there is likely to be some double counting in transit stations. This is because people exiting the stations and who go to workplaces or homes are potentially also counted at those workplaces and homes.

21. Transit stops have been weighted by the number of passengers using the stop on a typical day; homes and workplaces by residents and employees accordingly using data from the Massachusetts Bay Transit Authority (MBTA), Census 2000 and Environmental Systems Research Institute (ESRI) Business Analyst.

22. Arup. (2016). *Cities alive. Towards a walking world.* Retrieved from https://www.arup.com/perspectives/publications/research/section/cities-alive-towards-a-walking-world?query=cities%20alive%20toward; Transport for London. (2014). *Annual Report and Statement of Account 2013/14.* Retrieved from http://content.tfl.gov.uk/annual-report-2013-14.pdf.

23. Iyer, E. S. (1989). Unplanned purchasing: Knowledge of shopping environment and time pressure. *Journal of Retailing, 65*(1), 40–57.

24. Freeman, L. C. (1977). A set of measures of centrality based on betweenness. *Sociometry, 40,* 35–41.

25. The *Betweenness* measure is defined as follows:

$$Betweenness\,[i]r = \sum_{j,k \in G-\{i\}} \frac{n_{jk}[i]}{n_{jk}}$$

where the betweenness of location "i" within the search radius "r" is the number of shortest paths from origin "j" to destination "k" that pass by "i" and "n_{jk}" is the total number of shortest paths from "j" to "k." *Betweenness* is computed by considering all origin-destination pairs that are within a distance "r" from each other. It is not computed by considering all pairs of buildings that are within a distance "r" from "i" itself.

26. Carter, C. C., & Vandell, K. D. (2005). Store location in shopping centers: Theory and estimates. *Journal of Real Estate Research, 27*(3), 237–265.

27. Luberoff, D. (2019). Reimagining and reconfiguring New York City's streets. In D. E. Davis & A. Altshuler (Eds.), *Transforming urban transportation: The role of political leadership* (pp. 27–61). Oxford, UK: Oxford University Press.

28. Porta, S., Strano, E., Iacoviello, V., Messora, R., Latora, V., Cardillo, A., & Scellato, S. (2009). Street centrality and densities of retail and services in Bologna, Italy. *Environment and Planning B: Planning and Design, 36,* 450–465; Sevtsuk, A. (2014). Location and agglomeration: The distribution of retail and food businesses in dense urban environments. *Journal of Planning Education and Research, 34*(4), 374–393.

29. Freeman, L. C. (1977). A set of measures of centrality based on betweenness. *Sociometry, 40,* 35–41.

30. Takeuchi, D. (1977) Hokō-sha no keiro sentaku kōdō ni kansuru kenkyū (A study on pedestrian route choice behavior). *Doboku Gakkai no Yokou shū* (*Proceedings of the Japanese Society of Civil Engineers*) *259,* 91–101; Li, Y., & Tsukaguchi, H. (2005). Relationship between network topology and pedestrian route choice behavior. *Journal of the Eastern Asia Society for Transportation Studies, 6,* 241–248

31. Sevtsuk, A. (2018). *Urban network analysis. Tools for modeling pedestrian and bicycle trips in cities.* Cambridge, MA: Harvard Graduate School of Design. Available digitally from City Form Lab website: http://cityform.mit.edu/projects/una-rhino-toolbox.

32. It is also possible to weigh the paths by their qualities, such that more pleasant or more interesting routes attract more trips.

33. A *detour ratio* variable in the betweenness tool controls these pedestrian deviations in the Urban Network Analysis toolbox.

34. Walking patterns also change throughout the day. Morning commuting hour, evening commuting hour, and lunchtime typically constitute the most important peaks for pedestrian movement.

35. This is achieved by multiplying the betweenness values of locations with the same distance decay function as in the gravity index.

36. Sevtsuk, A. (2014). Location and agglomeration: The distribution of retail and food businesses in dense urban environments. *Journal of Planning Education and Research*, 34(4), 374–393.

37. My data included a total of 1,941 individual businesses: 1,258 retail establishments and 683 eating or drinking establishments in both towns. Geographic coordinates, as well as an address field associated with each establishment, allowed me to match each business to a specific building. Each building thus obtained a binary dependent variable (0 or 1) showing whether it contained retail or food establishments. The original dataset had 26,983 individual buildings in Cambridge and Somerville, but not all of these were suitable candidates for stores. I eliminated zoning blocks that were designated as single-family housing from the dataset and kept only those buildings that were commercial, industrial, multifamily, or mixed. Out of those, 834 buildings contained a retail or food service establishment as shown in Figure 57.

38. Anselin, L. (1988). *Spatial econometrics: Methods and models*. Dordrecht, Germany.

39. The clustering coefficient rho is constrained between negative one and positive one. If retailers are strategically attracted to each other, controlling for other location factors, then rho is positive and significant; if retailers are strategically repelled from each other, then rho is negative and significant. If no interaction in the location choices of retailers is observed, the coefficient is expected to be zero or insignificant.

40. When I set the model's dependent variable to represent the presence or lack of a particular type of store (e.g., a clothing store), then rho can also represent how the probability of encountering clothing stores in a building is affected not merely by all other retailers nearby, but by the same type of retailers—clothing stores—in neighboring buildings. In this case, the model captures the effects of competitive clustering with like stores. Table 6 illustrates competitive clustering results for the same dataset in Cambridge and Somerville, MA.

41. The proposed model offers a cross-sectional view of strategic interaction in retailers' location choices, as inferred from their observed spatial pattern at a particular moment in time. In reality, retail location choices are of course a sequential not a simultaneous process, where the conditions of adjacency change over time. In order to accurately represent the true adjacency conditions when each of the location choices historically occurred, the neighbor relationships would need to be specified individually for every establishment according to the situation at the time of each location choice. At present, such longitudinal data describing the opening date of each store, as well as the overall pattern of all other stores at the time, is difficult to find.

42. Since an average study-area building has 26 neighbors within a 100-meter reach, we divide 28% by 26 to get about 1%.

43. Harvard University itself constitutes another major anchor for the area, attracting not only students and staff, but also daily tourist groups, who are important patrons of clothing and apparel stores.

44. For instance, "boutique du coin" in French, "nurgapood" in Estonian, or "Laden an der Ecke" in German.

45. Caplin, A., & Leahy, J. (1998). Miracle of Sixth Avenue: Information externalities and search. *The Economic Journal*, 108(446), 60–74.

46. Sevtsuk, A. (2014). Location and agglomeration: The distribution of retail and food businesses in dense urban environments. *Journal of Planning Education and Research*, 34(4), 374–393.

47. The probability P of a demand point *i* to visit a particular center *j* is given as a ratio between accessibility to that particular center and the sum of accessibilities to all available centers, including center *j*:

$$P_{ij} = \frac{\left(\dfrac{W_j^\alpha}{e^{\beta D_{ij}}}\right)}{\sum_{j=1}^{n}\left(\dfrac{W_j^\alpha}{e^{\beta D_{ij}}}\right)}$$

Having assigned a visiting probability from each origin to each destination, the patronage of a specific destination is estimated by multiplying the visiting probability with the weight of each demand point and summing across all demand points:

$$S_{jr} = \sum_{i=1}^{n}(W_i \cdot P_{ij})$$

where S_{jr} represents the patronage of center *j* within a demand search radius *r*, W_i is the weight of a demand point *i*, for instance the number of people in a building, and P_{ij} is the probability of the demand point *i* to visit center *j*. Each demand point can have a weight W to model differences in household or building size or in its purchasing capacity. Only those demand points that are within a specified network radius *r* from the destination affect the destination's patronage; those that are farther are assumed to be too far to visit that destination.

The Huff model generally assumes that all patronage or purchasing power in the model is fully spent among available stores. If there are 10 people on the demand side, then the sum of patronage across all stores is also 10. Under such conditions, the overall shopping frequency in the system is not affected by the spatial configuration of stores—all demand is always cleared and the overall patronage is identical with different store patterns.

In order to account for the accessibility differences between customers, I have added another element to the equation, which discounts the patronage allocated to each store by the same inverse distance decay function as used in the gravity model. Since the store attractiveness is already accounted for in finding patronage probabilities, this decay effect only focuses on an inverse distance effect, with an enumerator of "1." Customer *i*'s patronage of a store *j* is thus given as function of (a) demand point's weight, (b) its probability of going to *j*, and (c) its distance from *j*:

$$S_{jr} = \sum_{i=1}^{n}\left(W_i \cdot P_{ij} \cdot \frac{1}{e^{\beta D_{ij}}}\right)$$

Due to the third element in the summation, demand points that are located at a distance from stores do not allocate all their weights between stores. Using "1" in the numerator and factoring in only proximity in the denominator ensures that the overall patronage across all stores is always less or equal to the sum of demand weights W_i. Only in a scenario where all demand points are located at the same location as stores, facing zero transportation costs, can the totality of demand weight be allocated to stores.

As a result of the additional distance decay effect, the overall patronage of stores in the system depends on the spatial configuration of stores and patrons. Changing the location of stores will affect overall store visits in the system. The probability of visiting a destination increases if the destination is more attractive or closer to the demand point, depending on what alpha and beta parameters are used to dampen the size and proximity effects.

48. Tobler, W. (1970). A computer movie simulating urban growth in the Detroit region. *Economic Geography*, 46(2), 234–240, 234.

49. We learned from talking to a Dunkin representative that the Cambridge market is a bit of an oddity for Dunkin Donuts, which typically focuses on vehicular access.

Chapter 6

1. Corbusier, L. (1973). *The Athens charter*. New York, NY: Grossman Publishers; Gropius, W., Shand, P. M., & Pick, F. (1965). *The new architecture and the Bauhaus*. Cambridge, MA: MIT Press.
2. Though notably lower in population density than Singapore.
3. See, for instance, Pelevin, V. (1998). *The life of insects*. New York, NY: Straus & Giroux; Pelevin, V. (1998). *Omon Ra*. New York, NY: New Directions.
4. The quote comes from a debate about how to reconstruct the Commons Chamber in British Parliament, which was badly damaged as a result of German Blitz bombings. Churchill favored the restoration of a rectangular space over an alternative semicircular auditorium that we see, for instance, in the US Congress or the German Reichstag. Asserting that the shape of the old chamber was responsible for the two-party system that is the essence of British parliamentary democracy, Churchill sided with those in favor of reconstructing the historic rectangular hall. According to long tradition, Members of Parliament can only transfer their allegiance from government to opposition, or vice versa, if they openly cross the floor of the chamber. During debates, members speaking on opposing sides are also expected to refrain from stepping over the red lines on the carpet, which are said to equal the length of two swords. With Churchill's approval, the debate was settled in favor of rebuilding the original rectangular space that is still used by the Parliament today. *Churchill and the Commons Chamber*. Retrieved from the UK Parliament's website: https://www.parliament.uk/about/living-heritage/building/palace/architecture/palacestructure/churchill/.
5. For instance, in 2014, an Apple Store bought a 17,500-square-foot space for $100 million—$5,700 per square foot—on the Third Street Promenade in Santa Monica. This amount would be extremely rare in a shopping center, given that an Apple store is perceived as a small anchor that attracts lots of customers at all hours of operation. Malls would typically reward the customer spillovers that an Apple store produces for other stores with a bargain lease contract.
6. Untermann, R. (1984). *Accommodating the pedestrian adapting towns and neighborhoods for walking and bicycling*. New York, NY: Van Nostrand Reinhold; Ewing, R., Hajrasouliha, A., Neckerman, K. M., Purciel-Hill, M., & Greene, W. (2016). Streetscape features related to pedestrian activity. *Journal of Planning Education and Research*, 36(1), 5–15; Hoehner, C. M., Ramirez, L. B., & Elliott, M. B. (2005). Perceived and objective environmental measures and physical activity among urban adults. *American Journal of Preventive Medicine*, 28(2S2), 105–116.
7. Whyte, W. H. (1980). *The social life of small urban spaces*. New York, NY: Conservation Foundation.
8. Guo, Z. (2009). Does the pedestrian environment affect the utility of walking? A case of path choice in downtown Boston. *Transportation Research Part D*, 14(5), 343–352.
9. New York City Department of Transportation (2008). *World class streets: Remaking New York City's public realm*. New York, NY: New York City Department of Transportation. Retrieved from New York City website: http://www.nyc.gov/html/dot/downloads/pdf/World_Class_Streets_Gehl_08.pdf.
10. NACTO. (2013). *Urban street design guide*. Washington DC: Island Press.
11. Malls, after all, are also pedestrian-only environments.

12. Coleman, P. (2006). *Shopping environments: Evolution, planning and design*. Abingdon-on-Thames, UK: Routledge.

13. *Urban design guidelines for developments within Singapore River planning area*. Annex A, Appedix 2: 1st storey UD Guide Plan (1st Storey Pedestrian Network) & Activity Generating use. Retrieved from the Singapore URA website: https://www.ura.gov.sg/~/media/User%20Defined/URA%20Online/circulars/2013/nov/dc13-17/dc13-17_App%202.pdf.

14. Cox Castle & Nicholson LLP. (2013). *Proposed formula retail ordinance: Comparison to other ordinances*. Retrieved from https://www.malibucity.org/DocumentCenter/View/4882/PC130729_Item-6D_Correspondence_DWaite2.

15. Lynch, K. (1984). *Good city form*. Cambridge, MA: MIT Press.

16. Sevtsuk, A., & Mekonnen, M. (2012). *Urban network analysis: A new toolbox for measuring city form in ArcGIS*. 2012 Proceedings of the Symposium on Simulation for Architecture and Urban Design. Ed. Nikolovska, L. & Attar, R. (pp. 111–121); Sevtsuk, A. (2014). Analysis and planning of urban networks. In R. Alhajj & J. Rokne (Eds.), *Encyclopedia of social network analysis and mining* (pp. 2–13). New York, NY: Springer.

17. Accessibility to stores in grid layouts depends on the block sizes. Blocks that are too long or short can reduce accessibility. For detail, see Sevtsuk, A., Kalvo, R., & Ekmekci, O. (2016). Pedestrian accessibility in grid layouts: The role of block, parcel and street dimensions. *Urban Morphology, 20*(2), 89–106.

18. Environmental Systems Research Institute (ESRI) Business Analyst Data 2006 and 2017. See more at ESRI website: https://www.esri.com/en-us/arcgis/products/arcgis-business-analyst/overview.

19. Thadani, T. (2018, July 24). Proposed SF law could force tech workers to actually go out for lunch. *San Francisco Chronicle*. Retrieved from https://www.sfchronicle.com/business/article/Tech-industry-s-coveted-office-cafeterias-could-13101014.php.

Chapter 7

1. United States Securities and Exchange Commission. (2018). Form 10-K Target Corporation. Retrieved from https://www.sec.gov/Archives/edgar/data/27419/000002741918000010/tgt-20180203x10k.htm.

2. Gruen, V., & Baldauf, A. (2017). *Shopping town: Designing the city in suburban America*. Minneapolis MN: University of Minnesota Press.

3. In 1967, three nights of rioting followed an incident of police brutality on a black woman. The event led to the looting of hundreds of stores and drew the National Guard to the city's streets.

4. Gruen, V., & Baldauf, A. (2017). *Shopping town: Designing the city in suburban America*. Minneapolis: University of Minnesota Press.

5. Southdale had more than 120 stores and 4 anchors in 2018. Simon Property Group L.P. (2018). Southdale Center property fact sheet. Retrieved from https://business.simon.com/mall/leasingsheet/Southdale_Center_Brochure.pdf.

6. Cavanaugh., P. (2006). *Politics and freeways: Building the Twin Cities interstate system*. Minneapolis, MN: Minneapolis: Center for Urban and Regional Affairs (CURA) and Center for Transportation Studies (CTS), University of Minnesota.

7. Avila, E. (2004). *Popular culture in the age of white flight: Fear and fantasy in suburban Los Angeles*. Berkeley, CA: University of California Press.

8. Cohen, N. E. (2002). *America's marketplace. The history of shopping centers*. Lyme, CT: International Council for Shopping Centers, Greenwich Publishing Group. (p. 56).

9. Jackson, K. (1985). *Crabgrass frontier: The suburbanization of the United States*. New York, NY: Oxford University Press.

10. Leinberger, C. B., & Lynch, P. (2014). *Foot traffic ahead: Ranking walkable urbanism in America's largest metros*. Retrieved from https://www.smartgrowthamerica.org/app/legacy/documents/foot-traffic-ahead.pdf.

11. National Trust for Historic Preservation. (2017). *Millennials and historic preservation: A deep dive into attitudes and values*. Retrieved from https://nthp-savingplaces.s3.amazonaws.com/2017/06/27/09/02/25/407/Millennial Research Report.pdf.

12. Sisson, P. (2017, July 25). "Seniors want walkability, too, survey says." *Curbed*. Retrieved from https://www.curbed.com/2017/7/25/16025388/senior-living-walkability-survey.

13. Ehrenhalt, A. (2012). *The great inversion and the future of the American city*. New York, NY: Alfred A. Knopf. (p. 3).

14. Kneebone, E., & Berube, A. (2013). *Confronting suburban poverty in America*. Washington, DC: Brookings Institution Press.

15. I am referring specifically to census tracts that are at least partially within a 1.5-mile radius around Seventh Street and Nicollet Avenue in downtown Minneapolis. US Census Bureau Tiger Shapefiles for Census Tracts in Minnesota. Retrieved from https://www.census.gov/cgi-bin/geo/shapefiles/index.php?year=2016&layergroup=Census+Tracts.

16. Luberoff, D. (2019). Reimagining and reconfiguring New York City's streets. In D. E. Davis & A. Altshuler (Eds.), *Transforming urban transportation: The role of political leadership* (pp.27–60). Oxford, UK: Oxford University Press.

17. Bloomberg, M. (2015, September/October). City century. Why municipalities are the key to fighting climate change. *Foreign Affairs, 94*(5). Retrieved from https://www.foreignaffairs.com/articles/2015-08-18/city-century.

18. Florida, R. (2002). *The rise of the creative class: And how it's transforming work, leisure, community and everyday life*. New York: Perseus Book Group.

19. Benfield, K. (2012, March 14). How Amazon got the urban campus right. *Citylab*. Retrieved from http://www.citylab.com/work/2012/03/how-amazon-got-urban-campus-right/1485/.

20. Who We Are. (n.d.). Haley House website. Retrieved from. http://haleyhouse.org/who-we-are/history/.

21. The authors used the Local Origin-Destination Employment Statistics (LODES) dataset by the US Census Bureau, where all states but Arizona, Arkansas, Mississippi, New Hampshire, and Massachusetts, as well as the District of Columbia, were represented. Hartley, D. A., Kaza, N., & Lester, T. W. (2016). Are America's inner cities competitive? Evidence from the 2000s. *Economic Development Quarterly, 30*(2), 137–158.

22. Ibid., 138.

23. Kolko, J. (2017, May 22). Seattle climbs but Austin sprawls: The myth of the return to cities. *The New York Times*. Retrieved from https://www.nytimes.com/2017/05/22/upshot/seattle-climbs-but-austin-sprawls-the-myth-of-the-return-to-cities.html?_r=2. Urban and suburban zip codes were distinguished primarily according to population density. Based on a survey of several thousand Trulia users, Kolko determined that the common threshold between urban and suburban neighborhoods that respondents personally identified was around 2,213 people per square mile. Other factors also had significant but minor predictive power for defining what urban and suburban meant for respondents, but population density alone was the strongest predictor.

24. Alofsin, A. (June 6, 2018). A defense of the suburbs. *The Atlantic*. Retrieved from https://www.theatlantic.com/technology/archive/2018/06/a-defense-of-the-suburbs/562136/.

25. Suburban employment also grew faster than inner cities in the South Atlantic region, but in those states, both suburban and inner-city job growth was superseded by jobs growth

in the Central Business District, where it was highest. Interestingly, these states largely also overlap with the Metropolitan Statistical Areas where Kolko observed largest average residential density decreases, rather than increases, over the same period.

26. Hartley, D. A., Kaza, N., & Lester, T. W. (2016). Are America's inner cities competitive? Evidence from the 2000s. *Economic Development Quarterly, 30*(2), 137–158.

27. Baum-Snow, N., & Hartley, D. (2017). *Accounting for central neighborhood change, 1980–2010* (No. WP 2016-09). Federal Reserve Bank of Chicago. Retrieved from https://www.chicagofed.org/~/media/publications/working-papers/2016/wp2016-09-pdf.pdf.

28. Pogash, C. (2015, May 22). Gentrification spreads an upheaval in San Francisco's Mission District. *New York Times.* Retrieved from https://www.nytimes.com/2015/05/23/us/high-rents-elbow-latinos-from-san-franciscos-mission-district.html.

29. Zip codes with fewer than 2,213 and 102 or more households per square mile. Kolko, J. (2017, May 22). Seattle climbs but Austin sprawls: The myth of the return to cities. *New York Times.* Retrieved from https://www.nytimes.com/2017/05/22/upshot/seattle-climbs-but-austin-sprawls-the-myth-of-the-return-to-cities.html?_r=2.

30. Li, W. (2012). *Ethnoburb: The new ethnic community in urban America*. Honolulu, HI: University of Hawaii Press. (p. 29).

31. Spivak, J. (2018, July). Retail realities: Rebuilding economic resiliency as brick and mortar goes to pieces. *Planning Magazine,* (July 2018), 16–21.

32. BBC News. (2014, November 11). Alibaba's Singles' Day sales exceed predictions at $9.3bn. *BBC News.* Retrieved from BBC News: https://www.bbc.com/news/business-29999289; Reuters. (2017, September 26). Alibaba Says It's About to Build Up a Massive Logistics Network. *Fortune.* Retrieved from: https://fortune.com/2017/09/26/alibaba-jack-ma-global-logistics/.

33. According to Piper Jaffray, approximately 60% of US households have Amazon Prime memberships. Among high-income households who make over $112,000 a year, Prime penetration is as high as 82%. Piper Jaffray. (2016). Teens are "snapping" up denim, sneakers and beauty, according to survey of 10,000 teens [Press release]. Retrieved from http://www.piperjaffray.com/2col.aspx?id=178&releaseid=2211939&title=Teens%20Are%20%22Snapping%22%20up%20Denim,%20Sneakers%20and%20Beauty,%20According%20to%20Survey%20of%2010,000%20Teens.

34. Stone, B. (2010, November 24). What's in Amazon's box? Instant gratification. *Bloomberg Businessweek.* Retrieved from https://www.bloomberg.com/news/articles/2010-11-24/whats-in-amazons-box-instant-gratification.

35. Retail Strategy for the City of Cambridge: Market Analysis. Larissa Ortis presentation at Cambridge City Hall in May 2017 as part of a retail study commissioned by the city.

36. Vaccaro, A., & Pohle, A. (2016, April 21). Amazon offers same day delivery to every Boston neighborhood, except Roxbury. Boston.com. Retrieved from https://www.boston.com/news/business/2016/04/21/amazon-roxbury-same-day-delivery-boston.

37. Cohen, N. E. (2002). *America's marketplace. The history of shopping centers.* International Council for Shopping Centers. Lyme, CT: Greenwich Publishing Group. (p. 10).

38. Smith, S. (2012, September 1). Big-box store has new life as an airy public library. *The New York Times.* Retrieved from https://www.nytimes.com/2012/09/02/us/former-walmart-in-mcallen-is-now-an-airy-public-library.html.

39. Christensen, J. (2008). *Big box reuse.* Cambridge, MA: MIT Press.

40. *Urban Design Guidelines for Developments within Singapore River Planning Area.* Annex A, Appednix 2: 1st storey UD Guide Plan (1st Storey Pedestrian Network) & Activity Generating use. Retrieved from the Singapore URA website: https://www.ura.gov.sg/~/media/User%20Defined/URA%20Online/circulars/2013/nov/dc13-17/dc13-17_App%202.pdf.

41. Space sharing can be a practical option for businesses that don't hold significant inventory on site—coffee shops and eateries, personal service providers, pop-up stores, etc. It may not be a practical solution for retailers that store significant quantities of goods on site.

Conclusion

1. Smith, A. (1776). *An inquiry into the nature and causes of the wealth of nations.* London, UK: W. Strahan and T. Cadell.

2. Mayor of London. (2014). *Action for high streets.* Retrieved from https://www.london.gov.uk/sites/default/files/GLA_Action%20for%20High%20Streets.pdf.

3. Ibid.

4. Ibid.

5. Ibid.

6. Whyte, W. F. (1943). *Street corner society: The social structure of an Italian slum.* Chicago, IL: University of Chicago Press; Whyte, W. H. (1980). *The social life of small urban spaces.* New York, NY: Conservation Foundation; Jacobs, J. (1961). *The death and life of great American cities.* New York, NY: Random House.

7. Jacobs, J. (1961). *The death and life of great American cities.* New York, NY: Random House.

8. Anderson, S. (1978). Studies toward an ecological model of the urban environment. In S. Anderson (Ed.), *On Streets* (pp. 267–307). Cambridge, MA: MIT Press.

9. Sennett, R. (2018). *Building and dwelling.* New York, NY: Farrar, Straus and Giroux.

10. It is important to note that both metrics, as well as the population density metric, depend strongly on the aerial units of analysis. The numbers in this table correspond to city-wide densities. If measured at a neighborhood scale, urban block scale, or even individual parcel scale, the same metrics yield much higher numbers. At a block scale, for instance, we can find FAR results greater than 15 in some parts of New York City. This is known in the literature as the Modifiable Aerial Unit Problem or MAUP. See more in Openshaw, S. (1984). *The Modifiable Areal Unit Problem.* Norwich, UK: Geo Books.

11. Amindarbari, R., & Sevtsuk, A. (2019). Spatial structure of American metropolitan areas. Forthcoming article.

12. Eliel Saarinen, quoted by Eero Saarinen, "The Maturing Modern," in *Time*, July 2, 1956:51, cited in Saarinen Houses by Jari Jesonen and Sirkkaliisa Jetsonen, p. 11.

Index

Page numbers in italics refer to figures.

access, independent, 155–157
accessibility measures, 121–140, 202–203; betweenness metric, 128–134, 134–140, 223n27, 224nn34–35; gravity index, 122–128, 134–140, 222nn10–12; Huff model, 140–143, 225n47; reach metric, 167, 222n13; retail patterns in Cambridge and Somerville, MA, 134–140, 222nn15, 17–18, 224nn37–44, 226n49
Action for High Streets program, 197
activity generating uses, 166, 192
adjacent buildings, relationships between, 157
Alibaba, 185–186
Alofsin, Anthony, 181
Alonso, William, 63
Amazon, 179, 185–186, 187–188, 189–190, 191, 192; Prime, 186, 229n33
American Express, 177
American Planning Accreditation Board, 8
Americans for Tax Fairness, 111
Americans with Disabilities Act, 117
Anderson, Stanford, 199
Annelinn, Estonia, 144–150, 152, 154–155
Apple Store, 226n5
arcades, 159
architectural typologies. *See* built environment, affects of
area median income (AMI), 48–49
Arkády Pankrác shopping mall (Prague, Czech Republic), *82*
Artesia, California, 184
Assembly Row (Somerville, MA), *108*
Associated and Federated Stores, 176
Athens Charter of 1933, 69
Atlanta, Georgia, 15, *19*, 209–212
Austin, Texas, 112

Bahnhofstrasse (Zurich, Switzerland), 162, *163*
bankruptcies, store, 186–187, 190

Barnes & Noble, 186
basement stores, 147–149
Baum-Snow, Nathaniel, 182
Bed Bath & Beyond, 139
Berry, Brian, 42
Bertoia, Harry, 173–174
Bettencourt, L. M. A., 11
betweenness metric, 128–134, 134–140, 223n27, 224nn34–35
Beverly Hills, California, 153, *154,* 188–189
Big Box Reuse (Christensen), 192
big box stores, 150, 187, 190, 192
Biltmore Square Mall (Asheville, NC), 108
Bleecker Street (NYC, NY), *47,* 47–48
Bloomberg, Michael, 159, 178–179
Bolling Municipal Building, 180
Books Actually, 32
bookstores, 77, *78,* 90, 112, 186
Borders bookstores, 112, 186
Borough of Hackney (London), 102
Boston, Massachusetts, *19,* 178; Boston Public Schools, 180; Dudley Square, 179–180; MIT, 87–88, 156, 169–171, 218n17; Newbury Street, 154–155, *156,* 193; Public Works department, 193; Roxbury, 179; Waterfront District, 164
Boston Properties, 170, 171
boundaries, 96
Bourke Place (Melbourne, Australia), 162
Bourke Street Mall (Melbourne, Australia), 56
branding, influence on retail density, 71–73
Brattle Street (Cambridge, MA), *158*
brick and mortar stores, intertwining with e-commerce, 189–190
Broadsheet Coffee Roasters (Cambridge, MA), *75*
Bronx (NYC, NY), 48
Brooklyn (NYC, NY), *81*

Bugis District (Singapore), 163, *164*
built coverage metric, *202,* 203–204, 230n10
built environment, affects of, 7, 111, 123, 144–171, 201–202; Annelinn, Estonia example, 144–150; double-sided streets with easy crossings, 159–162; floor areas of shops, 150–153; ground-floor heights, 153–154; independent access and circulation, 155–157; linear density of entrances, 162–166; permeable facades, 152–153; shape of retail clusters, 166–171; sidewalk quality, 157–159
Burlington, Vermont, 117
business improvement districts (BIDs), 93–98, 118, 197, 219n2, 220n26; defining, 94–96; effectiveness of, 96–98
Byzantine Latino Quarter (Los Angeles, CA), 180, 198

Cambridge, Massachusetts, 51, 90–92, 117–118, 123–124, 126–129, 140–143, 169–171, 196; Brattle Street, *158*; Broadsheet Coffee Roasters, *75*; Darwin's sandwich shop, 124–126; Harvard Square, 119, 163, 169; Kendall Square, 169–171, 196; Massachusetts Avenue, 119; retail patterns in, 119, 134–140, 222nn15, 17–18, 224nn37–44, 226n49
Campo di Siena, Italy, 65
Caplin, Andrew, 139
Car Free Days, 193
Carluccio's Café, *35*
Carnaby Street (London), 167
central business district (CBD), 16, 78–79, 178, 199
Central Place Theory, 33, 58, 62, 65, 71–73, 77, 80, 83; spatial distribution of competing stores and, 39–42
Cervero, Robert, 56
Chicago, Illinois, *20,* 26
Chinatown (NYC, NY), 66
Christaller, Walter, 39–42, 77
Christensen, Julia, 192
Churchill, Winston, 150, 226n4
Church Street (Burlington, VT), 117
circulation, 155–157
City Form Lab, 131, *167*
Civic Economics, 112
Clarksville, Tennessee, 100
class demographics, 109, 177–178, 179, 185, 191
Cleveland, Ohio, 115–116
clothing stores, 78, 90–91, 188
clusters, retail, 77–92, *183,* 202–203; clustering coefficients, 90–92, 135–140; competing stores, 83–92; complementary stores, 79–83; distribution of, 183–184; five types of, 78–79;

isolated store cluster, 78; shape of, 166–171, 219n27. *See also* coordinated clustering; predictability of retail cluster distribution
coffee shops, 34–35, 70, 74–75, 112–113, 119, 123–124, 140–143, 215n3
"Commercial Lasnamäe" (Ljadov), *148*
commercial planning, 8, 213n8
community benefit, 50–51, 193, 214n8
comparison goods. *See* search goods
competing stores, clustering of, 83–92
complementary stores, clustering of, 79–83
complexity studies, 11
Concord, Massachusetts, 112, *113*
condoization, of commercial space, 116
convenience goods, 89, 92
cool factor, 72–73
co-ops, 100–102, 220n17
coordinated clustering, 93–118; beyond the mall, 104–107; malls, emulation of main streets, 107–114; municipal government role in, 114–118; store mix, 98–104. *See also* business improvement districts (BIDs)
Copenhagen, Denmark, 159, *160,* 205
Corbusier, Le, 144
core based statistical areas (CBSAs), 14, 29
corner shops, 137
corridor typology, 156–157
costs of retail and service businesses, 33–35, 39, 215nn2–3; labor, 34; operating space, 34; storage, 42–43; time, 51, 79–80, 88; transportation, 40, 42–43, 51–58, 79–80, 83, 86–87, 187–188, 216n24; utilities, 34, 215n2; variable costs, 33–34. *See also* fixed costs
creative class, 179
crime, 97
crossings, pedestrian, 159–162
Crossrail, 197
cultural shifts, 74–76

daily patronage, 141–143
Darwin's sandwich shop (Cambridge, MA), 124–126
Davis Square (Somerville, MA), 133, 219n26
Dayton, Donald C., 172–176
Dayton, George Henry, 172
Dayton Company, 172–176, 178
Dayton-Hudson Corporation, 176
Dedham, Massachusetts, 108, 109
demand, inelastic, 84, 86–87, 218n14
demographic shifts, 9, 136, 151, 172–184, 193–194, 227n3; class, 109, 177–178, 179, 185, 191; gentrification, 8, 31, 32, 48, 94, 118, 201; Minneapolis, MN example, 172–176, 228n15. *See also* inner-city revival; racial demographics

density, of customers, 58–62, 65–66, 217n39
density, of development, 59–61, 62–74, 215nn12–14; accessibility, unequal spatial, 63–66; branding and marketing, 71–73; customer density, 58–60; population density, 58–59, *60*; prices, 73–74; regulations, 66–71; transportation, 52–54
density, of entrances, 162–166
density, of population, 66, 174–176, 202–204, 228n23, 230n10; effect on clusters, 25–26, 30
Desert Hill Premium Outlets, 73–74
design guidelines, 8, 164–166, 170–171, 195–208, 213n8; assessment of strengths and weaknesses, 196–198; equitable street commerce, 200–201; to include e-commerce, 191–194; influence on retail clusters, 30–31; no one-size-fits-all prescriptions, 195–196; public investment into community-oriented streets, 198–200; size and shape of street commerce, 206–207
Detroit, Michigan, 172–173
DiPasquale, Denise. *See* one-dimensional retail density model
discount outlet centers, 73–74
Donaldson's, 173
double-sided streets, 159–162
Dudley Square (Boston, MA), 179–180
Dunkin Donuts, 119, 140–143, 226n49
duopoly, 89

e-commerce, 9, 74, 151, 184–194; bricks and bits becoming more intertwined, 189–190; design guidelines to include, 191–194; experiences as part of the sell, 187–189; increase in dining establishments, 189; unequal restructuring of retail market, 190–191
economic multiplier effects, 4, 112–113, 207
economies of scale, 11, 15, 72, 114
Economist, the (magazine), 57
Ehrenhalt, Alan, 177–178, 182–183
employment, 9, 74–75, 97–98, 180–181, 182, 198–199, 228n25
endogenous externalities, 7, 77, 83, 87, 90, 214n8
end parcels, 137
en route shopping. *See* unplanned purchases
enterprise zones, 213n8
environmental benefits, 4–5, 201
Environmental Systems Research Institute (ESRI) Business Analyst software, *18–22, 99, 103, 183,* 223n21
Essex Road (London), 35–37, *37,* 116
ethnoburbs, 184
Evergreen Cooperative, 116
Evergreen Cooperative Laundry, 115

exogenous qualities of built environment, 7, 77, 83, 90
experiences, in-person, 187–189

facades, permeable, 152–153
Facebook, 73, 107
F-Building (Tallinn, Estonia), 105–106
Federal Aid Highway Act of 1956, 174
Federal Housing Authority, 176
Federal Reserve Bank of Chicago, 180
Finger Plan of 1947, 205
first-mover's risk, 139
five-foot-ways, 158
fixed costs, 34, 45–48, 217n44; policy innovations to address, 48–51
Flatiron 23rd Street Partnership BID (NYC, NY), 96
flea markets, 145–146, *147*
floor area, 58, 150–153; Floor Area Ratio (FAR), *202,* 203–204, 230n10
Florida, Richard, 179
food-related businesses, 37, 45–48, 72–73, 77–78, 90–91, 189, 190–191; space-sharing among, 189, 192–193, 230n41
Freeman, Linton, 128
free-rider incentive, 95
Future Streets Incubator Fund, 197

Galleria Vittorio Emmanuele (Milan, Italy), 173
Garment District (Los Angeles, CA), 93–94
gas stations, *88*
Gehl, Jan, 56–57, 158
Genesis Plus, 180
Gensler architects, 178
gentrification, 8, 31, 32, 48, 94, 118, 201
geography, 7; first law of, 140
George Washington University School of Business, 176
gerobak food vendors, 45–47
"Get Stuffed" taxidermy store, *37*
Gilbert Jeune bookstore, *78*
Gobbi, Pascal, *78*
Good Jobs First, 111
Google Places Data, *70*
Granovetter, Mark, 3, 199–200
grants, to stores, 117–118, 180, 197
gravity index, 122–128, 134–140, 222nn10–12
Greater London Authority (GLA), 197, 199
great inversion, the, 177–178, 182–183
Great Inversion and the Future of the American City, The (Ehrenhalt), 177–178
Green City Growers, 115
grid layouts, 167–168, 227n17
grocery stores, 87–88, 92, 111, 187–188, 217n37

Gropius, Walter, 144
ground-floor spaces, 119–120, 150, 152–154, 157, 164, 170–171
"Growth, innovation, scaling, and the pace of life in cities" (Bettencourt et al.), 11
Gruen, Victor, 172–173

Haabu, Andres, *55*
Hägerstrand, Torsten, 124–126
Haji Lane (Singapore), *164*
Haley House Bakery Café, 179
Hall, Peter, 213n8
Hampstead Heath (London), *35*
Hansen, Walter, 121, 222n10
Hartley, Daniel A., 180, 182
Harvard Graduate School of Design, 141
Harvard Square (Cambridge, MA), 119, 163, 169
Haute Coffee (Concord, MA), *113*
Hemmings, Paul Barker, *72*
hierarchical hexagons, 40–41, *42*
high-end blight, 48
higher-order goods and services, 39–40, *41*
high streets, 197
hipster effect, 72–73
Hollywood Boulevard (Los Angeles, CA), 17, *18*
Hong Kong, 58–60, 90, *91*
Hotelling, Harold, 84–86
household vacancy rates, 137
housing, affordable, 48–49, 177, 201
Housing Development Board (HDB), 68–69, 144
Houston, Texas, 26
"How Accessibility Shapes Land Use" (Hansen), 121, 222n10
Hudson Company, 172–173, 176
Huff, David, 122
Huff model of retail patronage, 122, 140–143, 225n47
Hurd, Richard, 121

ice-cream carts, 84–86
impulse purchases. *See* unplanned purchases
inclusionary retail programs, 8–9, 49–51, 216nn21–22
individual stores, survival of, 32–76; central place theory, spatial distribution of competing stores and, 39–42; density, of customers, 58–62, 217n39; fixed costs of running a business, 45–48, 217n44; market areas, for frequently and infrequently purchased goods, 33–39; policy innovations, to counter high fixed costs, 48–51; purchase frequency, 40, 42–43, 43–45; social, cultural, and technological shifts, 74–76; transportation costs, 51–58, 216n24. *See also* density, of development

Infogroup Business Listings, *18–22, 99, 103, 183,* 219n26
infrastructure, 53, 57–58
inner-city revival, 177–184, 228n21; inequality of, 181–184, 228nn23, 25
International Council for Shopping Centers (ICSC), 5, 60
International Downtown Association (IDA), 94, 99
intersections, 17, 55, 64–65, 77, 123, 129, 168–169, 179

Jacobs, Jane, 6–7, 62
Jacobs, Marc, 47–48
Jaffray, Piper, 186, 229n33
Jenks, George Frederick: Jenks' natural breaks, 24–25, 210, *211,* 215n12
jitneys, 54–55
Johnson, Boris, 197
joint lease coordination, 110
Jokowi, 47, 196–197

Kant, Edgar, 42
Kaza, Nikhil, 180, 182
Kendall Square (Cambridge, MA), 169–171, 196; Urban Renewal Plan, 171
Keong Saik Road (Singapore), 73
Khan, Sadiq, 197
King, Rodney, 93
kiosks, 145–146, 196–197
knowledge workers, 179
Kolko, Jed, 176, 181, 228n23, 229n25
Kruusamägi, Ivo, *149*

labor costs, 34
landscaping elements, 158
land use, 57, 61, 69–71
Langovits, Peeter, *146*
Lasnamäe housing district (Tallinn, Estonia), *148*
latent social ties, 4, 70, 199–200, 207
LaVerde's (MIT campus), 87–88, 218n17
Lawless, Seph, 107–108
Leahey, John, 139
Legacy Business Registry, 50, 114–116
Legacy Place (Dedham, MA), 108, *109*
Le Marais (Paris, France), 78
Lester, T. William, 180, 182
Li, Wei, 184
Library Bar (Singapore), 73
lifestyle centers, 107–114
limited liability corporation (LLC), 101
Lincoln Square (NYC, NY), 66
linkage funds, 50

Ljadov, Vladimir, *148*
lobby space, 155
local economy, effects on, 4, 110–115, 171, 179
Local Origin-Destination Employment Statistics (LODES), 228n21
location. *See* accessibility measures
London, England, *161*; Borough of Hackney, 102; Carnaby Street, 167; Essex Road, 35–37, *37*, 116; Greater London Authority (GLA), 197, 199; Hampstead Heath, *35*; Outer London Fund, 197; Transport for London, 128, 197; Upper Street, 1–3, 80
Los Angeles, California, 25–26, 153–154, 178, 190, 217n44, 219n1; Byzantine Latino Quarter, 180, 198; clustering in, *85*, 97–99, 102–103; Fashion District, 93–94, *95*, 219n2; Garment District, 93–94; Hollywood Boulevard, 17, *18*; Neighborhood Initiative, 180; store survival in, 53–54, 62–63, 73–74; Zipf's Law, 209–212
Lösch, August, 39–40
lower-order goods, 40, *41*, 80–83
Lynch, Kevin, 166–167

Macy's, 176
Magnolia's Bakery, 47
Manhattan (NYC, NY), 53–54, 65–66, *67*
market, unequal restructuring of retail, 190–191
market areas, 61–64, 77, 84, 87, 121, 215n1, 216n13; density models of, 39–42, *43*; purchase frequency in, 33–36, 40, 42–43, *43*–45
market dynamics, 6, 195, 198, 208
marketing, influence of, 71–73, 98–99
Massachusetts Avenue (Cambridge, MA), 119
Massachusetts Bay Transit Authority (MBTA), 223n21
Massachusetts Institute of Technology (MIT), 87–88, 156, 169–171, 218n17
Massachusetts's Tax Free Weekend, 193
McAllen, Texas, 192
McDonald's, 112, 217n46
Measure J, 114–115, 118
Melbourne, Australia, 56–57, 162
Melrose Avenue (Beverly Hills, CA), 188–189
Menino, Thomas, 179–180
metropolitan statistical areas (MSAs), 29–30, 180, 229n25
Miami, Florida, *21*
microdistricts, 149–150
middle-class movement, 177–178, 185
Milan, Italy, 162, 173
millenials, 177

Minneapolis, Minnesota, 100–101, 172–176, 220n17, 228n15
Mission district (San Francisco, CA), 182
mixed-use strategies, 61, 70–71, 157, 178
mobile communication, 74–75
Modifiable Aerial Unit Problem (MAUP), 230n10
Mong Kok (Hong Kong), 58–60
movement, of competing stores, 83–86, 139
multipurpose shopping clusters. *See* complementary stores
multistory retail environment, 163
municipal government, 164, 178, 191–194; role in cluster coordination, 102, 114–118. *See also* business improvement districts (BIDs); design guidelines
Myrtle Beach CBSA, 29–30

Nash, John: Nash equilibrium, 84–86
National Association of City Transportation Officials (NACTO), 161
National Establishment Time-Series (NETS) database, 97–98
National Household Travel Survey (2009), 4, 75
National Trust for Historic Preservation, 177
nearest-center patronage, 80
neighborhood business streets, 78–79
networks, 56, 163, 167; of people, 4, 94, 118, 174, 187, 196–198; of streets, 7, 17, 56, 63–64, 66, 78, 122–123, 167–169; of transportation, 54, 63–64, 174; of utilities, 11, 187, 190
Newbury Street (Boston, MA), 154–155, *156*, 193
Newton's gravitational law, 122, 222n10
New York City, New York, 122–123, 156, 183–184, 220n26, 222n13; Bleecker Street, *47*, 47–48; Bronx, 48; Brooklyn, *81*; Chinatown, 66; clustering in, 94–95, 97–98; Flatiron 23rd Street Partnership BID, 96; Lincoln Square, 66; Manhattan, 53–54, 65–66, *67*; Penn Station, 25, 215n13; PlanNYC, 178–179; Sixth Avenue, lower, 139; SoHo, 188; Times Square, *65*, 129, 159, 178; Zipf's Law, 209–212
Nike, 188
nonprofits, role in commerce, 95–96, 114–115. *See also* business improvement districts (BIDs)
Nordstrom's, 188–189
North American Industry Categories (NAICS), 12–13, *38*, 217n38, 219nn25–26
Northeast Investment Cooperative (NEIC), 100–101
Northland shopping Center, 172–173

North Randall, Ohio, 192
nuclear family, decline of the, 176–177

occupiable realm, 199
O'Day, Arthur, 176
Office for Metropolitan Architecture, 153, *154*
office workers, 125–128
older Americans, 177
oligopoly, 89
one-dimensional retail density model (DiPasquale and Wheaton): additional factors to consider, 62–65, 71–73, 77, 80, 83; explanation of, 33, 42–46, 51, 58, 215nn12–14, 216n13, 217n44
online pickup services, 189
Open Newbury Street, 193
operating space costs, 34
Orchard Road (Singapore), 167
organized complexity, 62
otherness, 200
Outer London Fund, 197
outlying business center, 78–79

Paaver, Toomas, *145*
parcel frontages, 162–164
Paris, France, 120
Park, Robert, 120
parking, 117; multistory garages, 162; parallel, 158
Pastéis de Belém (Lisbon, Portugal), 71–72
patterns of street commerce, 11–31; as emergent phenomenon, 6–7; scales of street commerce, predictability of, 12–15; uniqueness of retail clusters at the micro scale, 27–31. *See also* predictability of retail cluster distribution
Payless Shoe Source, 186–187
pedestrian studies, 155–156; crossings, 159–162; detours, 131–132; pedestrian-only environments, 161–162, 178, 226n11; safety measures, 161; walkability, 61, 177. *See also* walksheds
Pelevin, Victor, 146
Penn Station (NYC, NY), 25, 215n13
Phoenix, Arizona, 209–212
pilotis, 69
Pioneer Boulevard (Artesia, CA), 184
Place for Mom, A, 177
planned purchases, 80–83, 128
planners: advise for, 57, 191–194, 206–207; commercial planning, 8, 213n8; retail planners, 193. *See also* design guidelines
PlanNYC, 178–179
Pocket Parks Program, 197
podiums, 164–165
points of maximal demand, 120–122

policy innovations, to counter high fixed costs, 48–51
Porter, Michal, 213n8
Prada, 153, *154*
Prague, Czech Republic, *82*
predictability of retail cluster distribution, 15–27, 183–184; defining retail clusters, 16–22, 214n8, 215n9, 217n38; density, effect of, 25–26; figures, 19–22; tables, 22–27; Zipf's Law, 15–16, 24, 26–29, 40, 92, 209–212
predictability of scale, 12–15
prices, effects of, 187, 188; competing stores, 83, 86–87; retail density, 73–74
principal business thoroughfare, 78–79
Principles of City Land Values (Hurd), 121
private and public space, 155, 198–199; private management of public space, 94, 110–111; privatization, 147. *See also* business improvement districts (BIDs)
Proceedings of the National Academy of Sciences (journal), 11
property values, 98
Proudfoot, Malcolm J., 78–79
public policy, 7, 214n8
public-private partnerships (PPPs), 116–117, 162, 171, 198–199
public sector procurement, 115–116
public space. *See* private and public space
public transit, 61, 156, 162, 178, 223nn20–21; accessibility measures around, 126–128, 132–134, 136
Public Works department (Boston, MA), 193
purchase frequency, 33–36, 40, 42–43, 43–45

Quincy, Massachusetts, 184

racial demographics, 179–180, 182, 190–191, 201, 227n3; around retail clusters, 24; ethnoburbs, 184; white flight, 174, 176, 178
Rand Corporation, 97
reach accessibility metric, 167, 222n13
real estate economics, 7
real estate investment trust (REIT), 102, 104–105, 110
regulations, retail density and, 66–71
Renzo Piano Building Workshop (Paris, France), 120
repurposed buildings, 149, 192
residuals, 138–139
resource sharing between stores, 116–117
retail compatibility. *See* spillover
retail microeconomics. *See* individual stores, survival of
retail planners, 193

Rialto Bridge (Venice, Italy), 129
Riordan, John T., 5, 191
Rocca al Mare shopping center, 55
Rodeo Drive (Beverly Hills, CA), 153, 154
Romazur, 161
Roxbury (Boston, MA), 179
Royan, Jorge, 129
Rue Saint-Séverin (Paris, France), 77–78
Rue St. Michel (Paris, France), 77–78

Saarinen, Eliel, 208
sales, retail, 44
San Francisco, California, 21, 50, 114–115, 118, 179, 182
San Luis Obispo-Paso Robles CBSA, 29–30
Santa Fe Institute for Complexity Studies, 11
Santa Monica, California, 117, 167, 168, 226n5
Santee Alley (Los Angeles, CA), 95
scaling: scales of street commerce, predictability of, 12–15; scaling laws, 12, 30; sublinear, 11, 15
Schwietzer, Robbie, 186
Scitovsky, Tibor, 89
search goods, 89
Seattle, Washington, 179
Sendelbach, Henrik, 160
Senior Living Preferences Survey, 177
Sennett, Richard, 200
setbacks from the street, 154–155, 156
Severn, Charlie, 177
SF Heritage, 114–115
shared-space street crossing, 159, 161
Shibuya intersection (Tokyo, Japan), 169
shopping centers, 5–6, 73–74, 81–82, 89–90, 162, 191, 207
shopping malls, 82–83, 90, 107–114, 151, 172–176, 218n10, 226n11
shopping spines, 162, 193
sidewalks, 137, 157–159
Silicon Valley, California, 179
Singapore, 60, 66–69, 144, 189, 192, 217nn35, 44; Bugis District, 163, 164; Haji Lane, 164; Keong Saik Road, 73; Library Bar, 73; Orchard Road, 167; Urban Redevelopment Authority, 166; Yong Siak Street, 32
Sixth Avenue, lower (NYC, NY), 139
Small Business Commission (San Francisco, CA), 114–115
Social Explorer, 175
social shifts, 74–76
social ties, 3–4, 70, 199–200, 207
SoHo (NYC, NY), 188
Solo, Indonesia, 45–47, 46, 60, 196–197, 217n35

Somerville, Massachusetts, 90–92, 129; Assembly Row, 108; Davis Square, 133, 219n26; retail patterns in, 134–140, 222nn15, 17–18, 224nn37–44, 226n49
Southbank (Melbourne, Australia), 57
Southdale Center, 173–176, 227n5
Soviet Union, 104, 144–150
space between buildings, 149–150
space-sharing, retail, 189, 192–193, 230n41
spatial lag regression, 135–140, 219n25
spatial network, 167–169
speakeasy phenomenon, 73
Specialty Coffee Association of America, 74
spillover, of customers, 80–83, 100, 101, 110, 151, 157
spillovers, of information, 139
squares, 168
"Stability in Competition" (Hotelling), 84–86
storage costs, 42–43
Storefront Improvement Program, 117–118
store mix, coordination of, 98–104
Street Tree Initiative, 197
strip malls, 79
Strøget (Copenhagen, Denmark), 159, 160
subsidies, 100, 111–112, 114
Subway, 72, 217n46
supplemental zones, 213n8
Surabaya, Indonesia, 160
Sutton, Stacey, 97–98
Swanston (Melbourne, Australia), 56

tactical physical interventions, 214n8
Tajeda, Paula, 182
Tallinn, Estonia, 54–56, 104–107, 146, 147, 148, 190, 197–198
Tallinn Electrical Engineering Factory, 104
Target Corporation, 172–176, 188–189
taxation, 46–47, 159, 193, 215n3
taxidermy stores, 35–40
taxpayer strips, 152, 154
technological shifts, 74–76
Telliskivi Creative City (Tallinn, Estonia), 104–107
Third Street Promenade (Santa Monica, CA), 117, 167, 168, 226n5
timber column-beam structures, 152, 153
time cost, 51, 79–80, 88
time-space constraints, 124–126
Times Square (NYC, NY), 65, 129, 159, 178
Tiong Bahru, 32
Tobler, Waldo, 139
Tokyo, Japan, 169
Trader Joe's, 61–62
traffic-calming measures, 159

training, for business owners, 117–118
transaction counts, 50–51
transit-first policies, 56–57, 204–206
Transitional Employment Program, 179
Transit Metropolis, The (Cervero), 56
transportation costs, 40, 42–43, 51–58, 79–80, 83, 86–87, 187–188, 216n24
transportation mode share, 52–54
Transport for London, 128, 197
Trulia, 176, 228n23
Trunk Club, 188–189
Tunjungan Street (Surabaya, Indonesia), *160*
Two Rivers Company, 100

United States Census Bureau, 37, *175*, 223n21, 228n21
United States Department of Housing and Urban Development (HUD), 49
University Circle (Cleveland, OH), 115–116
University of California Los Angeles (UCLA) planning program, 180
University of North Carolina, 180
unplanned purchases, 60, 128–134, 223nn32–33, 224n34
Upper Street (London), 1–3, 80
urban empowerment zones, 213n8
Urban Network Analysis toolbox, 222n11, 223n33
utility costs, 34, 215n2

Vancouver, City of (Canada), 164, *165*
variable costs, 33–34
Venice, Italy, 129
Via Dante (Milan, Italy), 162

Victoria, State of (Australia), 56
Virginia Beach, Virginia, 26–27, *28*
void-decks, 69
voluntary business association, 95, 96
volunteer-based initiatives, 180

Walgreens, 112
walksheds, 22, 65–66, 122–126, 137, 162, 167–171, 202–203; maps of, *67, 124, 126, 133, 167. See also* pedestrian studies
Walmart, 111, 221n30
Washington, DC, 15, *20*, 215n11
Waterfront District (Boston, MA), 164
weak social ties, 3–4, 200
Webber, Oscar, 172–173
Westbury Village BID (New York), 100
Wheaton, William C. *See* one-dimensional retail density model
white flight, 174, 176, 178
Whole Foods, 187–188
Whyte, William, 156
work schedules, increased flexibility of, 9, 74–75

Xin Tian Di (Shanghai, China), 108–109

Yong Siak Street (Singapore), 32

zebra crossings, 159, 161
Zillow.com, 181
Zipf, George Kingley: Zipf's Law, 15–16, 24, 26–29, 40, 92, 209–212
zoning, 57, 69–71, 118, 192
Zurich, Switzerland, 162, *163*

Acknowledgments

I would first like to thank the researchers at the City Form Lab who helped me with background information, data collection, and figures: Alexander Mercuri, Matt Schreiber, and Kevin Chong. The subject matter of the book and particularly the chapter on location also benefited from joint research efforts and stimulating discussions with Raul Kalvo, Liqun Chen, Emily Royall, Onur Ekmekci, Reza Amindarbari, and Michael Mekonnen. All of these talented urban scholars have since gone on to establish successful careers of their own in universities, companies, and cities around the world.

I am also grateful to the incredible set of mentors that I had the opportunity to work with at MIT: Bill Mitchell, Bill Wheaton, Julian Beinart, and John de Monchaux, as well as Philip Steadman from University College London. The conversations we had years ago planted the seeds that turned into chapters in this book. Unfortunately, the world lost two of these incredible individuals—Bill Mitchell, who passed in 2010, and John de Monchaux, with whom I remained friends until his death in 2018.

Several of my faculty colleagues at the Department of Urban Planning and Design at Harvard read pieces of the manuscript and shared their generous feedback and suggestions as I revised and restructured the work: Alex Krieger, Peter Rowe, Diane Davis, Jerold Kayden, Rick Peiser, and Susan Fainstein. Funding support from Dean Mohsen Mostafavi and my colleague Rick Peiser helped cover the research assistants and image publication costs.

The comments and feedback from two anonymous referees engaged by the University of Pennsylvania Press, as well as the press's senior history editor, Robert Lockhart, were instrumental in my restructuring of a rather rough first full draft into the final manuscript.

On a more personal note, I am thankful to my parents and my brother's family for their continuous support and love over the years, and to Lily's family in Los Angeles for their warmth and love. I am also thankful to the staff at Diesel Café, Block 11, Broadsheet, and Darwin's that hosted me as a frequent guest, typing away with a cup of cappuccino.

I would like to dedicate the book to Lily, my partner in life and closest friend, and our four-year-old son Luukas, who was born soon after I started the manuscript. Much of the book was written during early morning hours or afternoon naps, while Luukas was sleeping and growing from a baby into a curious and fun boy. Luukas's curiosity and unfiltered love, combined with Lily's intellect and loving support gave me the energy to keep going, even when it seemed hard to open the keyboard again.